ADVANCE PRAISE

"*In 2005, Diane Harsha strapped on a pack and took her first steps on the Appalachian Trail at Springer Mountain, Georgia. She completed her 2,200-mile odyssey atop Mount Katahdin, Maine, thirteen years later. With humor and unvarnished honesty, she tells us how she carried out her quest, section by section, to hike the AT while also fulfilling her roles as wife, mother, and FBI agent—proving we don't have to put off our dreams until we 'have the time' to pursue them. Sometimes solo and sometimes accompanied by Smokin' Goat, Kim Commando, She Who Falls A Lot, or other strong, colorful women, 'Sticks' (as she became known) encounters bears, rattlesnakes, unfriendly Bubbas, storms, and other dangers that threaten to derail her plans. But always, the beauty of the AT that she writes of so reverently calls on her to strap on her pack and tackle the next challenge. Whether you have also answered the call of the wild or prefer to live it vicariously, you'll find much to laugh about and love in this delightful coming-of-middle-age memoir.*"

—GERALD D. SWICK, AUTHOR OF THE *WEST VIRGINIA HISTORIES* SERIES

"*Few of us have the imagination, fortitude, courage, or pluck to tackle a 2,200 mile hike. But the intrepid Diane 'Sticks' Harsha is not most of us. For thirteen years, she entwined her life with the Appalachian Trail. Now, she offers an enthralling memoir that transports us across dramatically beautiful landscapes, through ever-changing weather, into triumph and despair, enlivened by memorable characters and quirky landing zones. As she crawls through sleet across New Hampshire's White Mountains, your skin will sting and your knees ache. While she jokes about 'nature...rolling in the aisles at (her) antics,' we just marvel at her grit. A truly gifted writer with a talent for evocative phrasing, Sticks reminds us what being alive is truly all about. We may not share her admirable perseverance, but we can all revel in Sticks' captivating story."*

—LESLEY WISCHMANN, AUTHOR OF *FRONTIER DIPLOMATS* AND *THIS FAR-OFF WILD LAND*

"For 2,200 miles from Georgia to Maine, over mountains and into valleys, through forests and fields, we walk the entire length of the Appalachian Trail with Diane 'Sticks' Harsha. She takes us with her on this finely written memoir, and the details put you right there with her throughout this amazing journey. We see, hear, and feel the rain, snow, hail, heat, bear, deer, snakes, and danger, and then suddenly, we are given glimpses into the soul of a hiker: 'In reality, these miles would reduce me to a ragged winter bone from which all the marrow had been sucked until even the hungriest dog would disdain it.' That's good writing! Go buy this book, then go home, sit down, and enjoy the hike with Sticks."

—GEORGE SPAIN, AUTHOR OF *LOST COVE* AND *SUNDANCING WITH CRAZY HORSE*

STICKS AND STONES

STICKS AND STONES

HOW TO HIKE THE APPALACHIAN TRAIL IN THIRTEEN YEARS

DIANE "STICKS" HARSHA

HOUNDSTOOTH
PRESS

STICKS AND STONES
How to Hike the Appalachian Trail in Thirteen Years

ISBN   978-1-5445-2209-8 *Hardcover*
       978-1-5445-2208-1 *Paperback*
       978-1-5445-2207-4 *Ebook*

This book is dedicated to all Angels, on and off the Trail.

CONTENTS

PROLOGUE

The Appalachian Trail stretches for almost 2,200 miles from Springer Mountain, Georgia, to Mount Katahdin, Maine, along the spine of the mountain chain that gives this iconic footpath its name. The path, as a rule, is about eighteen inches wide, lined with fragrant pine needles and musky fallen leaves, bordered by clingy bramble bushes or the jade-green leaves of laurel and rhododendron, meandering up and down, switchback by switchback, under a canopy of hardwoods and evergreens. It is marked with four-by-six-inch white blazes painted on trees every fifty feet or so. But the many exceptions to these rules give the Trail its appealing diversity and its maddening challenges.

Sometimes the path widens along old foresting roads or narrows to crevices between boulders, it often crosses rivers and streams without benefit of bridges or stepping stones, and occasionally it marches itself right down through the middle of a small town. It goes through tunnels, over bridges, and along highway overpasses. It winds its way through state parks, national parks, city parks, and privately owned lands. It traverses or skirts meadows, cow pastures, and fields of crops—corn, barley, soybeans—cultivated in the eastern United States.

The mountains themselves consist of rolling hills, craggy peaks, and sunny balds. At the southern end of the AT, the Smoky Mountains are covered in dense forest, and at the northern end, the White Mountains rise up above tree line as great slabs of granite. The change in elevation along the Trail is over 460,000 feet, and if you have walked the entire length, you have climbed the equivalent of sixteen Mount Everests.

The four-by-six-inch white blaze can be found on trees, rocks, sidewalks, telephone poles, road signs, and bridge railings. As the AT crosses meadows and fields, posts have been set into the ground at steady intervals for the sole purpose of bearing a blaze to guide the hiker. There is a blaze painted on the bottom of the rowboat which ferries hikers across the Kennebec River in Maine to verify the authenticity of this method of crossing the dangerous waters.

For over two thousand miles, the Appalachian Trail constantly contradicts itself. It is brazen but respectful, remote yet accessible, harsh and then forgiving. There are few rules on the AT other than universal camping or hiking etiquette, and there are no scorekeepers or officials. The Appalachian Trail Conservancy is a benevolent overseer, and dozens of hiking clubs staffed by hundreds of volunteers provide general upkeep and maintenance. The Trail—while crafted by human hands and tended to with human hearts—is a wild place, constantly on the precarious lip of returning to nature.

It attracts thousands of visitors annually, and most of those will hike for only a few hours or a day. Of those who attempt a thru-hike (the entire Trail in one hiking season, usually four to six months), only one in four of those will complete the trek. Those who do will tell you it was the best time of their lives and the hardest.

Then there are the section hikers. We are those who, periodically and sporadically, hike over a stretch of time and miles—a weekend here, a week there, twenty, fifty, a hundred miles. My journey began on a September weekend in 2005 at Springer Mountain, Georgia, and ended on a September weekend in 2017 at Mount Katahdin, Maine. For thirteen years, I had one foot on the Trail and one foot off—my heart always in two places. But this was a blessing and a gift, a pleasure doubled rather than halved.

❋ ❋ ❋

Over those years, whenever my mind called for peace, when sleep would not come, when worries of work or family troubled me, my thoughts turned to the hike. I saw the narrow soft trail under my boots, rising and falling with my breath. I smelled the sharp clean pine needles and heard the small animals scuffle away at my approach. I felt the heaviness of my pack and the sweet relief of rest. The utter simplicity of hiking—eat what you have, drink when you can, sleep when it's dark, follow the blaze—called to me and I would go.

Then at the end of a hike, a section, I went home to the security of my family and the routine of my work, refreshed and recharged. My need for the solitude of nature had been answered, and now I could get on with my busy life, balanced and clearheaded. Weeks and months would pass happily filled with appointments and schedules, with work travel and family vacations, with household chores and social obligations. Then eventually a vague feeling of displacement and restlessness would come upon me, and I would once again study the maps, gather up my gear, and travel east to the mountains of Appalachia.

CHAPTER 1

2005 (51 MILES)

SPRINGER MOUNTAIN, GEORGIA, TO WOODY GAP, GEORGIA

WOODY GAP, GEORGIA, TO NEELS GAP, GEORGIA

NEELS GAP, GEORGIA, TO UNICOI GAP, GEORGIA

On the Appalachian Trail, there is a revered tradition for long-distance hikers to adopt trail names. The origin of this practice has been lost to time and conflicting claims, but it has been practiced for decades. As far as I know, this is the only sport or activity (except for perhaps professional wrestling) where the participant is known almost solely by his or her alias.

Who chooses this moniker? It is customary for fellow hikers to bestow the name; it is rare that it is self-imposed. For example, someone might call a hiker "Chips" because he eats a lot of them or "Barefoot" because she rarely wears shoes. I suppose some people try to name themselves, but it seems the ones that stick are those that evolve organically. You might start your hike thinking you're going to earn a trail name like "Superman" or "Blazer," and then you become something like "Squirrel Nuts." And—fair warning—these things are hard to undo.

So you can call me "Sticks" now. But it would not be until halfway through a thirteen-year section hike on the Appalachian Trail that this name was assigned to me. When my hike and this story first began in 2005, I was still known by the name given to me at birth in 1959 small-town Alabama.

I was not born into a family of adventurers or into a community of outdoor enthusiasts. There was a smattering of nature-bonding experiences—Girl Scout camps and backyard sleepovers—but these were hardly the stuff of the wild. My parents did take my siblings and I, first as eager young children and then as sullen adolescents, on occasional car-camping trips in the hot summer months to Elk River in nearby Lauderdale County. Daddy fished and drank Schlitz, Mom read Harlequin romances while reclined under a tall sycamore, and we kids waded in the creek to look for crawdads under rocks. The Swiss Family Robinson we were not.

I grew up and moved away, as some people do. My interests outside of work seemed to be mostly urban-centered, and there was no time and space in my life to appreciate nature or take to the outdoors. What vacation time I had (and with what little money I had) was spent at the beach or visiting family.

As my twenties gave way to my thirties, I met and married my husband. We bought a small tent and a camp stove for weekend getaways in the Ozark Mountains of southern Missouri, a short drive from our home in Kansas City. That gear was packed away with the birth of our daughter, which happened to coincide with our transfer to Detroit. Neither of those two events were conducive to outdoor activity.

When said daughter was in kindergarten, we moved once again, this time to Nashville. By then, we figured she was old enough that we didn't have to worry obsessively about plucking her from a campfire or lake. So we dug out the old camping gear and introduced our only child to nature.

For several years, until this daughter reached the eye-rolling stage, we enjoyed an annual tradition of camping at one of Tennessee's state parks. We hiked on easy trails or canoed on placid rivers or boated on still lakes. These weekends were about family harmony and simple pleasures; there were no attempts to conquer the wilderness or take on physical hardship.

As our daughter grew and our lives became more settled in some ways and more complicated in others, I began to be drawn to the idea of the peaceful serenity of the silent woods and yet also to the challenges of serious hiking. I craved quiet strength, physically and emotionally.

Long walks, for several hours, became a habit on the weekends. (As a lifelong habit, at least as an adult, I also ran a few miles several days a week, but this was more about staying fit for my job and my vanity than as an enjoyable pastime.) The idea of hiking the Appalachian Trail, or at least part of it, began to seep into my mind. I don't know how this idea came about or even when I first heard of the Trail. I suppose, on some level, I was always vaguely aware of it. After all, the southern portion of it is not far from our home, and I occasionally read news reports about an event on the Trail or a certain hiker's accomplishments or woes.

I read Bill Bryson's *A Walk in the Woods* (as anyone who appreciates biting humor, intelligent wit, and piercing insight should) and found it so beguiling that I searched out other books about the AT and long-distance hiking. *How lovely*, I thought, *strolling along a pine-needle-covered path bordered by wildflowers and moss-covered trees, listening to birdsong, breathing the clean, fresh air.* I suspected perhaps Bryson, in his wry manner, had overexaggerated the difficulties of such a hike. Really, how hard could it be?

A thru-hike was impossible; I had neither the desire nor the means to leave my family and career for several months. *But*, it began to occur to me, *there's no reason in the world I can't at least try it for a few days. If I like it, I can go back from time to time.* These were my thoughts at the very beginning of the twenty-first century. But I was an FBI agent and the world had other plans.

* * *

In the months and then years of the early 2000s, during those sad, scary times that followed 9/11, my job required dedication and frequent travel. There was no question of pursuing this vague and unformed dream of hiking the Appalachian Trail. But life sometimes offers other opportunities, and occasionally, I walked or hiked on other trails in places far from our eastern United States.

On a rare free weekend in 2002 while on an assignment to Turkey, I day-hiked with a group of tourists in the northern mountains of that country. Our guide, a middle-aged Turkish gent with a walking stick, met us at the base of the mountain and gently led us on a quiet, almost reverential, seven- or eight-hour ramble. This was in February, the weather chilly and the path occasionally crunchy with snow. The terrain was Alpine-like, with open vistas and small, stunted trees, nothing like the deep woods of Appalachia. There seemed to be no trail, but we trusted our guide, who led us from hummock to hummock and signaled when it was time to stop for lunch.

I sat on a rock, ate my sandwich, and shared my M&M's while gazing at views of brown, snow-patched hills and small, crumbling villages. The air was cold and clean, the taste of chocolate was sweet. *See, this isn't so hard*, I told myself. *In fact, it is lovely. Someday when the world regains its sanity—not that it ever had an abundance—maybe I will hike the Appalachian Trail.*

* * *

The late summer of 2005 found us living in a furnished apartment on the outskirts of Nashville. By *us*, I mean my forty-six-year-old self, an unemployed husband, a daughter who was at that delightful age of fourteen, and one high-maintenance dog. We had just returned from North Africa, where my job had taken us, and our own house, a rambling old Victorian in nearby downtown Franklin, was currently occupied by subletters who were reluctant to be dislodged.

A sense of unsettledness hung heavy over our lives as if we were in a holding pattern between past and future. I drove to Nashville every day to reacclimate myself into my stateside career, Tim surfed the internet in search of a job, and Melanie began her freshman year of high school. The dog just seemed confused.

"Tim," I said one evening as he and I sat in the charmless living room, Melanie in her small beige bedroom, no doubt furiously IMing her friends to complain about our current state of affairs.

He looked up from the newspaper.

"You know next weekend is Labor Day, and I'm thinking I might go over to Georgia and hike the Appalachian Trail."

A quiet, patient man, he looked at me blankly for a minute. "The Appalachian Trail? Isn't that like a thousand miles long?"

"Uh, no. It's like two thousand miles long, and I'm not planning to hike the whole thing now. *God*."

"Well, you've had crazier ideas."

I had to admit this was true. But I had mentioned hiking the AT to him several times over the years. (He had always been encouraging but noncommittal as if I were saying something like, *Honey I might like to try parachuting someday.*)

"Just a short trip, a couple of days. You want to go with me?"

"No, thank you. Think I'll pass." He returned to his newspaper.

✳ ✳ ✳

A trip to our neighborhood REI provided me with maps and guidebooks as well as with some very basic gear: a pack (which turned out to be way too heavy and inappropriate), first aid kit, knife, compass, rain poncho, and some decent boots. My simple plan was to hike for two days, ten miles each day, with a motel stay in between. Water bottles and a few snacks would suffice for nourishment.

The official AT maps produced by the Appalachian Trail Conservancy (ATC) can be ordered online, and some outfitters carry them as well. A good state highway map is also a necessity for section hikers because of the need for road access. There are many guidebooks available. *Exploring the Appalachian Trail: Hikes in the Southern Appalachians, Georgia, North Carolina, Tennessee* by Doris Gove is a very reliable source, particularly for day and section hikers. This book thoughtfully breaks down the Trail into manageable day hikes, with road directions to trailheads. Gove also provides interesting details about the flora, fauna, and features of any particular section. State or national parks will also offer maps, which can be very helpful. There are also excellent hiking phone apps available now, but in my early years of hiking, these were nonexistent.

The question of logistics was a bit trickier. On Friday I would make the five-hour drive to the Appalachian Trail's southern terminus at Springer Mountain, Georgia, find a cheap motel, and begin the hike bright and early on Saturday morning. But how to get back to my car after each day's hike? This problem, at least for my first few years of hiking, was the bane of my AT existence. A thru-hiker at least doesn't have this complication, no matter how arduous his or her journey may be. He or she can simply step on the Trail, begin walking, and then in five or six months consider how the hell to get home.

My guidebook provided the telephone number of a young couple who ran a small hostel in the area and who agreed (for a reasonable price, of course) to meet me at the end point of each day's hike and shuttle me back to my car.

Do you see the flaw in this plan? It meant I would have to be at the end point at a prearranged time to meet the driver. We did have cell phones in those days, but coverage in the mountains was often spotty or nonexistent. As this was to be my first hike on the AT, and I had no firsthand knowledge of the terrain and how quickly (or slowly) I would cover the miles, I could only estimate my finish time. This meant I would arrive sometime before the driver and have to wait at the side of the road, wishing for a grape Nehi and a bag of chips. Or more likely, the driver would have to wait for me, no doubt wishing she had charged me by the hour.

Lesson learned: do it the other way around. Leave my car (preferably with a stocked ice chest inside) at hike's end and have the shuttle driver take me to hike's beginning.

* * *

Amanda, a friend and neighbor with whom I run several times a week, agreed to accompany me on this little adventure. Forty-year-old Amanda, beautiful and gregarious, was recently divorced and had three young children, who would be spending the weekend with their father. (I've always thought a selling point for divorce is that the ex gets the kids every other weekend.) Amanda was happy to get away and eager to try something new—but although fit, cheerful, and fearless, Amanda gives not one whit about nature, flora, or fauna. Couldn't tell the difference between a possum and a polecat. No matter: off we went on a road trip to Georgia.

The official southern terminus of the Appalachian Trail is at the summit of Springer Mountain, Georgia. For most of the near hundred-year history of the Trail, the only feasible way to get to the starting point was to walk the strenuous 8.1-mile Approach Trail from Amicalola Falls State Park. Many thru-hikers even now consider this route as part of the overall Appalachian Trail experience, but it has never been and is not now an official white-blazed section. (A blaze is a mark on a tree or pole or sometimes a rock that indicates you are on the right track; in the case of the AT, the blazes are four-by-six-inch white rectangles.) I felt no compunction in skipping this Approach Trail; I would have enough of a challenge doing the real thing.

In recent years, United States Forest Service (USFS) Road 42 was extended to provide closer access to the Springer Mountain terminus. This is where Amanda and I began our adventure on a pleasant and sunny September Saturday.

This was late in the hiking season for northbound thru-hikers to be starting their journeys, and the parking lot was relatively empty. In March and April it is jammed with worried parents or slightly pissed-off partners dropping off their starry-eyed loved ones and waiting for them to make the U-turn at Springer and come back through.

Why come back to the parking lot? Because here is another AT quirk (already two, and we haven't even started): the road crossing here is still almost a mile to the official beginning of the Trail. You are required to walk a mile south on the AT, slap the plaque depicting the universal symbol for hiker, and then retrace your steps for the same mile back to where you started. I have been told some people just give up then and there.

After that little redundancy, we began our true journey through mixed forest on a soft trail of pine needles and fallen leaves. The day was not excessively warm, and soft breezes cooled the sweat on our backs and brows. There are some ups and downs on this nine-mile section but none that truly tested us. After the convolutions involved in actually *getting to* and then *getting on* the Appalachian Trail, it seemed to make amends now with a gracious and hospitable welcome.

This is exactly *what I had hoped for and expected.* The woods were hushed except for sweet sharp bird twitter and the sound of twigs snapping under our boots. The sun's rays rarely penetrated the dense green canopy above our heads, and yellow dapples danced with small white flowers growing in the shade of gnarly roots. Through the summer aroma of spruce, there was the smell of something wild, of prey in flight, or of blood spilled by a predator. We were caught in that season between summer and autumn which only migratory birds and burrowing animals can define.

Amanda moved with athleticism and speed, but I was happy to walk slowly with reverence and appreciation, savoring this first hike and already beginning to feel and hope there would be many more. We crossed small streams on charming little footbridges and stopped to admire sparkling waterfalls which had flowed through the millennium down slick and shiny cliff faces. Chipmunks and squirrels scattered and scolded at our approach. Deer, foraging in small clearings, froze and stared at us before turning to lope, heartbreakingly elegantly, into the deeper woods. Bear tracks in the mud around a drenched campfire gave us reason to pause and wonder.

Arriving at Hightower Gap to meet our driver, I was stunned by the accomplishment of this day. The smell of the Georgia pines, the sight of the little wildflowers and bright-green ferns lining the trail, and the sound of the easy conversation with my companion made for a simply glorious day.

The next day, as warm and pleasant as the day before, proved just as magical. Each step and then each mile along the soft, musky-smelling path reaffirmed my decision to hike the Appalachian Trail. This weekend was the true beginning of the journey, the hazy reasons for doing it no longer important. The Trail itself was reason enough.

* * *

I could not stop extolling the virtues of the Trail.

"Oh, Tim," I gushed to my husband. "It is simply beautiful, so quiet, so peaceful. So much wildlife. You've got to see it!"

He was a little hesitant. Tim is an athletic person and will walk for miles if it involves chasing a little white ball, but hiking nine or ten miles up and down mountains while carrying a pack and swatting at bugs did not, to him, seem like a purposeful way to spend the day. But, happy for me with my newfound pastime, he agreed to try it.

Three weeks after my first hike, I was back on the AT, now with Tim in tow. I have no recollection of where we stashed our daughter while we were gone—we were still living in the beige apartment, and she was, alas, still fourteen. We drove to North Georgia on Saturday, the weather sunny and cool.

The seven miles from Woody Gap to the base of Blood Mountain is a beautiful woodland walk along a smooth, easy trail. I wouldn't have been surprised to see Bambi or Thumper disappearing around a bend. Gorgeous views of Southern Appalachia spread out below and around us when the trail opened up out of the hushed forest. The ascent of Blood Mountain (at 4,500 feet, the highest point on the Georgia section of the AT) challenged our stamina but left us with a glorious feeling of accomplishment.

I believe also that Tim was somewhat reassured when we came upon the sturdy two-room Blood Mountain Shelter. This, and the fact that we encountered numerous friendly hikers—families, Scout groups, apparent neophytes like ourselves—helped allay his concerns that his wife would be flinging herself out into a solitary wilderness with no place to lay her head or seek shelter from the ravages of weather. Over the years, I would try not to disabuse him of this illusion.

The AT is close to 2,200 miles long from nose to toe. The official number of shelters can vary from year to year. New ones are occasionally added; old ones can burn down or be otherwise destroyed. But let's say, on average, there is a shelter every eight to fifteen miles for a rough total of about two hundred.

The vast majority are wooden, crudely built, three-sided structures that can accommodate four to eight hikers. The floor is usually made of wooden planks and raised a few feet off the ground. Some shelters are a little larger, with an upper level to accommodate a few more sleeping bags. There might be a window or a stone fireplace, but those are rare. In a very few instances, you will find what are called "Hiker Hiltons," such as the Blood Mountain Shelter, relatively grand affairs sleeping twelve to fifteen people.

There are no provisions or furniture, just a ziplock-bag-encased hiker's log and maybe a whisk broom. There is usually a campfire ring and often—but certainly not always—a picnic table.

Because they are three-sided, the shelters are open to the fresh air and never smell musty; body odors are not contained as they would be in an enclosed room, for which all hikers can be truly thankful. Although the shelters have a notorious reputation as mice havens, this seems to be an exaggeration. I have rarely seen evidence of rodents, although I have often seen homemade mice deterrents in the form of empty tuna cans tied to several inches of rope. These contraptions dangle from the ceiling, the theory being that you hang your food bag on the rope below the can, which blocks the mouse on his quest for your granola. Possibly.

The shelters are usually located near a water source, such as a stream or spring, and are almost always nestled in the deep woods, sometimes up to several hundred yards off the Trail itself. Some boast a nearby privy. I will spare you detailed descriptions of these outhouses; suffice it to say, they are rudimentary but usually very clean.

Always remember you probably won't be alone in a shelter. If you are opposed to sleeping next to a complete stranger who may have been hiking for weeks without benefit of a shower, you're going to want to bring along your tent. If the sound of roof-raising snoring bothers you, don't forget your earplugs.

After coasting the last three miles from Blood Mountain to Neels Gap, Tim and I were further rewarded with the Walasi-Yi Inn, perched just off the Trail as it crosses US Highway 19. This establishment is well known to thru-hikers. It is the first outfitter a northbounder will come to, and it signals the final push for those southbound.

Inside the little store, hiking boots—worn, destroyed, abandoned—are flung over a wire hanging from the ceiling. My boots had only twenty-eight AT miles on them, but already, they were beginning to show the first signs of wear. I was proud of the mud in the treads and the scuffs on the toes—an early testament to my resolve.

* * *

I was already beginning to go through hiking companions fast. Two short weeks after Tim and I made it to Neels Gap, I enlisted my cousin to join me for a twenty-mile walk to Unicoi Gap at GA 7.

Teresa, thirty-five at the time, is not particularly athletic, but she has a sense of adventure and is willing to try almost anything. She looks like a stereotypical librarian—brown bobbed hair, no makeup, sweaters adorned with reindeer or a symbol of whatever holiday is approaching—but in fact, as of this writing, she runs a saloon in Livingston, Montana.

The initial ascent out of Neels Gap is challenging, and our bodies warmed up quickly in spite of the nip in the air on this sunny Columbus Day weekend. Twenty miles is a very long hike by almost anyone's standard, and we moved quickly, hoping to reach our car at the highway before dark. After the first climb, the trail levels out for several miles and becomes a green magic carpet through the woods. We descended steeply to Tesnatee Gap at about five miles in, and then the trail becomes kind again with only gentle rises and falls.

The simple and stunning beauty of this hike rendered us almost speechless. We felt no need to remark on the startling color of the leaves or point out the intricate fungi on the side of a tree. Walking single file, we were each held rapt by these gifts of nature and the gift of each other's company. Conversation was pointless.

That evening in the charming town of Helen, known for its Bavarian architecture and its celebration of Oktoberfest, we sipped our beer at a little street café. Now was the time for talk, and we rehashed our glorious day as if we were Edmund Hillary and company after a day on Everest. The feeling of accomplishment and pride at having hiked even a short section of this iconic Trail was enough cause for celebration.

＊ ＊ ＊

I fully intended to get in another weekend trip or two before winter closed in on southern Appalachia, but the responsibilities of my job intervened. Within a week after the trip with Teresa, I was en route to New Orleans. This was mid-October 2005, almost two months after the devastating combination of Hurricane Katrina, Hurricane Rita, and a failed levee. For three weeks I was joining agents from field offices across the country in an effort to assist our employees whose homes had been destroyed and damaged.

The route from Nashville to New Orleans is an easy day's drive through northern Alabama and the southern half of Mississippi, passing through Birmingham, Meridian, Hattiesburg, and countless smaller and lesser-known towns with lovely sounding names like Laurel and Picayune. This is true Delta country, and the cotton fields were white and full.

A hundred and fifty miles north of the Louisiana border, in DeSoto National Forest, I became distracted by acres of leveled-off trees alongside the interstate. More and more of the disaster became apparent as I drove on: huge billboards and giant green interstate signs in tangled heaps by the roadside, caravans of southbound supply trucks and FEMA trailers, hardly a building (those that were left standing) that did not have at least part of its roof covered with a bright-blue tarp. This was two months after the fact.

The FBI command post had been established at a National Guard armory in Slidell, north of Lake Pontchartrain. Our team of eight or nine agents operated out of old FEMA trailers that boasted lights but no water. Each morning, armed with MREs and Tyvek suits, we crossed the one usable bridge over Lake Pontchartrain into New Orleans. We cleared out the sodden contents from various employees' homes, salvaging what we could and dumping the rest for garbage trucks to haul away. We cleared downed branches and limbs from yards and sawed trees into sections to remove them from driveways. These homes had been underwater for weeks, trash left uncollected and rotting on the curbs. Occasionally, we saw bloated animal carcasses festering in ditches.

I thought of the clean beauty that was the Appalachian Trail and the simplicity that was hiking. Here, whole families now were confronted with ugliness and filth, the complications of disruption marking every moment of their lives. They lived in tents in their yards or in cars at the Walmart parking lot. Fathers stood in line with infinite patience at Home Depot to buy a chainsaw or some bleach or yet another blue tarp. Mothers stood in even longer lines at the grocery store to buy what bread and milk and produce were available.

My hikes over the years would teach me more of the forces of nature and what humans can overcome when faced with its arbitrary fury. At those times, I would think of these people in New Orleans and admire once again their stalwart resolution and grace.

CHAPTER 2

2006 (47 MILES)

UNICOI GAP, GEORGIA, TO DICKS CREEK GAP, GEORGIA

DICKS CREEK GAP, GEORGIA, TO TIMBER RIDGE TRAIL, NORTH CAROLINA

TIMBER RIDGE TRAIL, NORTH CAROLINA, TO ALBERT MOUNTAIN, NORTH CAROLINA

W ho can leave jobs, spouses, kids, aging parents, house, yard, and pets for five or six months at a stretch to go on a ramble? Although—and let's be honest here—many of us probably dream of it from time to time. This is why you rarely see forty-year-old thru-hikers. Even to leave for a week or two requires negotiation and compromise, as well as determination and persistence. As the spring approached and I studied the upcoming North Carolina section of the Appalachian Trail, I recognized that the logistics of this adventure were going to need a serious review.

* * *

After four months in the beige apartment and just in time to greet the New Year, we finally moved our belongings, the dog, and our daughter (Dear god, would she be fourteen forever?) back into our house in downtown Franklin. Busy with our jobs and school, with friendships and extended families, with obligations to home and community, it was June before I could take the time to visit the AT.

I planned what I thought would be a quite manageable weekend hike for me and Tim from Unicoi Gap (where Teresa and I had finished in 2005) to Dicks Creek Gap, still within the state of Georgia. We drove over on a Friday evening with a hot and sunny weather forecast. Tim would take me on Saturday morning to Unicoi Gap, and then he would play golf while I hiked four-and-a-half miles to Tray Gap. He would pick me up there after his game, and we'd return to the town of Helen for postexercise rest and relaxation. On Sunday, we would hike the twelve miles from Tray Gap to Dicks Creek Gap together.

Part A of the plan went swimmingly. Tim dropped me off for my first solo AT hike, and I couldn't have been happier. I scuffled along in no particular hurry, enjoying the strenuous ascent to Rocky Mountain summit and then the lovely sloping descent. Tall summer flowers—blue, red, yellow, orange—carpeted the old abandoned farm clearings skirting the Trail. I scampered across rock scrambles and skimmed babbling brooks, besotted by the beauty of this place and smug in my decision to hike it. I approached the end of this glorious jaunt, serene in the knowledge that my wonderful, sweet husband would be patiently waiting for me with a smile and a cold beverage.

Except there was no wonderful, sweet husband waiting when I got to Tray Gap. But I was earlier than anticipated, so I stretched out on a patch of grass close to where the Trail crosses the road and basked in the late afternoon sun. My careful instructions to Tim had been for him to take USFS 698 from GA 349 for ten miles to junction with USFS 79.

USFS is the acronym for United States Forest Service. Be very leery when those letters precede a number. It denotes a seldom-used and sometimes impassable road. USFS roads are rarely paved and at best are graveled and graded; at worst, they are simply rutted dirt tracks. They can sometimes be closed, with metal gates prohibiting entry, to public traffic due to storm or flood damage. It's impossible for guidebooks to provide completely current conditions, but your ATC maps or state maps will provide phone numbers to the appropriate ranger station or Park Police authority, which should have up-to-date information about closures.

When Tim did eventually arrive, he was slightly irritated.

"What the hell was that all about?" he said. "You didn't tell me this would require an ATV. I've been on that road for an hour, almost lost the muffler a couple of times."

Perhaps I had not been entirely forthcoming about the possible state of USFS roads. I always tried to downplay any potential difficulties of hiking the AT so as not to discourage my companions. While a good intention, it sometimes backfired.

❋ ❋ ❋

Next morning the manager of the little family hotel where we were staying agreed to shuttle us from Dicks Creek Gap, an easily accessible Trail crossing at US 76, to the forbidding trailhead at Tray Gap. Tim thought his fee was pretty high, but we really had no choice. The area was so isolated we would have had little chance of hitching a ride.

The road seemed even drier and dustier (and longer) than on

Saturday. We bumped along in our chauffeur's old Cadillac, startling flocks of wild turkey and, once or twice, a white-tailed deer. The sun had burned off what little coolness the day may have started with and now hung hot and yellow in the white sky. Our arrival at the trailhead was marked by silence all around.

Most guidebooks describe the twelve-mile hike from Tray Gap to Dicks Creek Gap as "strenuous." I think Tim would tell you this is an understatement. Passing through the Tray Mountain Wilderness (capitalized because it has been officially designated as such by the US Forest Service), the trail is isolated and forlorn. Now, in June, masses of rhododendron and mountain laurel in full bloom crowd the trail and camouflage the danger of the rocky slabs and cliffs.

Two ascents that rise more than four thousand feet each, Tray Mountain and Kelly Knob, are separated by a five-mile ridgeline walk at three thousand feet. Two shelters, occasional campsites, and long-abandoned roads are the only signs of a human presence. The air was thick in the dense woods, and cloying spiderwebs strung across the path reminded us that no one had preceded us this day. The sweat dripped from our foreheads to entice tiny gnats and sting our eyeballs. I tried to sound cheerful and encouraging by pointing out a small animal or interesting flower.

"Oh look, honey, it's a chipmunk!" *Or mushroom. Or caterpillar.*

Tim's usual response was, "How much longer?"

I was dreading the Kelly Knob climb because my husband was becoming, as they say, not a happy camper. He wore heavy, outdated boots, and we stopped twice to doctor the rising red blisters on his feet.

The view from the Kelly Knob summit was indeed stunning, but for Tim, this was no compensation for the challenge of the ascent, the dense heat of the day, and the swarms of mosquitoes in our faces. He slung off his fanny pack (I was carrying most of our supplies), sat down on a log, and declared, "I'm through with this fucking trail."

Not for everybody, I thought to myself. "I'm sorry, sweetie. I really didn't know it would be this tough."

"Humph," he muttered with a glare.

"Only four more miles to the car and the cooler."

With an exaggerated groan, Tim refastened his pack and trudged north through the woods to finish what he thought was to be his last AT hike.

* * *

The rest of the summer—prime hiking season—washed over me with no chance to travel east to the Trail. My obligations at work did not allow for much vacation time this year, and what I did have was gladly spent with family. Also, this summer we were hosts to a Parisian exchange student who spoke very little English, and Tim speaks very little French. Melanie had turned fifteen (finally) earlier in the year and now had her learner's permit to drive. To leave Tim alone with this set of circumstances so I could go off, even for a few days, to commune with nature seemed more than a little selfish.

Labor Day weekend finally brought the chance to hike again. Two days hiking fifteen and a half miles from Dicks Creek Gap to Deep Gap and then about ten miles from Deep Gap to Timber Ridge Trail interspersed with a hotel stay near Hiawassee, North Carolina, was the game plan. And I had a new partner.

My friend Kelley looks like someone you would want on your Roller Derby team or on your side in a bar fight. Tall and rangy, with a headful of prematurely iron-gray hair although she is several years younger than me, she is actually a big old softie on the inside, kind-hearted and compassionate with an endearing little whine in her voice. She is also scared of snakes and spiders and things that go bump in the night, so she was apprehensive about accompanying me on this trip but agreed after quite a bit of persuasion.

Me: Oh, Kelley, you'll love it! It will be so much fun and so beautiful!

Kelley: But what if I can't do fifteen miles in one day? I have bad knees. What about bears?

Me: You can do it! Teresa did it.

Kelley: But I will slow you down. What about bears?

Me: I won't be in any hurry. You won't slow me down.

Kelley: What about bears?

Me: Hmm?

Kelley still had doubts about the entire undertaking as we headed east on Friday afternoon, but I tried to reassure her and keep things simple. Our end point on Saturday (and thus our starting point on Sunday) involved a dreaded USFS road, and I wanted to avoid the stress of trying to hitch a ride. We picked up a car at a local Rent-A-Wreck in Hiawassee, and so now we had two vehicles and could act as our own shuttle.

Saturday morning, in a misty fog, we drove tandem on US 64 to USFS 7, which dead-ended six miles later at Deep Gap. We consolidated our gear into the rental car, leaving my vehicle in the little gravel turnaround area. I noticed an untidy trash can at the side of the road. This concerned me. Trash cans are purposefully absent on the AT. They are unsightly and attract animals; you are expected to pack out your own garbage.

Kelley's concerns about bears had not diminished. During the drive from Nashville, at the hotel the night before, on the bumpy ride to the Trail that morning, she had whined and questioned. *What do we do if we see a bear? Are you carrying a gun? You think they hibernate?*

"Kelley, bear attacks are extremely rare. They will run away if they see us." I again tried to reassure her as we pulled out of the dead-end turnaround.

"I wonder how big they get?"

"Jeez, Kelley," I said loudly, turning in the driver's seat to face her. "Just relax. I am telling you for the thousandth time, we are not going to see any bears!"

My words were still hanging out there in the air as if in a cartoon bubble when a large—nay, huge—black bear moseyed out from the brush to our right. He stopped not five feet in front of the car's hood and looked at us calmly as if to say, "Why, this is a surprise. I thought you awkward creatures would be gone by now. I was just coming by to check if you left anything in the garbage there. Good day to you, mesdames," before scampering up a steep embankment on the left side of the road and disappearing into the Southern Nantahala Wilderness Area.

I could only glance at Kelley, who appeared to be in shock, and say in a tiny voice, "Except for that one."

The American black bear is the only bear species native to the Appalachian Mountains and can be found in every state through which the Trail passes. They live in the mountain woods but cover a wide territory. It's not unusual to see them alongside the road or even in a town park or neighborhood. They are dark brown or black in color and can weigh up to several hundred pounds. The male is usually a solitary wanderer, but a female will often have her cubs and yearlings with her. Bears are shy and unaggressive toward humans, but they have keen senses of smell and are not particular about what they eat. If they can smell it, they want it, and if they want it, they can usually get to it or will at least try. So the best way to avoid an unpleasant or dangerous encounter with these creatures is to be proactive. Keep your food wrapped in such a way that it doesn't emit a lot of odors; best case scenario is to carry a bear-proof canister. Don't leave food laying around a campfire or on a picnic table. Hang your food bag at night. If you see one in the distance, ignore or avoid him. If one crosses your path and stops to check you out, remain calm. Make some noise, but not in a startling or provocative way. Clap your poles together, sing a little song, or speak to her as one wanderer to another: "Good afternoon, my friend, you look magnificent today. I am going to continue on down the path now, and I wish you the best in all your endeavors."

Despite being confronted by the physical manifestation of her fears, Kelley was willing to bravely press on, and we traveled on to the trailhead at Dicks Creek Gap to begin our fifteen-mile-plus day. This is a very beautiful hike through a dark-green forest, but it is not easy. On the ascents, we rested often and took the time to admire the views from overlooks. There are three distinct summits on this section, each rising to more than 4,500 feet, including Yellow Mountain at almost five thousand feet. We walked through a misty rain most of the day, but we each had rain gear, and the temperature was mild. The deep woods were hushed, and we saw very few other people on this remote section of the Trail. Kelley was slow, as promised, but cheerful and uncomplaining.

But as the day wore on and Kelley's pace became slower, I began to worry about getting to the car at Deep Gap before dark. We had flashlights, but the trail was rocky and slippery in places. I worried that one or both of us might fall. We reached the intersection of Chunky Gal Road (how delightful a name is that?), and I encouraged Kelley to move faster; we still had three miles to go. Dusk quickly changed to dark as we navigated over, around, and through boulder fields and small streams. Kelley, almost in tears, was taking literally one step at a time. *Step, stop. Step, stop.* I knew her knees were hurting, and I wanted to be kind, but we really needed to get out of the woods.

"Kelley," I said gently. "This has been a really long hike, and you've been truly awesome. But you remember that bear we saw this morning?"

She moaned a bit and brushed her eyes with the back of her hand.

"Well, this is his territory, and I don't think we want to meet up with him again, do you?"

Kelley took a deep breath, stood up straighter, and grabbed my arm. She almost pushed me along the path, muttering, "Let's finish this son of a bitch."

✻ ✻ ✻

The next day, we did the two-car shuttle again. Deep Gap to Timber Ridge Trail is about eight miles on the AT, but hiking out on the access trail would add another two. The weather was perfect—cool and sunny. I was anxious to start. Finding the Timber Ridge trailhead at USFS 67 where we left a car had taken half the morning. We locked the car at Deep Gap, strapped on our packs, and stepped on the trail to begin the immediate ascent of Standing Indian Mountain, my first mile-high peak on the AT.

The Appalachian Trail was purposefully designed to be fairly accessible (except for the southern and northern terminals). The idea of the founders and planners was that people from the towns and cities along the East Coast could enjoy nature without having to travel too far from the urban centers and could dip into the woods and take a hike without convoluted arrangements. While it is true that once on the Trail you are almost never a day or two away from a road, there are some exceptions. If you plan to day-hike a section that doesn't cross a vehicle-accessible road for many miles, then you must study your maps and find an access trail. These are trails that go from a road where you can park a car and then hike in to the AT. These trails are usually marked with blue blazes, and if they are maintained by park authorities or hiking clubs, they will be included on maps. Its sole purpose may be in getting you to the AT, or it may be part of another trail system that happens to link up with the AT.

Once on the AT, you will also sometimes see blue-blazed trails leading to an interesting feature, such as a waterfall or nice viewpoint. Hikers refer to distance in points. You will not hear "The waterfall is a half mile off the trail," or "the overlook is three hundred yards away." They will say "point five" (.5) or "point three" (.3).

We walked for perhaps twenty minutes, and already Kelley lagged behind. I think she was sore from the long hike the day before, stressed because of the lateness of the morning, and worried she was slowing me down. Again, she was close to tears.

"I don't think I can make it," she said, looking at the stepping stones rising up the mountain path.

"Kelley, this is a very tough section of the Trail. You have done an amazing job. There is absolutely no shame in stopping."

"I've let you down, I'm so sorry." She hung her head, and my heart broke for her.

"No," I said firmly. "You are very brave. I will be absolutely fine. Go back to the car and the hotel. Get some rest. We'll celebrate tonight."

With relief, I'm sure, Kelley turned around and headed south on the Trail. I went on to have a fine hike, solitary and challenging yet peaceful and satisfying. I reached the side trail well before dark and easily walked the two miles to my car. *It all worked out okay*, I thought. Things usually do on the Trail.

Kelley never hiked the AT with me again, but we remain friends, and she has a great story to tell—which she does, proudly and often.

* * *

October arrived. My friend Jen agreed to accompany me on a one-day hike from Timber Ridge Trail to Albert Mountain, a seven-mile hike on the AT but over nine miles total when you factor in the access trail. (We would stay the nights before and after in a motel; this was probably really the draw for any woman with a busy career and young children, as was the case with most of my friends.)

Generous and amiable, Jen is probably the most outdoorsy of all my hiking buddies. Tall and lanky, she loves nature and knows the names of woodland flowers and what types of mushrooms are safe to eat. I like looking at the flowers but am hopeless about identifying them. As for mushrooms, I just steer clear of them all.

Jen approached this trip with near giddiness. For some time, she had wanted to hike the AT, and she had good basic gear and decent shoes. I told her, as I told all my hiking companions, "Just bring your food, water, and rain gear. I'll take care of the rest." I was happy to tote the first aid kit, maps, extra headlamps, and other necessities in exchange for the pleasure of company.

Jen and her husband, Chip, live down the street from us in Franklin, and a few days before our journey, they came by the house. Chip was excited for Jen, and I showed him on the map the route we planned to take.

"So see, we'll leave our car here," I said, pointing to where the AT crosses USFS 67. "Then we go back to Timber Ridge Trail and hike about two miles on it, which takes us to the AT, and then we hike seven miles on the AT to our car."

"Okay, cool," Chip said, but he seemed a bit confused as he squinted at the map. "How will you get from your car to Timber Ridge Trail?"

"Oh, we'll just hitchhike, no problem," I said cheerfully, trying to nonchalantly act like thumbing rides was something middle-aged suburban American moms did on a regular basis.

Chip got very still and then looked at Tim, who sort of shrugged and lifted a corner of his mouth in a half grin as if to say, "What can I do?"

"Look, it'll be fine. This is a popular section of the trail and beautiful time of year. There'll be plenty of folks about—locals who are used to giving rides to hikers." I tried to ease his mind.

Jen avoided eye contact with any of us.

Chip was not reassured. "Well, I don't know. Are you carrying a gun?"

"Oh sure," I lied and changed the subject. (My pack was heavy enough—I didn't need *that* extra four pounds.)

✻ ✻ ✻

The weather was beautiful with a little nip in the Saturday morning air as Jen and I bumped along USFS 67, traveling maybe twenty miles an hour to the designated end point. At first we chatted happily, but increasingly lengthy stretches of silence fell between us until finally I said what was obviously on both our minds.

"Gosh, not much traffic up here."

Silence for another minute. Then Jen, "Yeah. In fact, I don't think we've seen *any* cars."

My mind was clicking unpleasantly as I considered other scenarios and how we might save the day. *If we couldn't get a ride to the hike start and had to walk ten miles there and ten miles back, well, twenty miles is long for anyone, and we would be stressed, and we'd finish after dark and...*

"It's okay, I'm sure someone will come along," I said in what I hoped was a convincing voice as we reached the gravel parking lot at the crossing. A large, shiny pickup truck was parked here, which we took as a good sign. Sure enough, within a few minutes of our arrival, an angel strolled out of the woods.

This angel was a fortyish white man, so heavily armed that he looked like a character out of a sci-fi movie. This guy had shit hanging off him in every direction. Arrows poking up out of a quiver. Two or three bows over his shoulder. Knives of all sizes and descriptions lined up on his belt. He nodded at us and walked to his truck.

Jen and I hustled on our packs, locked the car, and approached Rambo Man.

"Hey, we are so glad to see you," I said with a big smile. "We're AT hikers and wonder if you could give us a ride south to Timber Ridge Trail."

He looked us up and down suspiciously, as if checking two skinny soccer moms for weapons. "Well, I don't know. I'm turning off at 83."

Was he refusing to give us a ride?

After another moment of consideration, he grunted. "All right, I guess. Get in the back."

We clambered into the bed and headed back down the mountain. Jen and I huddled together and bowed our heads against the chilly wind.

"Good lord," she whispered. "What's up with this guy? He must not have killed anything this morning."

Rambo stopped the truck at his turnoff and waited for us to clamber out, not offering a hand or good wishes. *No matter.* We had gotten this far and still had the whole day ahead of us. We walked quickly on the narrow dirt road and, within a couple of hours, made it to Timber Ridge Trail and turned into the woods away from all civilization.

Oh, happy day! We scuffled through fallen autumn leaves, knee-deep at times, and marveled at the colors still clinging to the trees. The path was soft under our boots, and the sheer exhilaration of walking steadily in the fresh air without care or concern of workaday worry made our steps light. We climbed Scream Ridge and Ridgepole Mountain, crossed Pickens Nose Trail at Mooney Gap, ascended Big Butt Mountain and descended into Bearpen Gap. (Did an eleven-year-old boy name the features on this section of the Trail?)

We climbed the rocky, almost vertical ascent of Albert Mountain, where we gaped in amazement at the views of the Smoky Mountains to the north. The late afternoon sun followed us down Albert Mountain as we descended to the parking lot where we had left our car.

It had been a long, glorious day. Jen and I stretched out on a blanket in the sunny clearing with a profound sense of well-being born of intense physical activity and self-sufficiency. We talked lazily of the hike, its difficulties and pleasures, and then, eventually, of our busy lives that were waiting for us at home.

✳ ✳ ✳

I had managed to hike a total of just forty-seven AT miles in 2006, even less than the fifty-one I'd completed in 2005. At that rate, if my math was correct, I would need forty-two years to complete the 2,200-mile Appalachian Trail. Now, that might not have been a problem had I started this lark in my twenties, but I was well into my forties and…well, you do the math this time.

I clearly remember standing on Springer Mountain's summit with Amanda that late summer day in 2005—my first day on the AT—brimming with energy and optimism. *I can knock this out in five years*, I thought at the time. *A couple of weekends a month, twenty-five to thirty miles a pop—hey, no problem.* In hindsight, the altitude must have been getting to me.

I had a job that required travel and long hours, and a family that required love and attention. This year had taught me that my approach to this adventure could be a bit more realistic and my aspirations scaled back to manageable. This realization in no way dampened my enthusiasm for the Trail or otherwise discouraged me. It did, however, serve as a wake-up call: I was in this for the long haul.

CHAPTER 3

2007 (127 MILES)

ALBERT MOUNTAIN, NORTH CAROLINA, TO WAYAH BALD, NORTH CAROLINA

WAYAH BALD, NORTH CAROLINA, TO TELLICO GAP, NORTH CAROLINA

STECOAH GAP, NORTH CAROLINA, TO FONTANA DAM, NORTH CAROLINA

TELLICO GAP, NORTH CAROLINA, TO WESSER, NORTH CAROLINA

FONTANA DAM, NORTH CAROLINA, TO CLINGMANS DOME, TENNESSEE

HOT SPRINGS, NORTH CAROLINA, TO TANYARD GAP, NORTH CAROLINA

MAX PATCH, NORTH CAROLINA, TO HOT SPRINGS, NORTH CAROLINA

A dolescence warily crept from our house like a cat banished to the outdoors. It occasionally turned to look back at us with narrow eyes and a hiss but eventually did slink out the back door. Melanie, as she turned sixteen, was becoming more independent and at the same time more tractable. She now had an after-school job at a nearby bakery and was involved with several school activities. These newfound responsibilities seemed to wash away the miasma of the early teen years and restore our daughter to a sweet and eager-to-help fifth grader. (But less gawky and without the braces.) Tim and I were grateful but still a bit leery; I sometimes thought of gently poking this beautiful creature with a stick to see if she would spring up and bite.

My responsibilities to my job and family had not decreased nor my commitment to them lessened, but the pathetic tally of forty-seven miles on the AT in 2006 was a nudging reminder that the years were passing us by. Melanie, with her increasing maturity, would not need my hovering presence as much, and no lengthy out-of-town assignments with the FBI were on the horizon. I resolved (always recognizing the caveat of flexibility) to take more hiking trips of, when possible, longer duration. The AT would not come to me; it was necessary that I go to it, and it was solely up to me to make the effort.

* * *

Late April would herald our hiking season of 2007, and I would begin at Albert Mountain in North Carolina. Two months earlier than the 2006 start, this was a positive beginning to my more-trips-more-miles objective. Two FBI friends flew to Nashville to accompany Jen and me on this particular AT adventure—Kim from New York and Diane from Detroit. My husband commented that I had blown through my local contacts and now had to recruit from farther afield.

I had first met Kim in 2004 while on assignment to Paris, and we had remained friends. A stunning woman with masses of black, curly hair, she is a sharp, funny, streetwise city girl. Having had some experience hiking in the northern Appalachian Mountains, she was eager to see what the South had to offer.

Diane and I were agents together in Detroit when we were both young women with small children, a construct that was still fairly rare in the late eighties and early nineties. Small with a red-haired pixie cut and the pale, lightly freckled face of an Irish lass, she is not terribly outdoorsy. In spite of her lack of hiking experience, she was happy to get away from the frigid Michigan spring for a walk in the sun.

Off we went: easygoing Jen, gentle Diane, firebrand Kim (whom Jen almost immediately dubbed "Kim Commando"), and their fearless leader, me. I think back now at how trusting my hiking companions over the years were and how much faith they had in me to lead them on this journey. I can see, even now, their eyes turned to me, shifting their packs, silently questioning, *Is this where we turn? Is it okay to get in the car with this complete stranger? Is this water safe to drink?* It was a blessing for us all they had no idea how clueless I was.

Our first day's hike, nine and a half miles from Albert Mountain to Winding Stair Gap, began with the familiar stress of finding a ride. We approached likely looking candidates—folks who looked like they could use twenty or thirty bucks to take us along these winding mountain roads to the trailhead—in the Circle K parking lot in Franklin, North Carolina, until we found a taker. Once we stepped onto the trail, the day turned sweet and easy.

We descended two thousand feet on this gorgeous section filled with early spring wildflowers, baby deer, and creeks rushing with winter runoff. On the pleasant treeless balds, we drank our cold water and ate our sandwiches. Then we blissfully stretched out to doze with our faces turned to the sun. The sky was cotton candy blue; the air smelled of clean sunshine and bitter spring grasses. Forgotten, or at least lingering as only a faint memory, was the dreary gray winter and the demands that came with it.

We reached our car at Winding Stair Gap, shared high-fives all around, and removed our packs and boots for the drive back into the town of Franklin, North Carolina. Then, all in one room with a couple of double beds, we lined up for the shower as we drank cheap red wine from Microtel plastic cups. After a huge dinner at a local Mexican restaurant, we returned to our soft mattresses and read our books until the last woman with the energy left to turn off the light did so. There is no rest better than that born from complete physical exhaustion and mental peace.

* * *

The next day, ten miles from Winding Stair Gap to Wayah Bald, was a little…harder. We again bummed a ride from a kind local and made it to the trail start at a reasonable hour. The trail here is quiet and densely forested. At this time of year, a pale-green carpet of mosses and ferns line both sides, and thick mountain laurel bushes rise overhead. This section includes three, five-thousand-foot-plus summits along sometimes rocky and slippery paths. We were aware of the aerobic challenge and our physical limitations, acknowledging them but not succumbing to them. At least until mile six.

After the descent from Siler Bald, we crossed USFS 69, an uncharacteristically well-maintained service road that takes vehicle traffic to Wayah Bald. With its beautiful stone observation tower erected by the Civilian Conservation Corps in the 1930s, Wayah Bald is a popular picnic site for car travelers.

When we got to the USFS 69 crossing, Diane was about done in.

"How much further, you think?" she asked.

I looked at the maps and figured we had about four miles to go. "It's mostly up," I said. "On the Trail, but taking the road here would be an even longer route."

I hesitated. "Unless you think we need to try to get a ride."

Jen and Kim Commando nodded. *Of course, of course, whatever we should do.*

Diane had not uttered a word of complaint all day and would certainly have continued on with us and walked the final four miles had not fate, in the form of an old rusty pickup, intervened.

This was ramp season in the southern Appalachian Mountains and a couple of local men were searching for the telltale double blades in the roadside ditch, their truck parked alongside the embankment. Diane is a gourmet cook and knew of ramps from the expensive and exotic food shops she frequents. We chatted with the men a while about ramp festivals, ramp queens, and ramp recipes. Diane mentioned she was pretty tuckered out and wouldn't mind a lift up to Wayah Bald if they could oblige.

Ramps, also called wild leeks, are delicate, edible perennials that are shy and rare, recognizable by twin pale-green shoots that grow two to five inches out of the soil on well-shaded embankments. They can only be harvested for a short period in midspring, when the bulbs, somewhat flatter than an onion or shallot, are pulled from the dirt. They have a smoky, haunting flavor—milder than garlic but reminiscent of earth, sky, and woods. They are very popular on menus in fine southern restaurants, and they're now considered a delicacy by many, although I suspect indigenous people as well as early white settlers gathered them without a thought.

Another edible root found in the southern Appalachians is the American species of ginseng, probably familiar to most of us due to its Asian reputation. However, this plant is endangered, and it is illegal to harvest ginseng except under some very narrow and controlled circumstances. Apparently, poaching this plant has been a somewhat widespread problem.

The beautiful greenish-purple leaves of the galax plant are also considered a commodity and were traditionally harvested by mountain-dwelling folks to sell as holiday decorations to commercial florists. The money this provided was no doubt a welcome and even necessary addition to the family coffers. However, this plant now, too, is considered endangered, but if you know what you are looking for, it can still be sighted in Western North Carolina.

Bottom line: Just don't bother picking anything, because even if your ecological conscience doesn't kick in, remember, these woods are also full of poison ivy.

"Sure, sure, no problem," they said. "Hop on in the truck. We'll run you up there."

The rest of us gals assured her that this plan was fine with us, and I gave her the keys to the waiting car.

"See ya up the trail!"

We waved goodbye to Diane as she turned around in the cab, wedged between her fellow ramp lovers, to give us a thumbs-up.

Jen, Kim Commando, and I turned back into the woods and trudged along in silence for a long while.

Eventually, I said, "Kim, did you happen to get the license plate on that truck?"

"Oh, my god, I was just thinking the same thing! No," she admitted.

Jen looked at us as if to ask, "What the heck kind of FBI agents are y'all anyway?"

Thinking of Diane's last backward look at us, I jokingly said, "Well, we'll never see her again."

We were sure she'd be fine. There was no reason to think those two local fellows were anything but chivalrous. Still, I think we were all relieved when we made it to Wayah Bald and saw Diane lounging in the grassy picnic area.

"Thought you'd never get here," she yawned. "Come on, let's head back into civilization."

And so we did. Jen and I to Tennessee, Kim Commando to New York, Diane to Michigan. We would meet many more times over the years, often in far-flung places, but we'd never again be all together on the Appalachian Trail.

* * *

As late spring gave way to early summer, I was once again on I-40 East with a plan to hike solo nine and a half miles from Wayah Bald to Tellico Gap. I had a work assignment in Cookeville, which was about sixty miles east of Nashville and therefore on the way to the Trail. I drove to Cookeville early Friday morning, assisted area law enforcement agencies with a training exercise, and then drove another few hours to the Franklin, North Carolina, area.

The hike Saturday was a nice, moderate walk under tall hemlocks and skinny beeches. The AT is soft and pleasant here, and the spring rains had fostered orange, red, and yellow fungi. It now grew in imaginative formations up and down the trunks of trees and in the hollows and stumps of fallen logs. The smell of musk and of something even more primeval rose from the layers of brown needles and slick leaves under the tramp of my boots. It was the rich and delicious odor of nature.

Less than ten miles is admittedly a short hike for a long weekend, but even one day alone in the woods is a chance for reflection and another page turned in a section map. I was beginning to see that if I chanced to be on a road leading to Appalachia, it was worthwhile to take the detour.

* * *

My next opportunity for a trip to the Trail came when my next-door neighbor, Jamie, invited me to join her and her family on an annual visit to their ancestral cemetery near Fontana Dam in North Carolina. Unless you are familiar with Southern customs, it might strike you as strange to be invited on an outing to a graveyard. We have a phenomenon here known as Decoration Day, a yearly tradition in which folks gather to clear gravesites of old faded flowers and to place new, brightly colored artificial arrangements at the headstones of their departed relatives.

On June 22, I drove solo to the North Carolina entrance to the Great Smoky Mountains National Park where I had a cabin reserved at Fontana Village, a "resort" originally constructed to house the builders of Fontana Dam, but which now serves as a way station for hikers, rafters, and family vacationers. Jamie was already in the area with her extended family and I was on my own for the first day's hike.

Because I had planned this hike based on proximity to the Hazel Creek Cemetery activities, I was skipping the section from Tellico Gap, where I had left off in May, to Stecoah Gap. I would knock out that section another time. On this warm Saturday, I had an easy seven-and-a-half-mile ridgetop ramble from Stecoah Gap to Yellow Creek Gap.

On Sunday morning, I left my car at the Fontana Dam parking lot, where I met up with Jamie and her kin for the cemetery visit. The day was again warm, and the waters of Fontana Lake were low. We took a ferry (really just a small motorboat operated by a park ranger) across the lake to the cove and Hazel Creek Cemetery. Jamie and I strolled along a gravel road, noticing occasional signs of long-departed humanity—the remains of a house foundation here, an old boarded-up well there. Damming the rivers forced many communities to relocate, as their homes, schools, and churches would be underwater forever. Cemeteries were also relocated, but in the case of Hazel Creek—either by sheer luck or the foresight of the original European settlers in the early 1800s—the graves were on a hill, high enough to escape the floodwaters.

After the rituals of flower laying and food consumption, we retraced our journey and returned to the mainland in the early afternoon. Jamie's brother Don agreed to drop me off at Yellow Creek Gap where the AT crossed and where I had finished the day before. I figured I could get in the eight-mile hike down to my car before dark. On the maps, it appeared to be easy ridge-walking for the first four miles and then a gentle descent to Fontana Dam.

We turned off NC 28 and wound our way down NC 1242 (Yellow Creek Mount Road) for several miles as I kept my eye out for a white blaze. Don and Jamie assumed there would be a sign. *Uh, no, probably not.* It is not unusual for there to be no markings when the AT crosses a road. Often, one must rely on simply spotting the two-by-four-inch white blaze, which can sometimes be quite faded or on a tree several feet off the roadway.

"Here it is!" I had finally spotted a blaze.

Don stopped the car. "I don't know about this, you going off all alone, all the way to the dam."

I assured him I would be fine and there would be plenty of people on the trail.

"You sure?" He seemed reluctant to leave but finally drove off with a shake of his head.

The terrain was as easy to hike as the maps indicated, but the warm day had turned downright oppressive. The woods were quiet, and I couldn't shake a certain spookiness, not altogether surprising considering how I'd spent my morning. I did not see another human being for the entire eight miles, and as best I can recall, this was the only hike I ever took on the AT where no other person (dead or alive) crossed my path for the entire day.

❋ ❋ ❋

Word had spread among my friends and acquaintances that I was *hiking the AT*. Many said to me, "Oh, I would love to go with you someday." That "someday" came for my friends, Denise Wolfe and Tammy, when they agreed to join me and Jen to hike the section I had skipped between Tellico Gap and Stecoah Gap, south of the Great Smoky Mountains National Park.

Both of these free-spirited and beautiful women are experienced hikers. I knew neither of them would have too much trouble with the physical challenges, although, according to the maps, we would have our work cut out for us.

On the weekend of July 13 in the very hot and dry summer of 2007, the four of us set off for Wesser, North Carolina. The route from Franklin took us between the Great Smoky Mountains and the Cherokee National Forest. In this wilderness, beware of the dragon—or at least an eleven-mile stretch of US 120 known as the Tail of the Dragon. My white-knuckled grip on the steering wheel took us along 318 curves, some of them veritable hairpins, on this most famous (dangerous) motorcycle road in the United States or, as some claim, the world.

Somewhat shaken, we made it to Wesser, and I refined our weekend itinerary. Our little motel was near the Nantahala Outdoor Center, a bustling recreation area mostly catering to water activities (rafting, kayaking, fly fishing) for which the Nantahala River is famous. Studying the maps, I decided we should do the fourteen-mile section from Wesser to Stecoah Gap on the first day and to do it north to south, in order to avoid the 3,500-foot climb out of the Nantahala Valley. We weren't really "avoiding" it. We were just going 3,500 feet down instead of up.

The climb out of Stecoah Gap is a series of rock scrambles with a few switchbacks through the thicket offering occasional relief. Friends, this hike is not for the meek, especially in mid-July of a drought-stricken year. We clutched and clawed our way up what can only generously be called a trail. It is really just a faint path hacked out of the wilderness, and we relied heavily on the white blazes to maintain our course. The ninety-degree heat forced us to frequently stop for long chugs from our water bottles. Each time we crested a hill and thought, *Well, surely this must be the summit at Cheoah Bald*, we met with another rocky scramble.

Tammy, quick and agile, scampered around like a mountain goat in the Rockies, bounding up ascents and picking her way down steep, dangerous rockslides. When we stopped for water and snack breaks, she'd light up a cigarette. She was forever after affectionately known to us as "Smokin' Goat."

We descended Cheoah Bald to US Route 19, a 3,500-foot elevation change. Down, down, down we went, which may sound easy but is very tough on the knees, as your weight and your pack unnaturally lean over your lower body. It's also hell on toes, as they are pushed into the tips of your boots. It would have been easier to slide down on our butts as we finished the last half-mile—a seven-hundred-foot drop in elevation. We limped across the black roadway and into the crowded and noisy Nantahala Outdoor Center. After a full day spent in the quiet solitude of the mountains, the hustle and bustle jarred our senses. We returned to the quiet of our little motel to nurse our wounds and marvel at our accomplishment.

The next morning brought another hot day, but the eight-mile, south-to-north section from Tellico Gap to Wesser proved to be moderate, with only one short ascent and then a long, gentle, six-mile descent to the Nantahala. We were all tired and sore, and Smokin' Goat's knees were done in after the previous day's tough downhill. We moved slowly and quietly, appreciating the relative ease of this day and encouraging one another when spirits flagged and the heat became unbearable.

I would go on many more hikes with these women, and it is to their credit that they didn't let this difficult weekend hamper our friendships. Each could have easily said, "Why didn't you tell us it was going to be so freaking hard?" On the other hand, while I was glad to have retained my friends, I did go home with a couple less toenails than I started with.

* * *

The time had come to backpack. I had, by this time, enough knowledge of the Trail and confidence in my abilities to plan a thirty-mile hike with two nights of camping. Jen agreed to accompany me for a mid-September adventure from Fontana Dam to Clingmans Dome, at 6,600 feet—the highest point on the Appalachian Trail. In the planning stages, this did not seem like an overly ambitious proposition. In hindsight, my naivete was shocking.

I bought a two-person tent, figuring this would be a selling point for my friends to join me on future hikes. *You won't even have to bring a tent. You can sleep with me. Just bring yourself.* I also bought a three-season, lightweight sleeping bag but told the salesperson I didn't need a pad—I was roughing it! This trip was to be my last without a sleeping pad. I'd rather go without food.

The choice of backpacks was overwhelming, as were the price tags. I opted to rent one for a very reasonable price, which turned out to be a good decision, and I rented for years thereafter. Hiking technology changes rapidly, and materials improve in durability and lightness. I figured that, as sporadically as I hiked, any purchase I made would quickly become outdated.

> The packing list for this maiden voyage looked something like this and actually stayed pretty consistent over the years with the addition of cold-weather gear when necessary: backpack, tent, tent poles, sleeping bag, boots, socks, shirt(s), underwear, shorts, raincoat, camp shoes, first aid kit, headlamp, insect repellent, watch, rope, knife, matches, fire starter, spoon, cup, water purification tablets, baby powder, comb, toothbrush, toothpaste, toilet paper, food bag, water bottles, maps, phone and charger, compass, toilet paper, wallet. It wasn't unusual at this time for a backpack with camping gear, food, and water to weigh forty pounds or more. Nowadays, with the popularity of ultralight gear, that weight would be considered ridiculous. Base weight now can be as little as eight pounds.

Our friend, Denise Wolfe, signed on for the adventure and asked if her niece, Heather, could tag along. *Perfect!* Because Heather lived in Raleigh, North Carolina, and she would be driving over solo, we would have two cars, solving the omnipresent shuttle problem.

Nervous and excited, we arrived at Clingmans Dome parking lot midday Friday. Heather—tall, sweet, shy, late twenties—was punctual to the minute. We enthusiastically loaded our gear into her car and headed to Fontana Dam to begin what I now call "a learning experience." Jen refers to it as our trip to the "Cussin' Mountains."

Have I mentioned the summer of 2007 was hot and dry? Hell-hot and bone-dry is a more accurate description. The parking lot at Fontana Dam was deserted, and heat waves rose up from the asphalt in silvery ripples like a desert mirage. The ranger station was closed, but we dutifully completed the backcountry hiking permit and dropped it into a wooden box nailed to the building. A handwritten sign had been taped to the door:

Warning—Serious drought conditions. Water sources are dry.

"What do you think? How much water does everyone have?"
We took stock. Each of us had a couple of bottles.
"Maybe we should get some more here. In case the springs are dry."
Even though our packs were already ridiculously heavy, we thought this would be prudent, and we each added a couple more bottles purchased from the station's vending machine.

Lack of water, or dehydration, is a serious concern for any hiker. A general guideline is that you should drink about half a liter an hour. More, maybe a liter an hour, should be consumed when hiking in higher temperatures or in direct sunlight. This is a lot of water and an impractical amount to carry if you are out for more than a day or two. The good news is that the Appalachian Trail (except in times of drought) is home to rivers, creeks, and springs. The bad news is that this water must be treated in order to avoid serious illness from bacteria. In my early days of hiking, I carried iodine tablets, which are effective but slow-acting; you have to wait for about thirty minutes, and by then the water is tepid. Additionally, the tablets cause the water to have an unpleasant taste. Up until fairly recently, thru-hikers filtered their water using a system of what was really just a very fine strainer, a hose, and a rubber pouch. I found this method cumbersome. Nowadays, there are many options in addition to these two traditional ones. Many hikers use straws (with various brand names) purchased from any outfitter that basically fits over your water bottle cap and filters the water as you drink it. Some people prefer small battery-operated pens which are placed in the water and emit electric shocks to kill the bacteria. The problem with all of these methods is that none of them work unless you have water to start with.

The four of us walked across the concrete, half-mile, five-hundred-foot-high Fontana Dam, our backs already wet with sweat against our packs, and then entered dense woods. Moving slowly and breathing heavily, we immediately started the 2,500-foot ascent of Shuckstack Mountain, pausing frequently to sip water and swat at the gnats swarming our faces. Encumbered as we were by the heaviness of our packs and the physical challenge of the climb, it was hard to appreciate the serenity of the peaceful woods or the magnitude of the ridgeline views.

The first major "What the fuck?" incident happened only a few miles into our hike.

"Ow! Shit! Oh, no-no-no!"

Jen, several yards behind me, had stepped into a yellow jacket nest. Yellow jackets construct their nests in holes or indentations in the ground, where they quite happily live a commune-like life-style—eating, working, making love—until some unsuspecting large mammal steps into their home.

I turned around at Jen's shouts to see her running toward me and slapping at her lower body.

"Run!" she yelled. "It's bees or something!"

Heather and Denise, who were just behind Jen, were forewarned and stepped off the path. A swarm of yellow jackets was actually *chasing* Jen down the trail. Several had landed on her exposed calves and shins, and some were clinging to her thick, wool socks. We encircled Jen and managed to help rid her of the demons, but not before they inflicted several stings, leaving painful red welts.

There was nothing to do but soldier on. At least this little diversion took our minds off the heat, our thirst, and the steep climb.

Dusk was falling when we arrived at Mollie's Ridge, where guidebooks will tell you there is a shelter and a stream. I don't recall the shelter. I assume it was there. But I can tell you for a fact that if there had ever been a stream, all that remained of it was a dry memory. We discovered a rusty pipe sticking out the side of a ditch and emitting a droplet of water every couple of minutes, so we placed a cooking pot under it and hoped for a yield. Then, exhausted, we made our first camp on the AT.

Denise and Heather had a cheap, heavy tent that someone loaned them. Jen and I set up my new blue High Sierra, and after a bite to eat and a rehash of the day's adventure, we crawled into our new accommodations.

I was tired and sore and simply could not get comfortable on the hard ground. Kind Jen (no doubt disturbed by my constant tossing and turning) offered to share her sleeping pad. Over my false protestations, she convinced me if each of us used half the pad maybe we could both get at least a little sleep. We placed the pad crossways instead of head-to-toe so that our bruised hips—the achiest part of our bodies because they had borne the brunt of our forty-pound packs on this ten-mile day—had at least a little cushion.

* * *

The canopy of dense tree cover, surrounded by tall mountains, blocked the dawn. I was reluctant to stir after the restless night, when finally my eyes and mind recognized daylight.

"Jen," I whispered softly. "You awake?"

"Yeah, sort of. Is it time to get up?"

The first decision of the day, and I wasn't sure I was ready to make it.

We had twenty miles remaining to reach the summit of Clingmans, and we were under no illusion they would be easy. We broke camp—later than we'd planned—and checked the maps for potential water sites. There were many possibilities, but we were not optimistic; the pot we had placed under the slowly dripping pipe fourteen hours earlier now held a half-inch of brown, mosquito-blown liquid.

We hoisted our packs, which felt like they had grown even heavier during the night, and began climbing what seemed to be a never-ending series of ups and downs on our fifteen-mile journey to Silers Bald. At least, that was our goal.

We hiked on, crossing Russell Field Trail, Eagle Creek Trail, and other spots where a tiny blue droplet on our maps indicated we'd find water, yet we found none, and the day continued to grow hotter. We trudged along at a very slow pace—maybe a mile an hour—over unnamed knob after unnamed knob, each of us lost in her own thoughts, the woods thick and close with humidity and the odor of musk. The Smokies have a sort of foreboding aura in late summer, as if the mountains do not want us there. They seem to say, "You have taken our native people, brought blight to our trees, dammed up our rivers, and hunted out our animals. Now leave us in peace."

Indeed, in late morning, we encountered a most unwelcoming creature. To be fair, he is a very misunderstood fellow and perfectly harmless if left alone. Still, there is probably nothing that says, "Go away," like a large rattlesnake coiled up dead center in your path. We all happened to be close together at the time, saw him more or less simultaneously, and came to a screeching halt. I am certainly glad to yield the right of way to all creatures (the snake was there first) and informed him and my colleagues of the plan.

"*Bonjour, mon ami.* We are just going to step off the trail here, give you a wide berth, and be on our way. *A bientot.*"

As we were gingerly moving forward, Heather, who was never able to later articulate her reasons for doing so, suddenly started spraying the snake with her water bottle.

"Heather, don't! What are you doing? You'll piss him off!" we all yelled at her.

I don't believe the water hurt the snake. He may even have enjoyed it. He certainly had no visible reaction. But later, as our thirst became more excruciating, Heather came to regret wasting even a few drops of water on a snake who was, after all, just minding his own business.

Snakes are very common on the Appalachian Trail. Rarely did a day pass on the Trail when I didn't see at least one snake. The good news is that most I encountered were small harmless black snakes that quickly slithered across the path and disappeared into the undergrowth. The bad news is that there are three species of venomous snakes indigenous to the Appalachians: the timber rattler, the copperhead, and the water moccasin. But again, like most things in nature, these reptiles are usually harmless if left alone. You have nothing they want, and they will not be aggressive unless provoked or startled. A bite from a venomous snake can be dangerous—although rarely fatal—and if you are bitten, you should of course seek medical attention. Some hikers carry snake-bite kits.

A friend told me about an incident that happened to her on the Trail as she squatted to pee in the bushes. A two-foot-long snake (my friend, in her shock, did not even attempt to identify the species) slithered whiplike between her legs, its tail flicking her ass. This is an image I cannot unsee in my mind.

A couple of hours later, another denizen of the forest quite literally crossed our path. I was in the lead with Heather close behind. As we rounded a switchback on the descent of Thunderhead Mountain, a black bear hurried left to right across the trail a few yards in front of us.

"Bear!" I hollered back to Jen and Denise, but our *Ursus americanus* friend had already disappeared into the woods. Not very big, this young lady was probably a yearling, and she seemed frightened. She did not look directly at us even though we were very near to her. Bears do not see very well anyway, or so I am told. I believe she heard us coming (or more likely smelled us) and was trying to get out of our way when we rounded the bend more quickly than she had anticipated. Maybe she had been told by her mother not to make eye contact with humans, as they can be dangerous and unpredictable creatures.

This day seemed interminable, and our pace slowed to perhaps a half mile an hour. At times, the steeply ascending trail seemed almost completely vertical, but descents offered no relief to our screaming thighs and calves. They only served to remind us we'd have to go back up.

The late afternoon turned into early evening, and with few landmarks to determine our exact location, I had no good way of knowing how far we were from the campsite at Silers Bald. Because of our slow pace, I couldn't count on the normal calculation of two miles an hour either. I was concerned about injury if we had to stumble along these rocky trails in the dark.

Just as dusk was truly setting in, we met up with a group of southbound hikers. Three or four twenty-something-year-old men cheerfully informed us they were out for a couple of days' ramble. With their tidy packs and expensive-looking clothes, they might have been models for a Patagonia catalog. We must have appeared disheveled and inexperienced with our cumbersome packs and mosquito-bitten legs. We chatted about the lack of water and the difficulty of the hike. Denise mentioned we planned to stay the night at Silers Bald. A startled silence followed, and I began to have a sinking feeling.

The guys sprightly went on their way wishing us good luck and safe travels. One of them said sotto voce into my ear as he passed, "You have a long way to go."

I drew back, and our eyes met, his kind and concerned. I don't know how he pegged me as the leader of this ragtag group, but I nodded, mouthed the word "Thanks," and silently conveyed to him, I hope, that we would be okay.

* * *

Occasionally, and without reproach, Jen, Denise, or Heather would wonder aloud, "How much farther, you think?" or "Surely just up this hill?"

Finally, as we were digging flashlights out of our packs at a fairly level and relatively wide section of the trail, I said, "Girls, we need to make a decision."

They listened quietly as I stated the obvious. "It's getting dark, the trail is not going to get easier, and I think we have a ways, maybe miles, to Silers Bald. We've been walking for eleven hours. We're hungry, we're thirsty, we're tired."

Great nods of agreement.

"So I think we can do one of two things: we can keep hiking tonight as long as we are able, or we can stop right here and make camp."

Heads tilted in consideration.

"The longer we hike tonight, the less miles we have to do tomorrow, and the sooner we make Clingmans Dome."

True, true.

"On the other hand, if we stop here, we'll be fresher in the morning, can maybe make better time, and Clingmans Dome is not going anywhere."

The vote was unanimous. With groans of relief, we slid our packs from our bruised shoulders and dropped them to the ground.

There are numerous options regarding where you lay your head for an evening on the Appalachian Trail. The first and most obvious option is the shelters and lean-tos. But sometimes these are small or crowded, and trail etiquette suggests that although they are technically available on a first-come-first-serve basis, thru-hikers have first dibs. Also, one may not be conveniently situated when you are ready to go night-night.

Almost all hikers, including thru-hikers, carry a lightweight tent in case shelters aren't available or desirable. Most shelter sites have a couple of flat sites or even a raised wooden platform in the area to pitch a tent. The AT goes through state parks or national parks where designated campgrounds offer numerous campsites and often bathhouses and other amenities. However, these are fairly few and far between. They usually charge a fee out of the range of many hikers' budgets.

All along the trail are what are known as primitive campsites. These can range from official sites with room for several tents to simply a tiny area flattened by the stamping of boots and cleared of rocks and roots by a hiker's hands. The former are usually marked on maps and described in guidebooks; the latter are not. These are usually (and hopefully) located near a stream or offer a nice spot to view a sunrise or sunset.

Stealth camping is a tricky term, but it is sometimes an option, and while usually not illegal, it is often frowned upon. It basically means to set up camp in an undesignated (and possibly unallowable) location either on or off the Trail.

To *cowboy camp* means to simply spread out your sleeping bag on the ground without benefit of tent or shelter and throw yourself to the mercy of the elements and night critters. I never personally exercised this final option.

To tent-camp anywhere except in a specific, designated site is not allowed in the Great Smoky Mountains National Park, for such valid reasons as the detriment to flora and fauna and the danger of wildfire. I do not recommend to readers they just stop and camp anywhere that pleases them, and I sincerely apologize to our park stewards for our transgression. Hopefully, in a small way, I can compensate for my crime by letting others know they can't be greedy in these mountains. If you normally hike a fifteen-mile day, just acknowledge that's not going to happen in the Smokies. Cut your ambition in half and plan accordingly.

Jen and I set up my tent just off the trail and unloaded our packs. Denise and Heather discussed cooking a freeze-dried meal, but we tried to dissuade them. I argued that it would take too much water, and we weren't even supposed to be sleeping there, much less cooking. Jen pointed out that the odor of cooking food would attract bears or other animals. This argument won the day, and we sat on the ground to eat crackers, dried fruit, and candy. Jen remarked that Denise and Heather had yet to set up their tent.

"Well, yeah, about that," Denise said softly, looking at the ground. "We don't have it anymore."

"What! Why? Where is it?"

"We left it this morning at that shelter we passed."

Jen and I were stunned.

"It was just so fricking heavy, and we knew there'd be no rain, so we figured we didn't really need it…" Heather's voice trailed off.

"But where are you going to sleep?" I asked.

"Oh, we'll just roll out our sleeping bags here next to your tent. We'll be fine!" Denise tried to sound upbeat.

Okay, whatever. Jen and I crawled into our tent, lay on top of our sleeping bags (it was too hot to even think about getting into them), and arranged ourselves over the shared sleeping pad. We heard Denise and Heather alternately giggle and groan as they settled in close by. Our conversations tapered off, drowsiness crept over us, and I believed we would all live to hike another day. Then our tent was pelted with what I first thought were hailstones.

What the heck?

"Heather, Denise, y'all okay?"

"It's nuts or berries from the trees."

Jen sat up next to me and leaned out the flap to look skyward. Nothing.

We were trying to relax back into sleepiness when—*pop pop pop!* Another round assaulted us. Acorns, we determined.

This went on all night. If you find it hard to believe acorns could make that much racket falling naturally and occasionally from the tree branches overhead, you would be right. They were being *launched* at us like rocket-propelled grenades by what, we eventually gathered, were either squirrels or chipmunks. We had no defense or even a right to a defense. We were in their territory, after all, and we were utterly defeated.

✻ ✻ ✻

On Sunday morning, after almost no sleep thanks to the squirrel bombardiers, we gathered our gear and, with moods somewhat lifted by the knowledge we were to reach our car this day, walked on. The water situation was dire by this time. Each of us had less than a full bottle and little hope of finding more. The temperature had not abated. We reminded each other to drink sparingly, and I offered a tip: take a small drink of water and hold it in your mouth for as long as possible before you swallow it. "This is what the Maasai people do in the desert," I pontificated.

We hiked several miles to Silers Bald, where the spring was dry, and then up and over and down a knob to Double Spring Gap. Nothing at either of its springs. Our final two and a half miles were the 1,100-foot ascent from the gap to the summit of Clingmans Dome. This hike is a series of undulating, deeply forested, unnamed mountains as far as the eye can see. I say these mountains are unnamed, but Jen forever christened them "The Cussin' Mountains," as in "You goddamn motherfucker! You son of a bitch! I hate you, mothertrucker!" Each time, especially in the last mile or so, we'd climb a mountain, thinking surely the next one would be Clingmans. Okay, then the next one. "You motherfucking piece of shit."

Occasionally, fat purple millipedes or centipedes inched across the trail at our feet, their pace seemingly faster than ours.

Denise mused aloud, "Those things look pretty juicy."

I believe she was actually considering eating one, and I wondered if thirst had driven us all somewhat mad.

In early afternoon, we rested briefly on a ridge that offered a stunning panoramic view.

"Look, there it is! There's Clingmans Dome!" I pointed to a tall peak in the distance.

We could just make out the observation tower on top of it. I tried to sound positive and upbeat, but really, I was afraid to meet my friends' eyes, because even though the sighting of Clingmans Dome was a good thing, we could hardly ignore the several mountains that stood between it and us.

"Way over there?" Denise asked almost tearfully.

"Hey," I said, only half-jokingly, "there's no crying on the AT."

We lifted our chins, straightened our shoulders, tightened our pack straps, and climbed onward and upward, arriving at Clingmans Dome a couple of hours later with self-conscious grace and dignity. We asked a passerby to snap our picture standing by the tower. He obliged, and as he handed my camera back to me, Denise stepped off the Trail and burst into tears.

※ ※ ※

We headed to my car in the parking lot, down a half mile paved road alive with tourists walking to and from the observation tower. I heard one woman say to her young son as we approached them from behind, "Some folks carry tents and stuff and come up here to hike and camp in the woods for days and days."

"Really?" he said. "Wow, that's so cool."

"Look, here's some now."

She gently pulled him aside by his shoulders, and they reverentially let us pass with our red and dirty faces, our legs scratched and insect-bitten, hair sweat-plastered to our foreheads, clothes and boots filthy. I never felt so proud.

We took Heather back to her car at Fontana Dam and stopped in the town of Cherokee for a meal. Perhaps because we had been in the fresh air for seventy-two hours, the restaurant and its occupants seemed sad and tired.

"You know, I don't think this place is very clean," Denise commented when she returned to our table from the salad bar. This from a woman who, not five hours earlier, had seriously considered eating a worm.

I laughed. *Well, there you go; it's all relative.*

I thought of this again the next week when I flew to New York for an overnight work trip. The crowded streets, the bustling airports, the hectic pace of my scheduled meetings and interviews stood in stark contrast to the solitary paths, the lonely peaks, the plodding boot steps, and heavy breathing. The AT and the biggest city in the US could not be more different from each other, yet each has its charms and its challenges. One is no better or worse than the other, just different.

* * *

For Tim's fiftieth birthday in early October, we took a weekend getaway to Asheville, North Carolina. The weather was early autumn crisp, and the trees were stunning in their peak of color. After quality time together on Saturday, we each felt a little less guilty for pursuing our separate interests on Sunday. Here was yet another opportunity for a hike.

Tim drove me to the Appalachian Trail near Hot Springs. This was some seventy miles north of Clingmans Dome, where my last hike ended, but I could fill in the skipped section at a later date. The hike I planned now from Hot Springs to Tanyard Gap was only a little over five miles, which meant I could meet Tim at the trail end in early afternoon after his golf game. I gave him careful directions about where to meet, and then he drove off to do his thing and left me to do mine.

I have never had a lovelier day or enjoyed a hike more. This is low-altitude walking, ascending about 2,200 feet out of the French Broad River basin to Tanyard Gap. I scuffled through fallen leaves, almost knee-high, to arrive at Lovers Leap, a popular day-hike destination for folks using the Lovers Leap Trail from Hot Springs. I sat on the ledge with my face turned up to the sun, watching hawks circle in the blue sky and glancing down at the shiny ribbon of the French Broad.

The words of John Muir ran through my mind: "Keep close to Nature's heart…and break clear away, once in a while, and climb a mountain or spend a week in the woods. Wash your spirit clean."

This little hike led to one joy after another—old logging roads, rhododendron tunnels, ponds teeming with turtles, amazing views, grassy meadows, and at the end of the hiker bridge crossing US 25, my husband patiently waiting, right on time.

❋ ❋ ❋

Heather and Denise had recovered from our great September adventure in the Smokies, and we planned a trip for November 10–11, Veterans Day weekend. Denise and I would drive over from Franklin, and Heather from Raleigh, so once again, we would have two cars and no shuttle worries. We chose to hike from Max Patch to Lemon Gap to Hot Springs, about twenty miles in two days, ending where my solo October hike had started. This would close part of the gap I had skipped after Clingmans, which would give me the satisfaction of checking off that section of the map.

After a long and confusing drive on rural roads from Newport, Tennessee, Denise and I met Heather at Lemon Gap. We left a car there and then drove several winding miles to the parking lot near Max Patch. From there, we walked half a mile up to the summit where the AT crosses. At 4,500 feet, Max Patch is a sunny highland field with clear views of the valley below and is very popular as a picnic site. Lovers lolled on blankets, families flew kites, and hang gliders gracefully floated about in the air currents like Icarian hippies. The trail is marked by posts set into the ground, as there are no trees on the bald, and we happily followed these until they disappeared into the northern woods.

The weather was mild for mid-November, and our packs were light without camping gear. The hike to our car at Lemon Gap was an easy six-mile descent where, in contrast to the revelry at Max Patch, we found serenity in the footbridges over streams, in the tunnels of rhododendron, and in the ridge views of the French Broad River. After the oppressiveness of the Smokies during the drought-stricken summer and fall, the North Carolina woods seemed open and friendly. The short hike was worth the long drive, we all agreed, and when we finished at Lemon Gap, we set off in good spirits for rest and refreshment in the town of Hot Springs.

We had difficulty finding accommodations for the night, maybe because it was a holiday weekend. We ended up being ridiculously overcharged for a shitty room in a dumpy one-story motel, which I feel sure has long since been closed by the fire marshal. There were two double beds with lumpy mattresses, flat pillows, and the kind of satiny coverlet that makes you glad you don't have a black light. Near the front door, a smoke detector, sans battery, hung from an exposed wire several inches from the water-stained ceiling. And not surprisingly, there was a prefabricated shower perched in a corner next to a tiny closet with a sink and toilet.

The one redeeming quality of this motel was that it was only steps away from what appeared to be the happening place on a Saturday night in Hot Springs. I know it was the place for us; the beer was cold and the pizza delicious. Young people played pool and old men sat at the bar. A very good-looking guy, dressed in the uniform of tight T-shirt and sliding jeans, flirted with Heather. By the time we finished our dinner, a five-piece band had set up, tuned up, drunk up, and was belting out some Tom Petty. They sounded pretty good, and we decided to stay for a few more minutes.

About four hours later, Denise and I, apparently remembering we had a fifteen-mile hike on the agenda for tomorrow, made our way through the detritus of two-wheeled tricycles, motorcycle parts, and old shoes strewn about on the narrow concrete strip outside the motel rooms. During the night, through uncomfortable sleep, we heard Heather saying good night to her new friend outside the torn screen window under the unshaded dangling bulb.

We hiked fourteen miles the next day from Lemon Gap to Hot Springs in quiet, shady solitude. Thankfully, in view of our somewhat hungover conditions, the weather was soft, the mountains gentle, the trail easy and forgiving.

This was the perfect setting for reflection on all the milestones this year had brought—on and off the Trail, particularly Melanie's sixteenth and Tim's fiftieth birthdays and my first camping trip on the AT, with its agonies and pleasures.

Melanie had survived quite well during my absence for seven separate hiking trips, and because none of these trips had been of long duration, I really did not take too much time off work. By taking the opportunities as they became available and combining hikes with other commitments, I was able to complete well over a hundred miles this year. While this was certainly an improvement, it was not lost on me that I still had a very, very long way to hike to Maine. But as I had said to my friends in the Smokies about Clingmans Dome, Mount Katahdin wasn't going anywhere. I would climb all the mountains between here and there, and if detours presented themselves along the way, I would take them also.

CHAPTER 4

2008 (135 MILES)

HOT SPRINGS, NORTH CAROLINA, TO ALLEN GAP, NORTH CAROLINA

HUGHES GAP, TENNESSEE, TO ELK PARK, NORTH CAROLINA

WIND GAP, PENNSYLVANIA, TO FOX GAP, PENNSYLVANIA

NEWFOUND GAP, TENNESSEE, TO LOW GAP TRAIL, TENNESSEE

LOW GAP TRAIL, TENNESSEE, TO MAX PATCH, NORTH CAROLINA

ALLEN GAP, NORTH CAROLINA, TO DEVIL FORK GAP, NORTH CAROLINA

DEVIL FORK GAP, NORTH CAROLINA, TO SPIVEY GAP, NORTH CAROLINA f the circumstances of 2007 had begun to teach me that to survive is to adapt, then that little adage would ring true in a completely literal sense this year. My familiarization with the Trail would only increase my fondness for it even as some sections would remind me that more difficult hikes awaited. Also, there is nothing like an assignment to a war zone to remind one that, while the journey might be the adventure, coming home is the reward.

My ever-increasing circle of hiking buddies grew by two on the first hike of 2008. Heather, who is a physician assistant, called me as I planned a January trip.

"Hey, do you mind if my friend Cecilia comes along? She's a doctor I work with."

"Oh, by all means," I answered. "You can't have too much medical expertise on the trail."

"Oh," Heather went on. "Can I bring my dog too?"

Jen and I met the crew from Raleigh in Hot Springs on a mid-January weekend. Cecilia is a happy person with a wandering spirit. Sebastian was a medium-sized, sweet-faced border collie with a herding instinct.

On Saturday afternoon, we hiked five and a half miles from Hot Springs to Tanyard Gap. This was the same hike I had done the previous October, but it is a beautiful section of the AT, and to do it now in winter would bring a whole new perspective.

We walked along the snow-covered path, happy to be with old friends and meeting new ones. Sebastian was only comfortable when we four humans were all in front of him and reasonably close together. If we got too strung out on the winding path, he would block the passage of the leader to slow her down, hurry to the back of the pack, and gently nip at the heels of the straggler.

On Sunday we continued north nine miles from Tanyard Gap to Allen Gap. Both days' hikes were low-elevation ridge-walking at its finest. Major street access at the gaps made this a perfect choice for cold-weather hiking, because we didn't have to worry about impassable snow-covered service roads. The cold woods smelled of clean evergreen and things buried deep under months of fallen leaves. Our breath was foggy and white in the still air, and our boots tramped through small puddles still rimmed with fragile ice.

This was a peaceful and restful weekend, and I thought that the Trail, in spite of its potential dangers, had come to mean a safe harbor for me, a secure mooring to which I could always return. Here was a place of security where nature, even with her caprices, offered consistency and permanency.

* * *

In mid-February I learned an assignment to Iraq was possible. By early April, the possibility had turned into reality, and the departure date was set for May 2. I would be overseas for about a month—not a long TDY (temporary duty) by FBI standards but certainly long enough to merit a farewell party, hiking the AT for two days with my friends.

Two newcomers joined Jen, Smokin' Goat, Denise Wolfe, and me. Katie, Denise Wolfe's nineteen-year-old daughter, is an athletic nature lover, but our old friend Denise Miller is a city girl, a young woman with zero experience in the woods. Nevertheless, she wanted to show her patriotic support of me by, as she put it, peeing outside where any old bug or snake could bite her on the butt.

Our medics and our shepherd, Cecilia, and Heather and Sebastian, made the trip west from Raleigh, for a grand total of eight happy hikers and one delighted dog.

We began Day One at Hughes Gap and hiked nine miles from there to the Tennessee–North Carolina border at Carvers Gap. (The Trail often crosses and sometimes even follows the state line. At some points, you will have one foot in Tennessee and the other in North Carolina.) The weather was very cold for mid-April but clear, and the physical challenge kept us all warm. We climbed Beartown Mountain to five thousand feet and Roan High Knob to 6,300 feet. We broke it up nicely with a rest stop where a few foundation stones are all that remain of the famed Cloudland Hotel that operated from 1885 to 1910. Denise Miller, more at home in a shopping mall than in the great outdoors, bopped along with earphones cranked up to the tunes of Kanye. I believe she was pretending to be in an aerobics class.

We ended our day at Roan Mountain State Park, Tennessee, where we stayed in a fully equipped, very comfortable cabin with plenty of room for us all. We happily cooked and lounged about on the porch or, as the sun disappeared and the temperatures dropped, in the living room and bedrooms. Like teenagers at a slumber party, we giggled and gossiped until sleepiness overtook us. One by one, we dropped off, and Sebastian could finally relax.

* * *

On Day Two we hiked thirteen miles from Carvers Gap to US 19 near Elk Park. We stepped onto the Trail into what promised to be another very cold day. Denise Miller had already left in one of the vehicles to return to Nashville, where her two very young children and anxious husband were waiting. Smokin' Goat couldn't shake the chill and returned to the car after a half mile or so, promising us a hot dinner at the cabin when we returned that evening. Though sad to not have her with us, our disappointment was mitigated by the knowledge that, among her many other artistic talents, Smokin' Goat is an excellent cook.

We remaining six walked through a winter wonderland of frozen rhododendron tunnels and Fraser firs. The hard frost had crystallized every stem, branch, leaf, needle, and bud into delicate icicles that were just beginning to melt and drip onto the crunchy trail. This section of the AT is in and of itself the answer to the question of why someone would hike it. It is simply stunning.

We tramped across mysterious balds (including Jane Bald, which my Gove book endearingly tells us was named for a woman who died there of milk sickness), where no trees are found and the blazes are painted on posts. We strolled along ridges with our eyes trained to the panoramic views of Grandfather Mountain and his kin. Soaring falcons and hawks dipped their wings in tribute to us, and blueberry bushes nodded under coats of moisture. We passed a charming shelter converted from an old barn, hopped across occasional boulder fields, and skirted abandoned iron mines. It seemed we were always pointing out one interesting thing after another to each other, and such was the diversity of this section.

Evening found us once again in our cozy Roan Mountain cabin with supper on the stove and warm beds waiting. If contentment means being satisfied with what you have, then by god, I was one happy woman.

*　*　*

I left Franklin in early May, bound for the FBI training academy at Quantico, where I met the three teammates who would be my constant companions for the next thirty days in the Middle East. We were briefed on our assignment, outfitted at the local Gander Mountain, and provided with all the necessary forms and clearances. On Sunday afternoon, we managed to catch a Nationals baseball game—fittingly, that most American of sports—and then there was nothing to do but catch our flight to Kuwait City, where we stayed for a couple of days awaiting military transport to Baghdad.

Our FBI teams, plus thirty or forty military personnel and a handful of civilians, were corralled into a hangar at the American base in Kuwait to be dispatched to various posts in Iraq. In helmets and vests, we were herded onto a C-130 like so many cattle going to slaughter. Our flight attendants carried MP5 submachine guns instead of drink trays and wore glum expressions rather than perky grins. They let us know the flight would be loud, bumpy, and low, and if we puked, we would clean it up.

Once we landed at the airfield in Iraq, each of us humped our seriously overweight duffel bags crammed with boots and helmets, antiballistic steel-plated vests, laptops, training materials, and personal items to a transport vehicle that would take us to the American embassy in Baghdad. The days of shouldering a heavy backpack on the AT had slightly prepared me for this heavy burden, and now the familiar trepidation of upcoming hardships fluttered in my guts.

The intense colors of the mountains in my mind were replaced with the reality that is Iraq. The low, sand-colored buildings rise out of the sand-colored earth to meet the sand-colored sky. On the government bases, the squat, prefab trailers are topped with sandbags, and desert camouflage netting is draped over anything standing still. Off the military installations, the scenery is no brighter. The dark clothing of the native population offers no more variation in hue than the tan uniforms of the soldiers.

The occasional stunted tree or drooping bush appears to have just given up and surrendered to its fate of death by dust. On base, the paths from housing units to dining hall to gym are finely graveled to delineate them from the surrounding desert soil, just as erosion-resistant grasses are planted along sections of the Appalachian Trail to keep it from fading back into the forest.

Heat and thirst were constants. Daily temperatures easily reached 120 degrees, and we wore thick khaki pants and heavy vests. Sweat trickling down our backs was cruelly captured between skin and Kevlar, as it had been captured between our shirts and packs during the drought-stricken days on the AT. The oppressive heat mocked the miserable conditions. It is not enough that this country has suffered so many years of war, and its clinics, schools, stores, and houses are literally shells. No, it also has to endure a climate so inhospitable that even the stray, starving dogs can't find a shady spot to seek comfort.

Our military friends told us that to survive in a war zone, one must live in this moment while preparing for the next. Nothing is easy, but everything is simple. We were admonished to "Stay focused—one thing at a time." I rose early in the morning, lonely in my assigned trailer, and thought about the next right thing to do. *Brush my teeth. Okay, open a bottle of water, pour a little over toothbrush, squeeze out some toothpaste. Check. Get dressed. Check. Chapstick and knife in pocket. Check. Sidearm loaded. Check.*

This lesson has served me well on the AT, where tasks, though simple, are many, and if I don't concentrate on each one individually, things get done in an unorganized or slovenly manner. The actual hiking is usually an exception—picking up one foot and putting it down in front of the other is an accomplishment I managed to achieve at a relatively young age—and I can let my mind wander. But day's beginning and end require concentration because the mind and body are so fatigued it is tempting to just sit on a log and stare into the distance. *Take off boots. Put on camp shoes. Empty pack. Set up tent. Inflate sleeping bag. Check, check, check.*

Each day after breakfast, my colleagues and I loaded up our assigned vehicle with classroom materials and drove to an Iraqi police or military facility, passing through checkpoint after checkpoint. We taught interview and negotiations techniques in rooms where the electricity often failed, shutting down our PowerPoint presentations and leaving us to rely solely on our Arabic interpreters. Adaptation and flexibility here too were key.

At each workday's end, we returned to our base for a workout, a shower, dinner. The evenings were spent preparing the next day's lesson plan, reading, and responding to email from home, and on a few wonderful occasions, watching a movie or baseball game. Then—finally—to bed on the hard cot in the stuffy trailer, where my dreams were shot through with the smell of old boots and stale sweat. These odors were no different from what I would have found in my tent on the AT, but instead of the constant chirping of night insects, I heard only the whir of a departing helicopter.

❊ ❊ ❊

As the summer came on full force in Baghdad and our responsibilities there ended, we allowed our thoughts to turn stateside.

Reentry into my familiar world is always strange after a TDY. The reintroduction to color is the most striking example after spending months in the Middle East or North Africa. The grass is unbelievably green, as are the eyes of my husband. The white contrail of a plane is vivid against a cobalt-blue sky. Even the yellow stripes on the highway seem sparkling new and bright. I've often wondered aloud after returning from desert lands, "Did they just repaint this road?"

And, like when I return from a long AT hike, the rooms in my house seem big and spacious after staying in cramped quarters or in a small tent. Our domestic worlds shrink and expand to fit wherever we find ourselves.

❊ ❊ ❊

After catching up at work in Nashville, Tim, Melanie, and I headed to New York City, where Melanie was to attend, at no small cost to her parents, a summer journalism program at Columbia University.

We drove I-40 east to I-81 beyond Knoxville, then followed that interstate through western Virginia and central Maryland. This route roughly parallels about six hundred miles of the AT—the southern and middle spine of the Appalachian Mountains. I felt a new kinship with the mountains, a personal connection to and deeper appreciation for them instead of just being a passing admirer of the soft green ridges and peaks hazy with mists and clouds. This was mid-June, the height of the hiking season, and I was eager to join the community hidden in those woods.

After Melanie was safely ensconced in her Columbia dorm, Tim and I traveled to Yardley, Pennsylvania, to spend a few days with his brother's family. The AT is just a couple of hours' drive west of here, and I, of course, had brought along maps and gear. Leaving Tim to his clan, who politely declined the invitation to accompany me, I set out solo on a bright, sunny Tuesday morning to hike a section in the southeastern part of the state.

The eight miles from Wind Gap to Fox Gap looks fairly easy on paper, with almost no elevation change and a maximum altitude of 1,500 feet. I left my car at Fox Gap where the AT crosses a relatively well-traveled road. Surprisingly, I had some trouble getting a ride, although quite a few cars passed here compared to the isolation of road crossings in the Smokies. Perhaps these drivers weren't used to seeing hikers; this section is not known to be popular for day and weekend hikes. I soon realized why as I picked my way through eight miles of rocks varying in size from shoeboxes to Volkswagens. Every rock seemed to have been placed there by Lucifer himself—that one to stub your toe on, these to step between and break an ankle, this one to trip over and fall on your face.

For several hours, I stumbled, tripped, and fell—once fairly hard, face first, but thankfully onto what may have been the only patch of bare earth in the state of Pennsylvania—until I finally reached my car. This brush with the central Appalachian Trail left me apprehensive. I could only hope that my skills would improve, because I could clearly see that this adventure was not going to get any easier.

* * *

In mid-July, Denise Wolfe and a new recruit headed east from Franklin with me to whittle down some of the fifty-five miles I had skipped between Clingmans Dome and Max Patch. Allie, a neighborhood friend, fortyish at the time, is pretty, petite, and remarkably cheerful. Our medical support staff, Heather and Cecilia, would once again travel west from Raleigh to meet us.

We would skip the eight miles from Clingmans Dome to Newfound Gap because Jen really wanted to do that section, and I had promised I would wait until she could accompany me. We left Heather's car at Cosby Campground, twenty miles from Cherokee, North Carolina, on TN 32, and all five of us piled into my car to drive the winding roads back to Newfound Gap for the beginning of our twenty-five-mile hike.

Newfound Gap, with its scenic views and relative proximity to Gatlinburg, is a popular pull-off-the-road-and-take-a-picture spot in the Smoky Mountains National Park. Tourists milled about in the crowded parking lot as we tightened boot laces and hoisted packs, but few of the tennis shoe- or sandal-clad day travelers wanted to leave their air-conditioned SUVs and RVs for long on this very hot day. I couldn't blame them.

A *gap* usually describes a valley or low point between mountains, an obvious place for road crossings. In the case of Newfound Gap, it is something of a misnomer. Yes, at five thousand feet, it is a lower elevation than 6,500-foot Clingmans Dome to the south, but it is not in a deep valley or near a riverbed, where you would be more likely to find a geographically low point. On the other hand, a *dome* or *summit* will be your high points. A *ridge* is the line—at a fairly consistent elevation—between summits. Think of it as the crest or spine of the mountain. *Switchback* is a term used to describe a snaking path on the slope of a mountain. The path will double back on itself, often multiple times, to make the ascent or descent indirect instead of on a direct line. One dreaded word the AT hiker will hear is PUDS, an acronym for "Pointless Ups and Downs." This will describe a section of the Trail that seems to go on forever, hill after hill, crest after crest, with no particularly glorious feature to break the monotony.

We made good time along a pretty and well-maintained trail at about an average of a 5,500-feet altitude, but I don't want to minimize the difficulty. The ridges make constant one- or two- or three-hundred-foot changes in elevation and are often rocky and steep. The heat and burdensome packs, heavy with extra water, made for unpleasant personal conditions, but our group, to a woman, was upbeat and determined. Allie, who is athletic and fit but not an experienced backpacker, did not utter a word of complaint or regret. After the painfully long day of fifteen miles, we camped at Tricorner Knob Shelter, relieved the day was over but dreading the next.

Day Two promised to be just as hot as its predecessor, but we had the consolation of knowing we only had ten miles to Low Gap Trail, which we would follow to the car at Cosby Campground. No problem.

Hah!

Again the heat. Again the thirst. Again the heavy packs. Added to these woes, we had symptoms of altitude sickness—headache, fatigue, mild nausea, shortness of breath, but nothing sundown, cooler temps, and getting off the fricking mountains couldn't cure.

When we finally reached Low Gap Trail in late afternoon, we high-fived one another and, knowing we had just two and a half miles to go, set off briskly—only to come to a screeching halt. Low Gap Trail runs alongside Cosby Creek, and it is not so much a trail as it is a rocky, dry creek bed, the sole purpose of which seems to be to get from point A (the AT) to point B (the campground) in a straight downhill descent that punished our knees and forced our toes into the very limits of our boots. I sidestepped a good portion of this trail to ease the pressure but was nevertheless often near tears. Adding insult to injury, this wasn't the AT! It didn't even count. It was like kissing your brother.

We finally made it to the campground, and, oh, the joy of car camping cannot be overstated. Plenty of food and drinks in the cooler and a picnic table on which to spread the bounty. Denise fired up her Jetboil for our prepackaged pasta dinners. Not knowing much about camp stoves, I dumped my mac and cheese concoction into the boiling water.

"No!" Denise yelled too late. "You can only put water in there. Anything else will ruin it."

"Oh, my god," I exclaimed. "I am so sorry."

We tried to clean up the mess, but the damage was done. All I could do was promise Denise I'd get her a new one.

Until I reached the White Mountains years later, this excursion reigned as one of the most difficult hikes I ever attempted. When I recently told Allie this, she grinned proudly and admitted it was the hardest thing she'd ever done. We laughed and agreed that the loss of a few toenails and one Jetboil was worth it.

* * *

In August, the mother of one of Melanie's friends joined Jen and me to hike twenty-five miles from Low Gap Trail to Max Patch, that delightful bald of hang gliders and jubilant picnickers. Lynn V. had the leanness and fortitude of a long-distance runner and the eagerness of a first-time AT hiker.

Cecilia, without Heather this time, met us at the Max Patch parking lot, where we dropped a car and headed back to Low Gap Trail, which I'd spent the previous four weeks dreading. To my surprise and gratitude, the reality was less dreadful than the anticipation.

Oh, it was up, up, up the rocky, seldom-traveled path, dense on either side with heavy undergrowth, but the aerobic huffing and puffing was easier to take than the aching knees and jammed toes of the July descent. We hiked two and a half miles unscathed to the AT, where we headed north.

We climbed gently along an enchanted pathway bordered by soft, emerald-colored mosses and patches of wildflowers at foot level; laurel, rhododendron, and blueberry bushes at hip or shoulder level; and above our heads, the magnolia and tulip trees with dense leaves the color of dark jade. Our world was a green room with occasional glimpses of blue ceiling above.

A couple of miles into the hike, we arrived at a blue-blazed trail leading to Mount Cammerer, which is a half mile off the AT and boasts a stone observation tower. I'm sure it offers magnificent views, but we unanimously voted to skip this little side trip. That is my standard course of action when invited to add extra mileage to my day (unless food and drink are involved, and then I'm sometimes willing to make an exception).

Davenport Gap, at two thousand feet, is the end of the Smoky Mountains for the northbound AT hiker. The descent to it is rocky and uneven, with boulders the size of armoires littering the path, but we pressed on to Painter Branch campsite, four miles north of the gap and two thousand feet higher.

Mercifully, on this hot August day, our tent sites were alongside a babbling brook. We sat on the banks and blissfully removed boots and socks and…wait…*what the heck?*

"Good god, Lynn, what happened to your feet?" I was horrified. "They are bloody stumps!"

Lynn smiled and then grimaced as she gingerly dipped her feet into the creek. "Yeah, I think I wore the wrong socks."

She had not uttered a word of complaint all day, but her socks, thin like those that runners wear, were literally dripping with bright-red blood. I, as ringleader, was ashamed I had not provided her with better information about footwear.

Blisters are a fact of life for a long-distance hiker and perhaps even more so for a section hiker. If you're only hiking every few months, your feet do not develop the calluses that thru-hikers build up. You would think this is largely a shoe issue, but there are as many different opinions about footwear as there are hikers on the Trail. I prefer a decent high-top traditional boot that provides some ankle support. This may just be a psychological crutch, but I'll take help wherever I can get it.

Anyway, I think it's all about the socks, and this is where you don't want to be chintzy. Get some good, name-brand wool socks designed for hiking, and don't forget liners. If at all possible, change your socks every day. Another tip: as soon as you feel a blister forming—a hot spot—stop walking and slap on a Band-Aid or some moleskin. You might think, *Ho hum, it's not so bad. I'll wait till we stop for lunch, la de da de da.* Too late; the damage will be done by then.

Okay, enough about *that.* Rest assured, I won't be giving you a lecture about underwear and chafing. Just two words: baby powder.

We nursed Lynn's feet as best we could and had a fine hike the next day, including two, four-thousand-foot peaks, Snowbird Mountain, and Harmon Den Mountain. Lynn, sporting borrowed socks and a chin-up attitude, hiked with determination and joy. Middle-aged women have a more cheerful stoicism than any other demographic; there's not much they can't do if they put their minds to it.

* * *

Our August finish at Max Patch had tied up some loose ends. Except for the elusive eight-mile Clingmans Dome to Newfound Gap section, I had hiked the entire AT from Springer Mountain to Allen Gap, a total of almost three hundred miles.

Jen and I were able to get away in September, but we wanted to hike more than eight miles. So we decided to continue north from Allen Gap and put off the Clingmans Dome descent once again. (It would in fact be several years before we finally managed to check that off the to-do list.)

We drove over on a Saturday morning and, having only one car, hired a shuttle driver at an outfitter in Hot Springs and were on the Trail by early afternoon. The AT from Allen Gap to Devil Fork Gap is a little over twenty miles through the Cherokee National Forest and includes two, four-thousand-foot peaks. There are several nice campsites and a couple of shelters along this long, lovely hike, and we stopped after a few hours, leaving the bulk of the hike for the following day.

On Sunday morning, we rose from our tent fairly early, looking forward to a long, quiet day with a hot meal and a soft bed awaiting us at the end. The weather was North Carolina mid-September perfection, but we encountered very few people in this remote area except for the occasional southbound thru-hiker.

These guys and gals are easy to recognize. Having walked 1,800 miles from Mount Katahdin in four or five months, they are vacant-eyed and inwardly focused, their packs and clothes dirty and worn. In this hot month, the heavily bearded men are shirtless, their stomachs concave. The women wear athletic bras and shorts, their long, tangled hair piled on their heads, their legs hard and muscled. We spoke with a couple about the Smoky Mountains they would soon face. They used as few words as possible. If a nod or shake of the head would suffice, there was no need to waste energy on speaking.

"Are they as hard as we've heard?" the young man asked.

"Oh, they're tough, really tough." I suppose I was not very encouraging.

These were people who had hiked from Maine. If I knew then what I know now about the White Mountains, I would have told them the Smokies were a piece of whoopee pie after what they'd been through.

The number of people who attempt to thru-hike the Appalachian Trail consistently rises, but the percentage of people who complete it has seen a recent decrease. In the decade of the 2010s, between two thousand and three thousand eager, excited hikers began their 2,200-mile journeys each year, and about one in four completed it within roughly four to six months. The majority start at Springer Mountain, Georgia, and hike north; they are known as northbounders or NOBOS. A lesser number, the southbounders or SOBOS, will start at Mount Katahdin, Maine, and walk south. There is also an option known as a flip-flop hike. This means that the hiker will start midway—usually at Harpers Ferry, West Virginia—and hike north to Katahdin. He or she will then go back to Harpers Ferry (via car or plane or bus) and hike south to Springer. There are many variations of the flip-flop hike. For example, you might start at Springer and walk halfway, then get a ride to Katahdin and walk back to your halfway point. A decision to choose this option is usually based on weather. Katahdin closes in early October at the latest, while the southern terminus (even though the weather can certainly be cold in late fall) remains open. It doesn't really matter what direction you choose. Anyone who walks the entire trail in one season has the honor to call him or herself a thru-hiker and is considered a part of the community.

Jen and I rhythmically hiked for seven or eight miles, lost in our own thoughts and at utter peace with the world. This euphoric zombie state was rudely interrupted by what sounded like the motor of a chainsaw.

I was a few yards ahead of Jen on a wide trail bordered by dense laurel and tangled undergrowth. The noise grew louder and seemed to be approaching from head-on. I stopped in my tracks, confused, then turned and pushed Jen into the woods. "Get off the trail!" I mouthed, the sound of my words lost in the motor roar.

I stepped aside but remained just at the edge of the path as two four-wheeled ATVs—one behind the other, the trail barely wide enough to accommodate them—pulled up in front of me. The drivers silenced the engines.

A thirtyish-year-old man with long, straggly brown hair and a thin, drooping mustache was driving the lead ATV; a strikingly good-looking teenage boy straddling it behind him. Two burly men sat astride the second ATV. Like the first pair, they wore camouflage jackets and pants. Two-way radios or GPS devices crackled from the handlebars.

These men were hard-eyed, unsmiling, and expressionless. After some silent consideration of the situation, the lead driver and apparent spokesperson of the group, nodded. "Hey."

"Hey!" I answered with what I hoped was a confident smile.

"What are you doing?"

"Oh, just out for a couple of days on the AT."

"You ain't on the AT." He leaned over, spat tobacco juice, and wiped his mouth with the back of his hand. "You on my property."

"Really? I'm sorry—are you sure? I mean, we've been following the blazes." Motorized vehicles aren't allowed at any point on the AT, so I thought these dudes were the ones who were trespassing.

"Yup, you went through a rhododendron tunnel about a mile back. AT makes a sharp turn there. Lot of people miss it." The unsaid words hung in the air: *But they don't make the same mistake twice.*

He spat again, and Jen took this opportunity to step quietly out of the woods behind me. He stared at her for a minute and then asked, bizarrely, "Are you real?"

"Uh, I hope so." She sort of snickered.

"I thought you was a statue."

We had no response to that. After a few beats, he went on to tell us that he and his buddies were looking for his dog. "Think he's hurt up here somewhere. Got into it with a bear."

Engines revved back up, and we stepped off the trail with relief to let them pass. After they roared off, Jen said, "What do you think?"

I didn't know. I felt like we'd been following blazes, but then again, we had been so lost in our reveries that I couldn't swear we were still on the AT. "Let's go a little farther, and if we don't see a blaze, we'll turn around."

Jen agreed, and we walked another few hundred yards until the woods opened up onto a plowed field. We saw no sign of blazes or even a continuation of the trail.

"This doesn't look right," I admitted. "Let's go back."

We turned around and trudged back uphill for at least a mile until we saw two blazes—one atop the other, which indicates a change in direction—painted on a waist-high post. The marker was obscured by rhododendron and pockmarked with bullet holes.

"Well, I'll be damned." We had just added two extra miles to what was already a long hike. Moreover, we had to thank Drooping Mustache Man for setting us straight.

Jen and I made it to the car at Devil Fork Gap by late afternoon and drove to Hot Springs for a well-deserved meal and a good night's rest. We checked into a nicely maintained fifteen- or twenty-room strip motel on Main Street and grinned with pleasure to see the neatly made beds and spotless bathroom.

After showers, hot and strong, we put on clean clothes and walked to the townie bar that Heather, Denise Wolfe, and I had visited last fall. The atmosphere was much more subdued on this occasion—it was Sunday night, after all—and we ate an excellent meal in pleasant silence, then retired to our immaculate room. There, we forced ourselves to stay awake until the sun went down over the mountaintops and we judged it late enough to reward ourselves with sleep.

✳ ✳ ✳

In the fall, Melanie started her final year of high school, and I escaped from the madness (and expense) of having a senior in our midst for one final AT hike of the year. In mid-October, Lynn V. (apparently in a forgiving mood, her feet having healed) accompanied me to North Carolina. Cecilia, Heather, and Sebastian met us for a two-day, twenty-two mile hike from Devil Fork Gap to Spivey Gap. The weather was already chilly, so we did not camp but stayed in a little roadside motel in Erwin.

This hike is mostly pleasant and scenic ridgewalking at elevations of four-thousand-plus feet, with the notable exceptions of windy and exposed Big Bald at 5,500 feet and a rocky descent to Spivey Gap. We climbed stiles and passed through cow pastures. (Some are still in use—watch where you step!) Rural roads and remnants of long-neglected orchards where small, hard apples littered the ground reminded us of the human activity and domesticity of these mountains.

We nodded and waved at the passing pickup trucks and children playing in farmyards. Goats, sheep, and horses placidly chewed the grass within the barbed-wire fences separating them from our path. Dogs barked and chickens clucked. Sebastian did her best to keep us safe and on track.

It was a relief to finish the hiking season with a serene weekend of pleasant days and idyllic Americana with no injuries, no extreme weather, no bizarre encounters with man or beast. This year had found me in the desert and in the mountains, but yet I felt grounded by my friends, my job, my family, and my hobby. It didn't matter—on the Trail or off, blisters or balm, Baghdad or Hot Springs—as long as I kept my head where my feet were long enough to make it home.

CHAPTER 5

2009 (155 MILES)

HIGHWAY 91, TENNESSEE, TO DAMASCUS, VIRGINIA

SHOOK BRANCH RECREATION AREA, TENNESSEE, TO HIGHWAY 91, TENNESSEE

DAMASCUS, VIRGINIA, TO HIGHWAY 600, VIRGINIA

ELK PARK, NORTH CAROLINA, TO SHOOK BRANCH RECREATION AREA, TENNESSEE

SPIVEY GAP, NORTH CAROLINA, TO HUGHES GAP, TENNESSEE

ELK GARDEN, VIRGINIA, TO HIGHWAY 603, VIRGINIA

HIGHWAY 603, VIRGINIA, TO MOUNT ROGERS, VIRGINIA

The onset of 2009 apparently ushered in an ambitious mind-set—the first AT hike of the year was planned for the weekend of January 10. Jen, Denise Wolfe, and I made up the Franklin contingent, and Cecilia joined us from the eastern flank. We rendez-voused in the little hiker town of Damascus, Virginia, and rented a rustic cabin as our headquarters for this winter adventure.

The Appalachian Trail occasionally marches itself right through the streets of small towns, where the white blazes are painted on sidewalks, telephone poles, and street signs. Many of these towns are known as "hiker friendly" or "good hiker towns." There is usually a hostel or two catering almost exclusively to thru-hikers or long-distance section hikers, and the motels offer reduced rates and laundry facilities. Sometimes the restaurants offer hiker specials: "Free milkshake with any hamburger-fries combo! All you can eat pancakes!"

Hiker-friendly towns might also boast a decent outfitter or, at the very least, a grocery store with reasonably priced items for resupply. Many thru-hikers will plan their "zero days" (days during which zero miles are hiked) or "nero days" (days you hike only a few miles) based on the proximity of these towns. This is where packages from home or mail drops are held at the post office; where you can catch up on your emails, phone calls, journals, and blogs; where you can eat in clean restaurants with real utensils; and where, above all, you can rest your weary body and mind.

Damascus may be the most hiker-friendly town on the Trail and totally embraces, even honors, the hiking community with its "Trail Days" cele-bration. This annual event is held in mid-May when many of the NOBOs who started at Springer Mountain in late March or early April are in the area. Tents are set up in a large field, and vendors of outdoor clothing and gear hawk their wares at booths erected just for the occasion. There is free music and entertainment, and everyone dons his or her favorite outfit for the premier event, the Hiker Parade.

Trail Days has become so popular it is now viewed as a venue for AT reunions. Hikers return year after year like migrant birds to relive the glory and agony of walking over two thousand miles with others who have walked those same steps.

With light packs and light hearts, we ventured from this cabin for twenty-two miles of hiking from TN 91 to Damascus. Although this was one hundred miles north of Spivey Gap, where we finished in 2008, I had chosen this section because of easily accessible roads for day hikes. My mind was untroubled with logistics, as we had two cars for the shuttle. Really, this was just a weekend of relaxation in a warm, comfy cottage with good friends to share a meal with at the end of each day—with a little hiking thrown in to justify our indolence.

Ridgewalking at 3,500- to 4,000-feet elevation can falsely lull you into a belief that a day or two on the AT is just a walk in the park—and it is if you happen to choose this section. Memories of the hardships in the Smokies are starting to fade and Pennsylvania with her rocks and New Hampshire with her weather are yet very far away.

I felt that the state of Virginia and I were going to be very good friends.

❋ ❋ ❋

The January trip—as pleasant as it has been—served to remind me of the miles I had skipped in Tennessee, North Carolina, and Southern Virginia. If flexibility and adaptation were key to hiking the entire AT, well, so was attention to detail. I did not want to shortchange myself by missing one inch of this treasure. I decided 2009 would be the year of catch-up. I had no plans or intentions of taking a long FBI TDY this year, and my travels would be limited to trips to the mountains and vacations with the family.

In mid-March, I met Cecilia and Heather for a two-day, twenty-mile hike from Shook Branch Recreation Area at US 321 to where the trail crosses at TN 91, contiguously south of our previous hike in January.

We stayed in the Elizabethton, Tennessee, area, which is several miles from the Trail but close to interstates and amenities. The weather for the weekend was damp but not unpleasant, with crunchy snow still on the ground. The first several miles of this hike took us up and down on sometimes a rocky trail from Shook Branch Recreation Area to Watauga Dam Road at Iron Mountain Gap. We occasionally caught glimpses of Watauga Lake shimmering in the valley below.

The remainder of the day's hike and all of the next day was spent ridgewalking at four thousand feet. The views of the surrounding Blue Ridge Mountains were spectacular—at least when the mists lifted and the clouds parted enough to let us in on their secrets.

The three of us did not always keep the same pace. Heather, with her long legs and the advantage of youth, was often in the lead, and I usually followed fairly closely in my solitary reverie. Cecilia trailed behind, pausing frequently to take pictures of flowers, butterflies, or some vulnerable insect on its own journey in the world. Over the years, we had grown accustomed to each other's rhythms, and now, as always, we were grateful to be together even in our separateness.

* * *

The first week of April coincided with Melanie's last spring break of her high school career, and she was on her way to Panama City. I had purposefully planned a hike for this time, knowing I would need a diversion from worry. This was the first time Tim and I had let her go on a trip with no parental involvement, and the sad realization was sinking in that each new adventure for Melanie would take her one step farther from us. As she headed off on a nine-hour drive to Florida with her girlfriends, I headed to Virginia to meet mine. I had again rented a cabin in Damascus, and Cecilia and Heather would be joining me as they had in March.

Virginia is home to well over five hundred miles of the Appalachian Trail, more than any of the other thirteen states it passes through. The words Grayson Highlands, Shenandoah, and Skyline Drive evoke images of soft, rolling hills, of pine needle-covered paths, and of woods cool and dense as a rainforest. All true, but 540 miles is still a helluva long way to walk, and it is quite common for thru-hikers to become afflicted with a condition known as the Virginia Blues. Fortunately, I was not a thru-hiker, and one person's Gethsemane is another's Eden. Each time I hiked in Virginia as a section hiker, the Trail was new to me, so there was never any opportunity for monotony. This hike with Cecilia and Heather was no exception.

The Virginia Blues is a condition to which many thru-hikers succumb at least temporarily. I am told this is the state where thru-hikers are most likely to abandon their quests. I have no empirical data to back this up, but it makes sense. Just the sheer amount of time required to hike the Trail in Virginia means there is more opportunity for illness, injury, or family emergencies to occur. Also, after the challenges of the Smokies for northbounders and the Whites for southbounders, some people might call Virginia, well...boring. Not me, but I can understand how you might get to a point in your journey when you are hot, sweaty, and tired, and you've already walked twenty to thirty miles a day for two or three months, you might just say to yourself, *How many more postcard-perfect views can there possibly be? I'd trade them all right now for a quart of Ben & Jerry's Chunky Monkey.* No, it's not the Stairways to Heavens, the Roller Coasters, the Mahoosuc Notches, or other notorious challenges of the AT that quashes dreams. It's the Virginia Blues.

We broke down the twenty miles from Damascus north to VA 600 into two days. The Trail rises from two thousand feet in town to this section's high point at Whitetop Mountain, which summits at almost 5,500 feet. It parallels the famous Virginia Creeper Trail, a bicycle path, for some miles, which may give you some idea of how mild it is compared to more demanding sections. And—to prove pleasant doesn't mean boring—there are plenty of diversions along the way. We hiked over the five-hundred-foot railroad bridge (no trains now, just hikers) and crossed Laurel Creek. The remnants of Creek Junction Station and the gorgeous rushing Laurel Gorge give way to the balds of Whitetop Mountain and the views from Buzzard Rock.

Damascus, to which we returned in the evenings, was at its charming best in its April finery, and our cabin also did not disappoint. Situated at the edge of the town center, the back deck overlooked a small pond, complete with ducks, frogs, and lily pads.

It was on this deck after our first day's hike that I received a call from Melanie. She let me know she and her friends had made it safely to Panama City, were checked into their hotel, and were strolling along the beach. I was relieved to hear from her, happy she was safe, and proud of her independence. Yet at the same time, I couldn't help but feel how very far away from our loving protection she was. Perhaps I *had* succumbed a bit to the Virginia Blues.

* * *

As summer came on, I remained determined to fill in the gaps I'd skipped on the Appalachian Trail between the Smokies and Watauga Dam. Cecilia joined me for a mid-June adventure from US 19, where we'd finished on the pre-Iraq hike, to the Shook Branch Recreation Area, where our March 2009 hike had begun. This would knock thirty miles off the to-do list, and I felt, even as the hike began, that comforting sense of tidying up loose ends.

The first day was mild and pleasant, alternating between woods and farmland, stiles over barbed-wire fencing marking the transitions between the two. We walked eagerly and purposefully for twelve miles to Moreland Gap Shelter, where we pitched our tents with a few other hikers in nearby campsites.

The conversation turned to the Bonnaroo Music Festival in relatively nearby Manchester, Tennessee. (Melanie happened to be in attendance at this event, camping in a dusty field cheek-by-jowl with sixty thousand other music lovers.) One young thru-hiking couple, radiant with health and happiness, told us they had wanted to go off-Trail temporarily for Bonnaroo—several of their friends were doing so—but that plan was unexpectedly derailed.

Bonnie, the female half of this partnership, leaned across the picnic table and said almost conspiratorially to me and Cecilia, "I'm pregnant." She grinned widely and patted her belly.

Her partner, standing behind her with his hands on her shoulders, beamed. "Yeah, we just found out. Took a pregnancy test and then went to the doctor. It's official."

"But that's wonderful!" Cecilia said. She told them she was a doctor and that there was no reason in the world they couldn't or shouldn't complete their thru-hike. "Take your vitamins, rest when you can, drink plenty of water. Let your partner here carry the heavy stuff."

I have no idea if they finished or not, but I like to think they did and then had a fat and healthy baby they named Georgia. Or Maine.

The next day's hike was over fourteen miles long, much of it on steep, rocky trail. The sun was hot, and we spent the morning looking forward to the eighty-foot cascade at Laurel Falls. When we reached this gorgeous spot, I was reminded that the AT is not just about putting one sweaty boot in front of the other. It's also about taking off those boots for an hour or so and just enjoying these gifts of nature.

Cecilia, a freer spirit than I, took off more than her boots and jumped into the icy-cold water at the base of the falls. As she happily skinny-dipped in the sparkling clear depths, I was perfectly content to take off my boots and socks, stretch out on a large rock, and feel the sun on my face and the misty spray on my feet and legs.

This was a happy interlude. I recall Cecilia's smiling face and dripping, tangled hair, and I think back to how, during my first several years on the AT, I often felt compelled to hike as many miles as possible per day. I'm glad I often had companions with me, which forced me to think of someone other than myself and to lighten up a little. As I got older and wiser (and slower), I began to set more realistic mileage goals. Fifteen to seventeen miles became my daily max, and that was if my pack wasn't too heavy and the terrain not too difficult. I learned to take more breaks and to enjoy the views, the solitude, and all the things that were the reasons I was doing this in the first place. *What's the hurry?* I had to constantly remind myself. The AT isn't going anywhere—and Springer Mountain and Mount Katahdin are just two points on it.

* * *

As the summer ticked by, the demands of work and family trumped, as they should, the indulgences of hobby and hiking. But finally, in early August, Helie (an exchange student who had spent several weeks with us) returned to France, Melanie went to Chicago for Lollapalooza, and I traveled to the Tennessee–North Carolina border. Tim was, I'm sure, happy to stay home alone and have the house to himself.

Nine weeks after my last hike with Cecilia, I drove east for a thirty-six-mile trek from Spivey Gap to Hughes Gap near Roan Mountain. This was the only uncompleted section south of Virginia (save the ever-elusive eight-mile Clingmans Dome to Newfound Gap section).

I hiked the first day alone, eight miles from Iron Mountain Gap to Hughes Gap. (This was actually the northernmost section of this three-day hike, but I did it first because of easy road accessibility.) It felt good to be back, solo, on the quiet Trail after what seemed like a noisy and crowded summer. It was also nice to carry only a daypack and that, combined with the relative ease of this section, made light work of the day.

I arrived at Roan Mountain State Park, where I had again rented a cabin, to hook up with the rest of the crew joining me from Raleigh and Durham: Cecilia, her college-age niece also named Cecilia (henceforth known as Cecilia the Elder and Cecilia the Younger), and Carolyn, a colleague of Cecilia the Elder.

I am always a little nervous about initiating new people into trail life, although in this case, Cecilia the Elder had invited the other two, so I felt she bore most of the responsibility for their well-being. Cecilia the Younger's inexperience and apparent lack of fitness worried me, but youth and enthusiasm go a long way, and I figured she'd be fine. Dr. Carolyn, a petite but sturdy-looking blonde, accompanied by a small gray-whiskered mutt, was on a whole other level.

She had arrived in a different vehicle from the Cecilias—in fact, she was driving a van that had been converted into a camper / medical clinic. I learned she had cancer and used the van as a sort of mobile personal treatment center. I admired her spirit but was somewhat concerned about her health in this heat. My concern turned to downright horror when I saw she was reliant on a portable oxygen tank.

"You do realize tomorrow is a seventeen-mile day?" I reminded Cecilia the Elder as the four of us sat on the front porch discussing logistics of the next day.

Carolyn piped up. "Oh, I know. I'll be fine. I just have to go a little slower than most people."

Okey-dokey, then. I outlined the plan. "We will leave my car at TN 395, Indian Grave Gap, drive Carolyn's—uh—vehicle to Spivey Gap and hike the seventeen miles north to my car. This is a very remote section of the AT, and I just can't figure out a way to shorten this hike without using long access trails and rough forest service roads."

We rose early the next day and drove the winding, confusing roads to Spivey Gap and stepped on the AT before midmorning. The first few miles were hot, dry, and slow, all of which we expected. We passed a few southbounders, some of whom acknowledged Carolyn and her oxygen tank—which was strapped to her waist—with a thumbs-up and words of encouragement. Her little dog, Toto, panted after her.

At about five miles in, we paused before we began the ascent to No Business Knob. There, on this rocky stretch of trail crowded by thick laurel and thorny shrubs, Carolyn announced she'd had enough.

"How much farther to the car?" she asked.

"At least eleven miles," I said. "mostly tough ones."

Cecilia the Elder kindly offered to backtrack with Carolyn to the van, leaving Cecilia the Younger to forge ahead with me.

I hugged Carolyn. "You have been an absolute trooper," I said. I felt small and uncharitable for having doubted this woman's courage and stamina. Yes, she was conceding midway through the hike, but sometimes admitting one's limitations is the most courageous form of bravery. To have even attempted this difficult challenge on a hot and dry summer's day while dealing with cancer and the ravages of its treatment—not to mention doing it with a cheerful and uncomplaining attitude—was something I, who took my good health for granted, would certainly not have even considered.

Cecilia the Younger and I continued our northbound trek over a moderate trail for a few miles with lovely views of the Nolichucky River below. The descent to the river was a series of challenging rockslides that brought us down to the Chestoa Bridge.

We stretched out on the grassy riverbank for a well-deserved rest. Cecilia the Younger was holding up pretty well, but she had some blisters on her feet that needed treatment. As she took off her shoes—low-top, faux leather sneakers—I noticed one sole was literally flapping in the breeze. We used some white adhesive tape from my first aid kit to wrap around the instep until the sole was reasonably well secured to the top. Hoping we could hold mind, body, and spirit—not to mention footwear—together for a few more miles, we walked on.

We ascended slowly out of the Nolichucky Gorge and reached the car at Indian Grave Gap in very late afternoon. (I saw no sign of Indians or graves in the area.) We were utterly exhausted. I knew I had pushed myself too hard, and I was ashamed to have done the same thing to my young companion. As we drove back to the cabin, air-conditioning at full blast, Cecilia the Younger was very quiet.

"Can you pull the car over for a minute?" she finally asked, her hand gripping the door handle. I quickly obliged. She stepped out of the car, bent over, and threw up in the ditch.

"Oh, Cecilia, I am so sorry." I felt terrible for her. "You might have some heat stroke or dehydration."

She shook it off, clambered back into the car, and we finished the last leg of this very long day's strange journey.

We were happy to see Carolyn's van safely parked in the cabin drive when we arrived. After practically crawling up the front steps, I opened the front door to smoke billowing out and Cecilia the Elder trying frantically to open a window.

"Oh, my god, what happened?" I rushed to the kitchen area where the smoke was most intense. A blackened frying pan with some unrecognizable charred bits in it had been tossed into the sink. There were no flames or visible damage to anything, and it appeared the crisis had been averted.

Cecilia the Elder explained that she and Carolyn had backtracked to the car without mishap, and she had decided to cook dinner, as she knew we'd be very tired and hungry. She was cooking tortillas, turned her back for a minute, and the next thing she knew, flames were leaping about the stove and threatening to overtake the cabinets.

Oh, Cecilia.

We managed to get through the rest of the night without further catastrophes. On Sunday morning, we bid each other adieu, and I never saw Cecilia the Younger again or Carolyn and her little dog, Toto. I later heard from Cecilia the Elder that Carolyn had won her battle with cancer and was holding steady in the war. This news did not surprise me; cancer had met its match with this intrepid woman.

❋ ❋ ❋

By the end of August, Melanie was officially a college student at the University of Tennessee at Chattanooga, and Tim and I were officially empty nesters. We joked that had we known how wonderful this state of affairs would turn out to be, we would have kicked her out long ago. This was said in jest, of course; the flippancy belied the fact that we actually missed our daughter very much. Melanie has a way of filling a house or a room, and now our house and all its rooms were filled with her absence.

Winter would soon force me to stow my tent, and I canvassed friends to see who could accompany me on a September camping trip. I had no takers in Tennessee, but Cecilia the Elder said she could drive over from Raleigh for one day and one night.

I left my car at Fox Creek near the town of Troutdale, Virginia, on a Friday morning. I don't recall how I managed to get to Elk Garden, where my hike was to begin. These were the days when, for the most part, I just looked at the maps, figured I needed to get from Point A to Point B, stuck out my thumb, and flung myself at the mercy of strangers.

This two-day hike would total about nineteen miles. Since Cecilia would not be able to join me until late in the day, I would begin the hike solo and meet up with her about twelve miles in at Wise Shelter (which she could access from a side trail), stay the night there, and the next day, we would hike the remaining seven or so miles to my car.

At Elk Garden, I began my solo trek north. The morning was cool and misty with occasional sprinkles of very light showers and a fore-cast of heavy rain for the afternoon. I hiked several miles uneventfully, ascended to the summit of 4,800-foot Pine Mountain, and then on through Rhododendron Gap.

The southern Appalachian Mountains are a wonderland when the rhodos (as thru-hikers fondly call them) are blooming in June and July, and I am told the meadows along this stretch are filled with the purple floral masses. Even though too late in the season for this spectacle, it was nevertheless a joy to amble along across the bald, which ascends gently to almost 5,500 feet. I nodded to the west in acknowledgment of looming Mount Rogers (at 5,700 feet, the highest peak in Virginia) and then descended gracefully to Grayson Highlands and Massie Gap.

I had seen several other hikers during the morning—Grayson Highlands State Park is accessible by car and home to a network of loop trails—but now, as I walked along the narrow trail crowded by tall pines and full-foliage blueberry bushes, I realized all had been quiet for some time. I was startled by the gruff bark of a dog in the not-too-far distance.

Dogs mean people, and I looked up the trail, expecting to see a person rounding the corner and coming toward me. Instead, maybe thirty feet ahead, coming from a bend to my right, a large, dark-colored horse appeared, prancing and turning his neck to look behind him.

Oh, my, I thought. *This horse has thrown his rider.*

He continued toward me on the narrow path, at a slow trot now. Almost immediately, another horse followed him around the bend.

Now that's really strange. Here's another one with no rider. No, wait a second! They have no saddles. No harnesses. My mind was slowly catching up to the situation at hand. *Good grief, these must be the wild ponies of Grayson Highlands!*

This section of the AT is known for a herd of horses that makes its home here, unowned by humans and free to roam. But I expected to see, if anything, small, shaggy, Shetland-like ponies grazing peacefully on the treeless meadows. These were full-size—even huge—horses, alternately trotting and running, right on the AT deep in the heavy woods.

Well, whatever they are, I better get out of the way, I decided rather belatedly, as the first two were almost upon me. I hopped to the edge of the trail, my backpack pushing up against the thick bushes. I was almost hidden by the underbrush and overhanging branches. More horses followed the first two until there was a steady stream of them passing inches in front of me. I gave up counting at fourteen and just enjoyed the parade.

Oh, and what a parade! Horses and ponies of all sizes hurried past with tails sweeping the ground and manes hanging down over soft, brown eyes with lashes as long as your thumb. Their feet were unshod, of course, and I noticed the hooves of many were protuberant and calcified. They trotted by, most ignoring me, but a few slowed long enough to nuzzle my hands and waist, looking for a handout.

About halfway through the procession came the smallest pony I've ever seen. He couldn't have been more than a few weeks old, the size of a not-very-large dog, barrel-shaped and fuzzy. His mama nudged him along gently. He trotted as fast as his short little legs could carry him and stared straight ahead, but just as he passed me, his eyes cut to his right for an instant and met mine.

I will never forget this tiny animal or the way I felt for those several minutes. Every mile I had walked on the AT, every blister, every moment of thirst and hunger had been irrefutably worth it. I never did see or again hear the dog that had warned me of oncoming traffic, but I figured later her barking must have startled the horses into their stampede through the woods. For that I will be forever grateful to her.

* * *

I descended out of the Highlands, still in a daze, now eager to get to the shelter to meet Cecilia and regale her with tales of the day's adventures. Very late afternoon now and the all-day on-again, off-again rain became a steady downpour. I was wearing a heavy plastic poncho with an ill-fitting hood that flopped about my face, blocking my peripheral vision—so that is what I will blame for missing a turn in the trail somewhere around Quebec Branch and blithely wandering to the west instead of continuing north.

Don't get me wrong: I wasn't lost exactly. I just wasn't where I was supposed to be. I was obviously on a trail, but not the white-blazed AT. This trail was six or seven feet wide, which is several feet wider than the AT normally is. It was clearly well traveled by equestrians, judging by the horseshoe prints in the muddy path, which was steadily getting muddier. When I eventually noticed I was no longer seeing white blazes on the trees, I backtracked a quarter mile or so with no luck. Looking at the map, I could not see where I had gone wrong. There were several equestrian and foot trails in this area, and I couldn't determine which one I was on, as I had observed no signage or landmarks.

It was getting dark, and the rain was really coming down. I had not seen any other people, equestrian or otherwise, since I'd strayed from the AT. I wasn't particularly worried about my safety. I had plenty of food and water, as well as a tent. I had dry clothes and the temperature was mild. I was worried, however, that Cecilia would be concerned when I failed to meet her at the shelter.

With night truly closing in, I came to an intersection with another wide equestrian trail. Again looking at the maps and my compass, I decided this trail might lead to the shelter within a mile or so. I took a right (northbound) turn—and almost immediately sank well over my boot tops into a viscous bog. I tried another few sucking steps before deciding this would not do at all.

As I stood there like a pig in a wallow, though much less happy than the pig would be, the rain suddenly stopped, and the clouds broke just enough for the very last of the day's sunbeams to shine through the thick branches. An omen or just plain luck, I didn't know, but I decided to not tempt fate any longer. Near where the trails intersected, there was a relatively flat area just big enough for my tent. I pitched it quickly, put sleeping bag and pad in place, and stripped out of my wet clothes. I no sooner got settled safely inside than the clouds closed up and again the hard rain fell.

* * *

All solo backpackers are often asked, "Don't you get scared sleeping out there all alone?" I can honestly say no, not really. I have from time to time been a little spooked by a sudden noise or had a little lingering concern about animals or strange people I may have encountered earlier in the day, but overall, I feel safe in my tent and the woods. When asked this question, I usually add that sometimes I get lonely. This was the case on that particular night. I wasn't frightened. I mean, good grief, I was in a virtual slough in the middle of a wilderness area. What were the chances of some nefarious creature stumbling upon me?

But as I munched on cheese and crackers, leaning out of the opening of my tent under the rain fly, gazing at nothing but wet blackness, I felt very blue. I think it had been such an emotionally intense day—the stress of hitching a ride, the incredible high of seeing the ponies, and then the discouraging and senseless meanderings—that I was just sad to not have had someone to share it with.

I thought of my husband and daughter, missing them. I thought about my hiking buddies, sorry they had missed the horses but glad I hadn't subjected them to my incompetence. Mostly, I thought of my brother and how he would have loved this adventure. A shy boy and an even shyer man, he had died violently and young. I could picture him, moving silently along the trail, efficiently making camp, even fishing for his dinner. He was better situated to the wilderness than to civilization.

The sad but cleansing rain fell all night.

❋ ❋ ❋

Things looked brighter in the morning, as they usually do, both literally and figuratively, and I broke camp quickly. I continued on the northbound side trail, now more navigable since the rain had stopped in the early morning. In less than a mile, the trail intersected with the AT and voilá! There was Wise Shelter.

A family was just packing up their gear, and they told me Cecilia had spent the night there without incident. She had asked them to pass on the word to me she was traveling north slowly and that I would catch up. She apparently had not been a bit worried.

All AT shelters have a trail log or register, which is really just a spiral-bound notebook, replaced seasonally by the various caretaking clubs. Here, hikers leave messages for one another or for the community at large. *Hey, Jumping Jack and Shiner, zero day in Troutdale tomorrow. Wanna hang out? Peace, Bulldog.* I checked the register, but there was no message from Cecilia. As I hoisted my pack, I noticed a large white owl silently watching me from a low beam in the back corner. We studied each other for a long moment, and when I turned to leave, he bid me adieu with a soft hoot.

Back on the AT, where I belonged, I shouted out Cecilia's name every so often and caught up with her within a few miles.

"There you are," she said with a hug. "I knew you'd be okay." She told me the owl in the shelter had watched over her all night, and she had somehow surely believed I was also safe wherever I was. We happily hiked north without further incident.

* * *

The camping season, for me, was over, but I took advantage of one last free weekend in November to meet Cecilia the Elder for a twenty-three mile, two-day hike. We would start from VA 603, just south of Iron Mountain, where we had finished together in September.

For this trip, we stayed in Marion, a hiker-friendly town conveniently located on I-81. From there, we ventured out on our day hikes, enjoying brisk autumn weather and light packs. We climbed Iron Mountain on the first day, ending at Dickey Gap near Troutdale. On our second day, we crossed the South Fork Holston River and then climbed Brushy Mountain.

This section of the Appalachian Trail is well marked even as it winds through seemingly impenetrable forest. Southern Virginia is (oxymoronically) a tame wilderness where one imagines Mother Nature sweetly smiling down on her more obedient children even as she firmly holds back her more unruly ones. I felt almost tearfully grateful for her mercy.

* * *

This year's goal of filling in skipped mileage had, by and large, been accomplished, and I could take some pride in my perseverance. But already the memories of this year's events carried a tinge of nostalgia—a tender wistfulness for a present which was becoming a past with every second and every step. Day-to-day responsibilities of parenthood were lessening and opportunities for personal freedom growing, but the trade-off was bittersweet. Hiking helped me to remember that moving forward means letting go of the bad stuff, but it also means that some of the good stuff won't last forever either.

CHAPTER 6

2010 (105 MILES)

MOUNT ROGERS, VIRGINIA, TO HIGHWAY 612, VIRGINIA

HIGHWAY 612, VIRGINIA, TO HIGHWAY 606, VIRGINIA

HIGHWAY 606, VIRGINIA, TO PEARISBURG, VIRGINIA

GARDEN MOUNTAIN, VIRGINIA, TO HIGHWAY 615, VIRGINIA

The AT and I did not live in a vacuum, and the world did not hold its breath while I crept along at my petty pace. Other people, rightfully, have their own agendas with their own desired outcomes. Commitment to work and responsibilities has to be a priority; the rent must be paid, after all. Weather, illness, and acts of nature are supremely indifferent to our little projects; the gods will merely snicker. The previous three years on the Trail had seen me averaging close to 150 miles annually; not exactly record-setting to be sure, but nevertheless fairly respectable for a middle-aged section hiker. Now this year would remind me of the mythical fellow whose eternal punishment was to endlessly push a boulder up a mountain. But even in that extreme case, there are lessons which I would—at first grudgingly and eventually gratefully—learn.

✳ ✳ ✳

Through the winter, I had no opportunity for a hike. In January, I traveled to Tel Aviv for a work assignment and, if I dreamed of walking a section of the Israel National Trail (685 miles north to south), it remained just that: a dream. My responsibilities were to the work at hand, but as I traveled the country with its sandstone cliffs and fertile valleys and tiny villages, I was reminded of how many other trails, with all their diversity, there are in the world. With the hot, dry heat in my face and the yellow-white sky all around, the lovely call of the early morning muezzin in contrast to the bustling noise of the cafés and trinket shops on the Mediterranean, I realized that in fact I would probably never be back here and would never hike this countryside. This knowledge left me feeling shortchanged and then ashamed at my greed.

In March, I traveled to Arkansas for a week's assignment to assist our Little Rock office in hosting a crisis negotiations course for local cops. As the week went on, several of our students came down with flu-like symptoms. The chills and body aches hit me on the seven-hour drive home. There was no question of following through on my intention of an AT hike that weekend; my only immediate goal was recovery. I was, however, grateful that I could be sick in the comfort of home with my own bed and my own bathroom.

I've never fallen sick on the trail, but that was probably just a matter of luck, because in my first years of hiking the AT, I wasn't as careful as I should have been about water consumption. I often drank straight from a spring if it was sparkling clean and cold. When I told my mother, she was horrified.

"Hey," I said, "Native Americans drank from these streams for thousands of years without filters or pills."

"Well, there weren't cows shitting upstream in those days," she responded. "Or factories dumping their chemicals any old where."

She had a point.

Sometimes you will hear rumors there has been an outbreak of norovirus or giardiasis on a certain section of the Trail. These viruses (fecal in origin) are spread through contaminated food or water or person-to-person through dirty hands. It has been my observation that hikers do the best they can to practice good hygiene and treat their water, but immaculate conditions are hard to come by. Symptoms of both these illnesses include stomach cramps, vomiting, and diarrhea, which can cause dehydration. I myself have a few times come across a hiker, sick and miserable, huddled in a corner of a shelter on a sunny day. There's not much you can do but offer some words of comfort and whatever salty food or fresh water you can spare.

Insects, particularly ticks, can also spread disease with their bites. The most common of these is Lyme disease, which can have serious and long-lasting consequences. The first symptom will be a rash at the site of the bite and that might not show up for days. The best defense against Lyme is a proactive one. Try to wear hats and clothes that cover as much of the body as possible, although this is often not practical during Appalachia's hot summer months. Apply powerful insect repellant often and liberally to any exposed skin. Above all, check yourself (and your partner if requested) for ticks.

With the end of March, a quarter of the year was gone and then the lovely months of April and May passed with no chance for a hike. With the advent of June—and before I had to acknowledge half the year gone without setting foot on the Trail—Cecilia the Elder and I set out on a forty-mile, three-day ramble through the woods.

We met in the Mount Rogers area where we left off in November. In high spirits and enchanted by the tiny wildflowers and mushrooms of all sizes and hues, we climbed Brushy and Locust Mountains, eventually arriving at VA 615. Here, a nineteenth-century farm village was being restored, and we meandered over the grounds, peering into the windows of the old schoolhouse and rustic farmhouse, thankful to those who care enough about Appalachian history to preserve it.

After a night of tent camping on the trail, we continued north. The temperature had risen considerably from the day before, and now our bandanas were soaked with sweat, our thirst unquenchable. The hike up Little Brushy to Tilson Gap was strenuous, and the humidity of the southern summer unrelenting. We descended to the banks of the North Fork Holston River and blissfully soaked our feet in the relatively cool waters. The final few miles took us to Knot Maul Branch Shelter and a night of dry rest, but morning brought sheets of rain. There was nothing to do but don our raincoats and trod on, feeling caught in the wet and tangled web of nature.

We trudged miserably up Lynn Camp Mountain, down into Poor Valley, and over countless PUDS. Seven or eight hours of slogging in the ceaseless rain brought us to the 4,500-foot summit of Chestnut Knob, where a squat, concrete block building is incongruously perched on the bald mountaintop. We hurried to seek shelter and joined several other hikers, ponchos and raincoats dripping, in the large dry room. I sat on a waist-high wooden platform built into the side of one wall and leaned back to rest my body without even bothering to take off my pack. I wasn't sure I would ever rise again.

We finally moved on, motivated by the knowledge we only had a few more miles to reach our car, and we could put this difficult section behind us. I consider any adventure successful if I'm sorry it's over, but I'm glad to be going home. This particular hike might have been weighted a wee bit to the latter.

* * *

The brutal dog days of summer marched on, and in early August, Tim and I settled Melanie into Chattanooga for her sophomore year. We were happy to have had her home for the summer, but even so, she was busy with her own increasingly independent life. There is nothing any parent could (or should) do to change this natural course of events, but it did occur to me as I wrote out the checks for tuition and books and board that she wasn't quite Lady Freedom yet.

* * *

At last, I sought the relative coolness of the mountains. Cecilia and her son joined me for a two-day, eighteen-mile section hike from VA 612 to VA 606. Sixteen-year-old Carson was sweet and shy, athletic and eager. He was, befitting a teenaged boy, somewhat awkward and probably a little embarrassed to be out hiking with his mom and her middle-aged friend. He walked quite a bit ahead of us, but that was okay. He forced us to keep a good pace with his strong, young legs and adolescent energy.

Mountain breezes and slightly overcast skies tempered a warm weekend, and we considered ourselves lucky to be out of the humid cement-and-glass cities. This relatively easy hike varies in altitude from two thousand to three thousand feet with a summit at Jenny Knob and two on Brushy Mountain. (We had already climbed two or three other Brushy Mountains on previous hikes. Perhaps Virginians weren't too imaginative when it came to naming their mountains. But you must applaud them for the appellation Lickskillet Hollow, the gap at VA 608.)

After two days and a night on the trail, we went in search of a decent hotel along I-81, only to discover this was the weekend of an annual NASCAR race at Bristol Motor Speedway that draws upwards of 150,000 fans who fill all the lodging for miles around. We finally secured a room near Wytheville in a small mom-and-pop operation that charged us a ridiculous amount. The solitude and vastness of the Trail leads us to forget how crowded the world can be and how it is often nearer than we think.

* * *

Disappointed in my pitiful tally—hardly more than fifty miles in only two trips for the year—and with autumn closing in, Labor Day weekend called for a twenty-two-mile, day-and-a-half trip from VA 606 to Pearisburg with Heather and her dog joining me from Raleigh.

By the time we got on the Trail early Friday afternoon, we were already hot and tired from our busy weeks and long drives. The weather was humid and close and, as always, our packs heavy. After only a mile or so, a .3 side trail to Dismal Creek Falls tempted us, but we opted out after considering how many miles we yet faced. I thought later, as the hot day wore on, we should have taken advantage of a short diversion to a cold, sparking waterfall.

Crossing branch after boggy branch of Dismal Creek was…dismal. Swarms of gnats and mosquitoes compelled me to keep my bandana pulled across my face. We often passed small, algae-covered beaver ponds, where darting dragonflies intermittently scattered the clouds of bugs. The surrounding chewed-off trees, knee high and several inches in diameter, reminded me exactly of large pencils whittled to points by a dull knife.

About seven miles in, we began our climb out of the valley. Just before the steep ascent of Sugar Run Mountain, we made camp at Wapiti (Elk) Shelter and crawled into our tents, too exhausted to talk or bark.

I felt unsettled as I thought of the miles yet to conquer, not only on this trip but in the many sections north. Stamina and resolution can only carry a body so far; fatigue—mental and physical—seeps into the soul, and this is when it is easy to justify laziness and then abandonment. But as a very experienced hiker once quietly advised me: "Never quit on a bad day. Because that's what you would regret. If you must consider stopping, do it on a gorgeous day when the Trail is gentle and the weather kind. Then you would be in a state of mind for a rational decision."

Next morning, Heather and I, trailed by the never-flagging Sebastian, climbed an exhausting 1,500 feet in less than a mile to reach the

4,100-foot Sugar Run Mountain summit. From there, we walked twelve grueling miles along the ridge to Angel's Rest, one of the AT's most well-known overlooks.

From View Rock at Angel's Rest you can see the valley below, highlighted by the substantial New River and the modest town of Pearisburg. Some locals make the two-mile climb from town to Angel's Rest for this view. They are hardy souls—hiking up the rocky, two-thousand-foot mountainside would be no easy matter. The lovely panorama combined with the effort it took to get there moved me. It's almost as if the mountains and the Trail were a bit shamefaced and apologetic. *So sorry*, they seemed to say, *we know it was a tough go, and we admire your tenacity—now here is a little gift of nature as a token of our goodwill.*

We made the rocky descent late in the afternoon to Pearisburg, where we had left Heather's car at the Dairy Queen. Among long-distance AT hikers, this DQ is no less iconic than Angel's Rest. Before heading home on our long separate journeys, we lifted our Peanut Buster Parfaits in a toast to this rugged and rewarding section of the Trail.

* * *

The sixteen-mile section I had skipped between the June and August trips bothered me like a pebble in my boot, and I decided to knock it out over the long Columbus Day weekend. I cajoled Tim and Melanie into going with me, framing the offer as a family getaway to beautiful Virginia. I also talked Tim's brother Tommy into meeting us there with his wife, Lynne, and daughter Ellen. They would be traveling from eastern Pennsylvania, and this would be a six- to seven-hour drive for both families.

"Oh, what fun!" I said. "Tim and Tom can golf, Lynne and I can hike, Ellen and Melanie can do whatever teenage girls do during the day (sleep), and at night we can play cards or build a bonfire!"

Manipulative, yes. But it worked. Saturday afternoon we arrived at a nice little cabin in the woods near Wytheville. However, Tommy's truck pulled into the driveway with only two occupants. Lynne did not feel well and had decided to stay home. *Okay*, I thought after momentary disappointment, *I can hike alone, and all other plans will still be a go.*

Tim and Tom had arranged a tee time for Sunday morning at a nearby golf course, but first they would drop me off at the trailhead and then pick me up in the evening. I planned to hike the entire sixteen-mile stretch—a bit long for me but quite doable since I would have a relatively light daypack, and the hike itself could be considered easy to moderate. Apparently, I had forgotten why I hadn't done this section on previous trips. The trailhead was extremely remote, and the access road included a seven-mile gravel stretch where we could scarcely drive ten miles an hour.

The moments ticked by as we drove along the winding roads on a perfectly pleasant fall day. The guys' tee time came and went. I apologized profusely, but they were very gracious and assured me they could find another golf course willing to accommodate them.

When we finally got to Garden Mountain, it was at least mid-morning, and I figured it would be impossible for me to hike sixteen miles before dark. I pointed out on the map to Tim and Tom where to pick me up—about nine miles north at VA 615—and they agreed to meet me there in late afternoon.

The terrain on this section is as easy as the guidebooks tout, and the Trail—this late in the season—was isolated. Meandering through rhododendron tunnels on this seasonably cool day, I descended Garden Mountain and ascended Brushy Mountain. (Another one?) I waded across numerous streams, including many branches of Little Wolf Creek, which twists and turns back on itself through the valley.

It took only a few hours to hike this beautiful section, so I reached the designated meeting place at VA 615 by midafternoon. As I stretched out on the lawn of a charming little country church, it occurred to me I still had time before dark to hike the easy seven miles to US 21, where I had originally told Tim and Tom to meet me. But I had no cell phone service to let them know the change of plan. I just sat there on my butt, wasting half a day and leaving a seven-mile unfinished stretch that I knew would irritate me like chigger bites I couldn't get at to scratch.

That evening as we sat around the fire pit, I admitted to myself that my stubbornness and inflexibility had created the very opposite of what I wanted my AT experience to be. Instead of relaxation and enjoyment, I found stress and regret. Moreover, I had forced my family into accommodating what was my obsession, not theirs. This weekend would not go down as one of my prouder moments.

* * *

I wanted one more quick hike before the year's end, and Jen happily agreed to accompany me over the November Veterans' Day weekend. We planned to pick up where we had left off at Clingmans Dome in 2007 and—at last—hike the eight-mile northbound descent to Newfound Gap at US 441. We were cutting it close this late in the season because an autumn snowfall could close the seven-mile paved road from US 441 to Clingmans Dome. It normally closes annually from late November until early April, but Mother Nature keeps her own calendar.

By early Friday afternoon, we were in Gatlinburg with light snow and mild temperatures. As we drove up 441, intending to leave our car at Newfound Gap and hitch a ride to Clingmans Dome, the snow cover became thicker and the highway slicker. Sure enough, a metal gate had been pulled across the road near the Sugarland Visitor Center, and a couple of park rangers' vehicles sat with lights flashing. *Dammit!* A ranger told us it was possible the road would be open the next day if the snow stopped falling and the plows could clear the streets.

I studied our maps while Jen, unconcerned, sat on the ground happily munching dried banana chips. I believe that girl would follow me through the gates of hell itself.

"Look," I said. "I think we can forget about the AT for today. It'll be dark in a few hours, and who knows what the roads will be like if we try to drive to another section?"

"Fine by me."

"Let's just take one of these short park trails around the visitor center here," I continued. "Then we'll get a hotel room and see what the morrow brings."

We left the car at the visitor center and walked on a wide, well-trodden path for a couple of miles back into Gatlinburg to check out the hotel situation. The establishment we chose was a run-down, concrete edifice touting "Hot tubs!" and "Balcony views!" This was the place for us, we decided, and retraced our steps to retrieve the car.

Our room was on the second floor with the promised balcony, a narrow ledge with two old, scarred plastic chairs and a waist-high railing, perched over the rushing Little Pigeon River. High branches of trees on the opposite riverbank were maybe twenty-five feet from us. For several hours, until dark and dinnertime, we sat drinking wine and watching a family of raccoons chase each other through the treetops. It was, as advertised, a fine balcony view.

The morrow brought sunny skies to Gatlinburg, but as we drove to the visitor center, the sunshine turned into gray cloud cover, and the temperature dropped steadily. The metal gate still blocked entry onto 441. Not even a park ranger was around. My heart sank. Here we were, probably the last chance for a hike this year, and it wouldn't even be on the goddamn Appalachian Trail. But as I looked at Jen with her ever-present smile and cheerful attitude, my spirits lifted. I would be to my friend what she always was to me: optimistic and present.

Okay, we have food and water, good cold-weather gear, and ten hours of daylight, but realistically, we can't walk to Clingmans Dome either on the road or side trails, hike the eight-mile section we had planned, and then get back here before dark. You know what? That's okay. We are in the Smokies. It's a beautiful day and there are plenty of other trails.

We set off into the wild, snow well over our boot tops at times, on a loop hike of about ten miles through the Great Smoky Mountains National Park.

There is something very satisfying, even rewarding about hiking in winter. If you are dressed warmly enough, you can be quite comfortable physically. Gloves and hat and layered clothing are key. You will see very few, if any, other people. When and if you do, you acknowledge one another quietly with a shared sense of pride as if to say, "Hello, comrade. Yes, we are the brave ones, the serious hikers. Let us leave all those fair-weather Sunday strollers to their afternoon naps and TV football games. *Salud!*"

Winter also offers the best opportunity to see wildlife up close and personal. No underbrush or bushes block the view into the forest. The trees, with their branches bare of leaves, seem taller and straighter and offer no hidden refuge to a fleeing creature. Animals are less camouflaged than in the seasons of foliage and shadow, and their tracks are more noticeable in the pristine snow. Small rodents and rabbits leave tiny, feathery tracks across the surface, but larger mammals easily break the fragile crust, leaving deep, round spaces like those made by a posthole digger.

Conversely, the animals seem less aware of us. Perhaps our scent doesn't reach their noses on a still, cold day, and the sound of our footsteps, muffled by the snow, doesn't reach their ears.

A couple of hours into the hike, we rounded a bend and noticed a churned-up swath just to the side of the trail, snow mixed with black soil and moldering leaves. We saw what we thought were hoof prints. Deer had apparently been pawing at the snow to get at whatever plant life was buried beneath. I bent over to peer more closely. Just as I straightened up to say, "Jen, I don't think this is deer," she, slightly behind me, clutched my right shoulder with her left hand and hissed, "What is *that*?"

Ten or twelve yards ahead of us, just off the trail to the right in a small clearing, was a stout, black creature the size of a very large dog. He was long-bodied and short-legged and snuffled at the ground. We stood stock-still for a few seconds. My mind at last registered what we were seeing. I whispered, "I think it's a boar."

He lifted his snout, swung his huge head toward us and froze for a few seconds. We could clearly see his yellow tusks through the dirty snow clinging to the black bristles. Then he was off, running awkwardly through the woods at a ninety-degree angle away from us. He never once looked back.

Boars, also called feral hogs or wild pigs, are rather common in the Appalachian Mountains, but I never saw another one in my thirteen years on the Trail. (My daughter told me years later, a sow and three piglets once approached her tent at dusk. She banged her cooking pot and they fled.) There are different theories as to how the boars came to be so prevalent in the woods of Florida, Tennessee, Georgia, and North Carolina. Perhaps they are descendants of the domestic pigs raised by early white settlers or of the hogs brought to America by Europeans for hunting sport. It's probably a combination of the two, but in any case, they have the reputation of formidable beasts. I have never heard of any hikers getting into a tangle with one, which is just as well because I suspect, with his sharp hooves and tusks designed to dig and gouge, the boar would win. Perhaps his very reputation and his unattractiveness protect us and him. No one wants to get too close.

Jen and I continued on our way, stopping frequently to observe tracks and then lift our eyes to search the woods. *Is this a fox? A bobcat? A coyote?*

"Look at this." Jen pointed to a huge track on a small embankment just to the left of the trail. We had no problem determining it had been left by a very large bear. The pad was five to six inches wide, and the indentations made by the four claws bit deeply into the snow.

We continued on and hadn't gone far when I saw, some distance ahead, a small, sleek, brown bear scampering out of sight over a ridge. Jen did not see him, but I was sure this young teddy bear was not the one who had left the huge tracks. Not a quarter mile later, we saw two cubs heading away from us to our left through the woods. Baby bears everywhere, but no mama in sight—which is not to say she didn't see us. We were motivated to finish this beautiful hike with pep in our steps, and we ended this perfect day and this imperfect year back in the land of "Hot tubs!" and "Balcony views!"

* * *

The often difficult and sometimes unsatisfactory hikes of this year were nevertheless part of the journey, and even miles hiked in resentment or frustration are steps forward. This final hike with Jen, even though it was not on the AT, had turned out to be full of adventure and joy. To have abandoned the weekend or to have driven further in search of the AT would have been to miss what both Jen and I later said was one of the best trips ever. If it seemed that, at times, I was pushing a boulder up a hill, well, I could remind myself that this was a boulder of my own choosing, and it was okay to sometimes set it aside.

CHAPTER 7

2011 (125 MILES)

HIGHWAY 615, VIRGINIA, TO US 21, VIRGINIA

HIGHWAY 624, VIRGINIA, TO HIGHWAY 311, VIRGINIA

PEARISBURG, VIRGINIA, TO HIGHWAY 42, VIRGINIA

HIGHWAY 42, VIRGINIA, TO ANDY LAYNE TRAIL, VIRGINIA

INDIAN GRAVE GAP, TENNESSEE, TO IRON MOUNTAIN GAP, TENNESSEE

ANDY LAYNE TRAIL, VIRGINIA, TO BEARWALLOW GAP, VIRGINIA

My Tennessee and North Carolina friends began to decline my hiking invitations. Driving to a starting point was now an all-day proposition, and I was forced to acknowledge that of the more than 1,500 miles of the Appalachian Trail that lie ahead of me, most of them would be hiked solo. However, I also realized that for almost any endeavor, it does indeed take a village. I had already begun to learn of the generosity that is sprinkled along the Trail, and this year I would also learn that angels and magic are everywhere. If I was to be alone most of the time, I would not be without support.

On Presidents' Day weekend, I was determined to do the seven-mile stretch I had skipped in the Wytheville, Virginia, area. This may seem, well, a little anal. Who would ever know or care if I skipped seven relatively easy miles of a 2,200-mile footpath?

Even thru-hikers occasionally skip some miles. Walking more than two thousand miles in one long hike, in a time frame dictated by weather, is a Herculean task by anyone's measure, and it's not like there's an official waving around a clipboard or blowing a whistle. To *yellow-blaze* means to walk (or even get a ride) on a road to get from a section of the Trail to another as a shortcut. This is not to be confused with hitching a ride into a town or a supply source. To *blue-blaze* means to leave the AT and use side trails. However, this is rarely efficient because most side trails are just as arduous as the AT itself and won't often save you many miles. The most frequently used alternative blazing system is probably a combination of the two just mentioned. You take a blue-blazed side trail off the AT, walk on a road, and then take another blue-blazed side trail to reconnect with the AT. *Aqua-blazing* means that you canoe or kayak on a waterway instead of a certain section of the Trail. It is popular on the Shenandoah River, but again, you probably won't save much time this way. Of course, you will have to make arrangements with an outfitter or a friend in the area, but it does sound like fun. (There are two other phrases that are used within this terminology: *pink-blazing* and *banana-blazing*. I will leave the definition of those to the reader's imagination.)

I wanted to hold true to my original goal of hiking every step of the entire Appalachian Trail. As a section hiker, it would be easy to skip a few miles here and there, but that could easily turn into more than a few miles, and before you know it, large chunks would be over-looked. My aim was not so much to seek self-acclaim in hiking every stretch; I was just afraid of missing out on something. To skip even these seven miles would be starting down a slippery slope, leading only to disappointment in myself.

So in mid-February, I parked my car at US 21 and walked the seven miles south to VA 615 where I had stopped in October, turned around and hiked back. This is known as an in-and-out hike, and normally, most hikers, including myself, eschew them. It's seeing the same stuff twice while only gaining half the AT miles, but in this case, I did gain some sense of closure.

The next day, I only had time for a short hike before driving home. I chose an interesting-looking section from VA 624 to VA 311. It was some fifty miles north, but the maps indicated those fifty Trail miles would be strenuous and difficult to access, so I decided to save them for a backpacking trip.

The day was cold and overcast but dry. I crunched merrily along through cow pastures, over stiles, and up and down the sawtooth ridges, completing the six-mile trek in only a few hours. As I drove home, I thought about how I'd spent the previous thirty-six hours and about what Royal Robbins, the legendary Yosemite rock climber, once said, "Getting to the top is nothing—how you get there is everything." Driving fourteen hours round-trip to add thirteen miles to my AT total—the second half of the in-and-out didn't count, remember— seemed a little counterintuitive to that idea. *Oh well*, I thought, *no one's ever confused me with Royal Robbins, and they're certainly not going to start now.*

* * *

June and summer heat arrived in full force, and equipped with a new backpack Tim had given me, I set off for a solo forty-mile hike from Pearisburg, Virginia to VA 42 near…well, not really near anything. Roanoke, just to provide a landmark, is some thirty miles to the west by road.

The weather was hot, and my pack heavy as I left my car at the start trailhead in Pearisburg on Friday. *Screw it. I will hike my hike, and when I finish, which should be well before dark on Sunday, I'll hitchhike back.* It would be a long hitch, but I was optimistic and determined to not let the stress of logistics dampen my enthusiasm.

A steep, rocky climb brought me to about 3,500 feet, and I stayed at that elevation most of the day as I crossed the Rice Fields meadow and wandered into the Peters Mountain Wilderness. Swamps and switchbacks dominate this stretch, and after almost fifteen miles, I was ready to camp. Setting up my tent on a solitary site, I was exhausted and content. But I was also a little worried that I still had a long way to my destination of VA 42, and when I did reach it, I would have to get a hitch back to my car.

Just stop it! Things will work out. Enjoy the peaceful night, the breeze in the trees.

Well, if I do sixteen to eighteen miles tomorrow, I'll only have to do eight or nine on Sunday, which I could easily do before dark—Go to sleep!

The next day kicked my ass with a rocky ascent of Big Mountain and then on to Peters Mountain. I slogged through the day, enjoying the views and the solitude but suffering from the heat and the heaviness of my pack. I intended to hike until at least dusk and set up camp at a shelter about seventeen miles in, a long day by almost any section hiker's standard.

About three miles short of my goal, in the very late afternoon, I came to a gravel road crossing where there was a parking area large enough for several cars. It was empty except for a midsize RV that looked hard-traveled and well used. I crossed the area and continued to follow the blazes north into the woods but had second thoughts and returned to the parking lot. Groaning with relief, I took off my pack and sat on the ground to gratefully lean back against a tree.

Within a few minutes, a small, gray-haired man, maybe in his late sixties, emerged from the RV's side door. He maneuvered himself slowly to the ground, where a couple of folding chairs had been set up in the camper's shade. He noticed me, small and dirty and immobile under the tree, and offered a broad smile and a wave.

"Hey, there," he called.

"Hi." I lifted a hand.

He puttered around a bit at the camper's edge before approaching me to introduce himself as Bill. He was very chatty and sweet and probably found me a bit standoffish, but I was literally too tired to hold up my end of the conversation.

Bill himself wasn't a hiker. "Bad knee. But I bring my wife and her sister up here every summer—we live in Florida, you know. They hike a section, and I drive around and pick them up. Help them out, you know, cooking and stuff."

About this time, two very fit-looking women, easily in their sixties judging from their long gray hair and weathered faces, stepped out of the woods into the clearing.

"Ah, here they are now." Bill grinned widely.

They nodded and smiled politely as they moved to the camper but made no effort to engage me in conversation. They probably were used to Bill serving as spokesperson for their little group.

"You hungry?" Bill asked. "We got plenty of food."

"Oh, no, no, I'm fine," I declined, thinking of the smashed Pop-Tarts and dry trail mix that had been the day's nourishment.

"You want to camp here? There's a clear spot just up in the woods there. Group of fellas stayed there last night."

"I need to push on a few more miles to the next shelter," I said, although the thought of strapping my pack on and taking one more step was almost more than I could bear.

"Okey dokey." Bill smiled and reached into a front pocket. He handed me a two-inch, wooden whistle carved to look like a little hiking stick-figure, complete with a drawn-on face and a perky acorn hull for a hat.

"I sit and whittle these while I'm waiting for the girls, give 'em out to hikers." He smiled and returned to the RV.

I studied the little work of art—I have it still—and thought of the kindness of strangers. The late afternoon started giving way to dusk. The shadow of the camper lengthened until it blended with those of the trees, and then the entire clearing was sunless and peaceful. I had yet to move. The camper door opened, and Bill, with the aid of a walking stick, made his way slowly to me carrying a bowl.

"Here you go. Gotta keep your strength up."

I might have had tears in my eyes as I accepted the scratched plastic bowl and spoon. Bill returned to his lawn chair, and I slowly ate the cool, slippery canned peaches and cheap chocolate cookies, which had been softened by the syrup. I am not exaggerating when I say that bowl of peaches was the best thing I have ever eaten.

I hiked no farther that evening. After returning the empty bowl to Bill and telling him we were going to be neighbors for the night, I set up my tent. I read blissfully by headlamp until all the windows of the RV went dark.

The next morning was overcast and cooler as I broke camp and stepped onto the northbound Trail. I hesitated with a backward glance at the sleeping RV, wondering if I should call out my thanks and farewells, but I did not wish to wake anyone. After a moment of watching for any sign of activity, I quietly moved on.

Trail Angels are people who provide assistance in a variety of ways to hikers. This assistance is known as Trail Magic. It can come in the form of giving a tired hiker a ride into town, leaving cold clean water or snacks at a junction, or even providing hot meals at a road crossing. Most of the time, Trail Angels never know the recipient of their charity or even if it was received. Complete anonymity embodies this purest form of altruism. My hope is that the Angels find some happiness in imagining the look of astonishment on a hungry or thirsty hiker's face as she beholds the magic. In recent years, there has been some criticism among the hiking community regarding Trail Angels and—more appropriately—hikers who fail to remove the trash (empty bottles, food wrappers, etc.) from goodies left at the roadside. In order to keep this lovely tradition alive and healthy, we have to police ourselves. Who wants to live in a world without angels?

Any hope this day would be easier than the last was shattered as I climbed Salt Pond Mountain, Wind Rock, and Lone Pine Peak. Between summits, I sidestepped down to creeks and gaps and in the afternoon; I again ascended and descended. Now up Johns Creek Mountain and Kelly Knob, then back down to Laurel Creek. The landmarks blurred into one another until I barely registered them. I simply walked from one mountain or stream to the next for twelve or thirteen miles, my mind focused on my footsteps, until I reached the paved blacktop of VA 42 in what had become a light, sporadic rainfall.

With groaning relief, I took off my pack, retrieved my rain poncho from it, and plopped down at the side of the road to face reality. It was late afternoon, and rain clouds continued to rumble as I looked at the maps to figure out how to get back to my car in Pearisburg, some sixty miles by road to the south. Well, there was no way around it. I simply had to stand up, stick out my thumb, and hope someone would stop. The relief I had felt at getting off the mountains was now replaced by the familiar anxiety of trying to get a ride.

After at least an hour with no luck, a small pickup truck with the bed full of miscellaneous bags and boxes pulled over. A young, free-spirited-looking couple peered at me from the open passenger window of the cab and asked, "Where you headed?"

I explained where my car was. They said they were headed to the interstate but for me to hop in the back, and they'd see how far they could take me. I awkwardly climbed in with my pack and made a little nest among the cargo, sitting atop an old Army duffle bag, with knees drawn up and my back to the cab.

The dark-haired boy revved the truck's engine and screeched out onto the two-lane blacktop, with his left hand sticking out the driver's window to give me a thumbs-up. Or maybe it was a warning. He drove like a man just released from a twenty-year prison stint, careening around hairpin turns and mountain-road curves.

It started raining in earnest, and I pulled my poncho over my head. After a few minutes, my chauffeur braked suddenly and pulled over. The passenger door opened, and the girl scooched over to let me in.

"Thank you, thank you," I gushed as I clutched my pack on my lap and tried to avoid getting water all over everything. The cab was no less cluttered than the truck bed. Oddly enough, there was a Beatles CD playing, and not so oddly I guess, a faint but unmistakable odor of weed.

The couple was maybe in their early twenties and appeared healthy but disheveled, as if they'd been traveling hard. She, open and friendly, explained they had been working on a commune in Pennsylvania but had heard there was plenty of work to be found in the tourist town of

Gatlinburg. They were on their way there, maybe to wait tables and hike in the Smokies. Boyfriend added they had tents and gear in the back and camped out most nights.

These Angels insisted (although I did not protest too much) on taking me all the way to my car, where we arrived well after dark and a few wrong turns. I gave them some food from the back of my car and insisted they take what little cash I had, perhaps twenty bucks. Whatever it was, it wasn't enough to thank them for getting me back to my little port in the storm after sixty hours at sea.

* * *

Twenty-five days later, in early July, I was back exactly where I had been picked up by my little hippie friends. It was again very hot, and I was again solo but buoyed by the knowledge the year was scarcely half over, and this forty-mile trip would bring my 2011 total to over one hundred miles thus far. This section of the Trail in the Blue Ridge mountain range offers some of the most beautiful views of the Appalachians and includes the iconic Triple Crown: Dragon's Tooth, Tinker Cliffs, and McAfee Knob.

My day began with a steep, two-thousand-foot ascent to Bruiser's Knob. The trail then levels off for several miles, culminating with Sinking Creek Mountain and a long, difficult descent to VA 621 and Craig Creek. Hiking at a good pace, although the heat was pretty extreme, I felt relatively confident I could do the next day's fifteen miles in a similar fashion and then move on to the next challenge. I was wrong.

After an achy and lonely night in my tent, I pushed north and skyward for almost four miles to the Audie Murphy Monument, a man-made, waist-high, stone edifice just a couple of hundred yards off the trail on Brushy Mountain. Murphy's chartered plane crashed here in 1971, and the marker was erected here a few years later by the VFW to honor his heroic actions in World War II. A few wilted and faded posies, placed by visitors and hikers, lay at the base of the monument. I set a small smooth stone among a pile of others and paused for a few minutes in appreciation.

There are several monuments along the AT that honor various heroes or are placed in tribute to preservationists or patrons. The locations of many of these sites—or at least of the more notable ones—can be found in guidebooks and will vary in size and grandeur. The imposing Laura Spelman Rockefeller Memorial at Newfound Gap is an example. You will also see humble acknowledgments to folks less famous or unsung— maybe just an understated plaque screwed into the side of a rock. These are usually placed by a family member or loved one in tribute to a fellow hiker or nature lover. However, for any artificial alteration or addition to the Trail, permission must be obtained from the Appalachian Trail Conservancy and/or the appropriate trail maintenance organization. Hint, hint, in case any of my future descendants wish to enshrine my accomplishment.

Back down the mountain to Trout Creek, and half the day gone when I hiked up (and down and up and down) Cove Mountain to the infamous Dragon's Tooth. This entire seven-mile section from Trout Creek to VA 624 is just one long obstacle course of rocks and boulders ranging in size from Volkswagens to Winnebagos.

Dragons Tooth is basically a forty-foot tall rock rising up from the rocky trail known as the dragon's spine or back. The sides of this beast slope down on either side into gnarled and twisty woods, where the scaly treetops eagerly wait to impel a careless or inexperienced hiker. Fortunately, the AT skirts the tooth itself, and I had absolutely no intention of hauling my butt up and over it. It was enough that I found myself on this jagged pile of rocks with the knowledge that one slip or misstep could mean utter disaster. *What the hell am I doing here?* I slowly picked my way down to the highway, discouraged and exhausted. I felt very old and out of my element.

The next day, after walking four miles and climbing a thousand feet in July heat, I reached McAfee Knob. "Knob" seems misleading in this case. On the 3,200-foot summit of Catawba Mountain, it is more of a rocky shelf that juts out ten or twelve feet, and below this shelf is a whole lot of air. As you step onto it, you can't help but think, *Gee, I hope this holds my weight.*

The views of the valley below and the surrounding mountains are almost literally breathtaking, and I struggled to fill my lungs with the clean, clear air. Several hikers who had walked in on the side trail from VA 311 were scampering about, pausing now and then to lift their faces to the sky and their cameras to each other.

After a little catnap on the sun-warmed slab (well away from the lip), I descended Catawba and walked five more miles to Tinker Cliffs and the blue-blazed Andy Layne Trail that was my ticket out. Tinker Cliffs seem to be the stepsisters of the iconic McAfee and Dragon's Tooth. They don't get the attention they deserve, even though they are part of the Jefferson National Forest Triple Crown. The views are stunning and the climbs challenging. But in my exhaustion after this long and difficult day, the sheerness of Tinker Cliffs failed to stir me as much as it deserved. I was just too tired to appreciate the beauty and audacity of this particular jewel of the crown.

The Andy Layne Trail to US 779 and my car was another test of endurance. I was short on water and very, very thirsty, possibly on the verge of serious dehydration, as I labored along, torturing myself with a menu of favorite cold beverages. *Sweet tea, Dr. Pepper, lemonade, Fanta orange...*

When I finally reached the highway, I drove as fast as I could to the nearest Kwik Mart. I staggered inside, sweaty and dirty, and lunged toward the soft drink station to gulp down cup after cup of liquid sugar. A uniformed police officer near the cash register watched me carefully, as if I might be a wanted or missing person. I could have easily been mistaken for either.

❄ ❄ ❄

The hiking trips of the year thus far had covered a lot of miles, but now in mid-August, I only had time for a short weekend trip. The eleven miles I had skipped in 2009 from Indian Grave Gap to Iron Mountain Gap near Erwin, Tennessee, would fill this bill nicely. My hikes of the year had also all been solitary, and now I longed for some company to share my hard-won wisdom and experience with. I enlisted Melanie and her friend Cade to be my devoted followers.

Melanie and I picked up Cade at the University of Tennessee in Knoxville on a Friday afternoon and continued southeast to Erwin, where we checked into an inexpensive roadside motel. A somber woman, dressed in a sari, eyes large and dark below a red bindi, presided over the lobby, where an aroma of cooking spices wafted in from a side room.

"I'm here to hike the AT with my girls. Do you know of anybody who could give us a ride from the trailhead at Iron Mountain Gap tomorrow?" I asked this matriarch.

The woman, clearly wanting to be helpful, fished around in a pile of old take-out menus and thin phonebooks beside the counter. Triumphantly, she handed me a sepia-edged index card that had several thumbtack holes, as if it had been displaced numerous times from a bulletin board. *Randy's Taxi Service* and a seven-digit phone number were handwritten in faded ink.

I wasn't hopeful the taxi service was still in business, but while Melanie and Cade took off to explore the nightlife in Johnson City, I called the number.

"Hello?" a male voice said in the same softly questioning tone people generally use when the letters "FBI" show up on their phone's screen if I call from my desk at work without using caller ID block.

"Yes, hello there. I'm looking for Randy."

After a brief, suspicious pause, "This is Randy."

Hallelujah!

We made arrangements to meet at 8:00 a.m. where the AT crosses TN 107 / NC 226 and agreed on what I thought was the very reasonable price of thirty bucks. With firm plans in place and the girls safely back to the motel, I slept soundly, lulled by the sounds of the trucks whining past on the highway.

Sure enough, a dented and rusted brown Buick LeSabre was waiting in the small parking area along the very rural road when we arrived on what was already becoming a hot, muggy day. Randy unwedged himself from behind the steering wheel, heaved himself out the driver's door and gave us a wave and a grin through a forest of beard. He was a mountain of a man, well over six feet tall, with curly black hair. Shirtless, wearing only farmer's overalls and, oddly, flip-flops, he had to weigh close to three hundred pounds—probably about the combined weight of us three girls. I took the front passenger seat, checking for interior door handles.

"We need you to take us down to Highway 395 where the AT crosses," I said. "Then we'll hike back up here to our car."

"Dang, that's a really long way. You know, I could take you farther up the mountain. Then you wouldn't have to walk for so long."

Randy didn't seem to grasp our purpose and seemed very concerned about our safety. As we drove along the dusty road, he warned us about snakes and bears and even told us a long story about a spider bite on his toe that had gotten infected—hence, the flip-flops.

I explained that I had already hiked a lot of the AT and was pretty familiar with its dangers. He asked how I normally got rides from section to section.

"Well, a lot of the time I just end up hitchhiking."

"What?" Randy turned in the driver seat to face me, incredulous. "Don't you never let me hear of you hitchhiking up here. These people are crazy. Call me. Where you girls from, anyway?"

When I told him Melanie and I hailed from Nashville, he replied, "I love Nashville! Went over there a couple of years ago and saw Rascal Flatts at the Ryman. I love me some Rascal Flatts. Was gonna go see Shania Twain last year, but transmission on my car went out.

"I love me some Shania," he added sadly.

Cade spoke up from the back, "I live in Knoxville."

"Knoxville?" he exclaimed. "There's crazy people there! I wouldn't give you a *nickel* to live in Knoxville."

(For years after, every time I drove through the fine city of Knoxville, I would say aloud, "I wouldn't give a *nickel* to live here.")

Fortunately, Randy again changed the subject, and we spoke of more pleasant things until he delivered us safely to our destination. After tsk-tsking us for several minutes—"Have you got plenty to eat? Water? First aid kit?"—he left us with some final words of caution.

"Now, y'all be real careful. There's crazy people up here."

I thought of the great travel writer, Paul Theroux, who said that to travel widely requires one to depend on strangers and to trust them. Now it occurred to me that the stranger must also trust us, and once that has been established on both sides, there is nothing strange about it.

Our hike was glorious. Cade had been a gifted athlete in high school and now effortlessly skimmed along the trail. Melanie stayed close by me to chat about all things daughterly and to marvel aloud at the ease and pleasure of this adventure. The day was hot but the woods gorgeous in their full-summer foliage as we climbed to Beauty Spot, a wildflower-dotted bald at 4,500 feet, and then to Unaka Mountain at over five thousand feet. Here we stopped for lunch and spread out our picnic on large, flat rocks surrounded by shady hemlocks.

Cade, enjoying a gas station sandwich, mused, "I wonder if Randy is still worried about us. I hope not."

As for Melanie, I think she was intrigued by her first visit to the AT and now had some understanding of the allure that had drawn her mother to it. She was deferential and even seemed impressed (to her novice eye) by my skill. It would take the most hardened skeptic to not appreciate the splendor of this section's beauty, and I believe, for Melanie on this day, a little seed was planted in her heart that none of us could have expected to take root and flourish in the way it eventually did.

* * *

In mid-September, again solo, I took what turned out to be my last AT trip of 2011. I drove alone to Virginia to hike a respectable thirty-two miles, broken into two-and-a-half days, starting from the Andy Layne Trail where I had finished in July and ending at milepost 90.9 on the Blue Ridge Parkway at Bearwallow Gap. I didn't like the sound of *that*. On some maps, this is named Bear*swallow*—not very reassuring in either case. But I parked my car there and, with a hopeful grin, stuck out my thumb to head west.

The days were still hot, though the nights were beginning to cool off. This section involves a few steep ascents, most notably the Peaks of Otter near the hike's end. The challenges, however, are easily mitigated by the loveliness of the path and the beauty of the views from the knobs. Tinker Cliffs lies to the west, small towns to the east, and almost always, one can see the black ribbon of the parkway itself stretching long and then recoiling. I walked alone and found serenity in the solitary rhythm of my breath and boots. The hours of daylight and darkness passed in a comforting routine of sleep and wakefulness and of sunshine and moonglow. I found the harmony—which surely nature intends, but often eludes us mere humans—in every mile and minute.

I slept two nights on the Trail in my little tent, and on Day Three, worn and dirty but happy and proud, I rounded a bend at a trail intersection and came upon two young men huddled over a paper map. I cleared my throat and jangled my pack a bit to alert them to my presence. (The Trail, often carpeted by pine needles and surrounded by dense woods, is very noise absorbent. I've had entire Boy Scout troops pass me as I've squatted mid-pee several feet off the path, and I never even heard them coming.)

The two fellows jumped as I approached, and one clutched the other's shoulder. "You scared us to death!" They wore jeans and carried no packs. I pegged them as car travelers taking a break from the parkway.

"I'm so sorry. I didn't mean to scare you," I smiled.

They apparently decided—after taking in my diminutive size and overall dishevelment—that I posed no threat, and we relaxed into conversation.

"We're looking for the Appalachian Trail," said the taller one, glancing at his map and then back over his shoulder.

"Oh. Well, you're standing on it."

"What? There's no sign." He sounded doubtful.

"No, but look, see the white marks painted on the trees?" I pointed to a large oak a few feet north and then behind me to another one. "That's how you know you're on the AT."

"Cool," one said. "We just wanted to take a little hike and see the sights. Which way's the best, do you think?"

"I haven't been north yet, but there's a really nice spot a couple of miles back with great views."

"Two miles!" the shorter dude exclaimed. They recoiled as if I'd suggested they walk barefoot across the Mojave. "Good grief, how far are you hiking?"

I explained that I was on the trail for a few days, and they seemed duly impressed. I wondered what their reaction might have been had they met up with a thru-hiker.

"So you sleep in a tent? What do you eat? Berries and stuff?"

"Uh, no, I carry food in my pack."

They seemed disappointed.

"Have you seen any bears?" one of them asked, maybe a little hopefully.

"Not on this trip. I've seen them other times, though, on the AT." Sorry to disappoint them again, I added, "Hey, but I did see a porcupine just a few minutes ago, all curled up on the side of the trail. Almost stepped on him."

"Oh, yeah," the taller guy nodded. "I just saw one too."

His companion stared at him, and then slowly and deliberately said, "You just saw a porcupine? You mean between the car and here?"

"Uh-huh. Didn't you see it crawling around under a big tree?"

"I can't believe you saw a porcupine and didn't even say anything!"

"Well, I didn't know I was supposed to point out every squirrel along the way. God."

"A porcupine is not a squirrel. It's not like you see a porcupine every day."

They obviously didn't need me any longer. "Okay, guys, nice chatting with you, but I need to push on."

"Oh, sure." They wished me luck, and I moved on, grinning.

Behind me, I heard a soft voice, chiding, "Gosh, give a guy a break. I still can't believe I missed seeing a porcupine…"

So, with humor and sweetness, this final Trail adventure of the year ended. I left the porcupines to their winter dens and the Blue Ridge Parkway to its weekend nature seekers, knowing I would see both again in the spring.

* * *

Whenever I returned from a hiking trip, even a short one, I was always aware of the contrast and yet also the parallels of career and hobby. One seemed to offset the other and made my life feel balanced. My job consisted normally of ringing phones, loud voices, case write-ups, boring meetings, paperwork drudgery, PowerPoint presentations, data upload, document analysis, contradictory regulations, training seminars, interviews, complaint resolution, and office gossip.

But there were many times—and it seemed particularly so this year—that this daily routine was interrupted by drama and spectacle: the late-night callouts, the early morning search warrants, the hastily written operation orders, the silence before the go-ahead, the whir of helicopters, the crackle of radio traffic, the shouts of SWAT teams, the clap of flash-bangs, the camaraderie of teamwork, the gratitude from victims, and the slow creaking sound of the wheels of justice turning.

Likewise, hiking long miles can be a monotonous routine. Step after step, hour after hour, you walk on a trail that goes on and on. The surrounding trees and bushes are a constant. The sun hangs steady and the woods are quiet. Your feet are tired and your back is sore. Then you round a bend, and there stands a coyote in your path, or you top a rise and see a vista of snow-capped mountains, or you leave the woods, and a flower-filled meadow stretches out like a colorful quilt. *Ahh*, then you think, *this is why I chose this path.*

＊ ＊ ＊

As the year wound down, I took two separate trips to Europe. In early November, Tim and I visited Melanie for a few days where she was spending a semester abroad at Maynooth University in Ireland. (She had chosen this destination in part because, in its setting and architecture, the university greatly resembles Hogwarts.)

Then in late November, I again hopped across the pond, this time to attend a work conference sponsored by the Metropolitan Police Service in London. (This organization—called the Met by the Brits—is perhaps more readily identifiable to Americans as Scotland Yard. However, that title really refers to the physical headquarters building, which is neither in Scotland nor in a yard.)

In Ireland, on a cold wet day, Tim, Melanie, and I hiked the eastern cliffs overlooking the Irish Sea. On another—slightly warmer, slightly dryer—day, we rambled for several miles through the countryside with its iconic thatched-roof cottages and bucolic sheep.

The diversity of Ireland (or anywhere, for that matter) can be remarkably observed if one opts to see it from a hiking path. By necessity, you are slow enough and close enough to see the small intricacies and smell the peculiar odors and even taste the local air. The salty spray of the sea on our faces as we carefully navigated the stony cliffside was left behind when we walked through the grassy fields where sheep grazed. The larger and braver of them softly butted our knees in curiosity, and the wool was soft and springy under our fingers. The tiny lambs in their pens bleated softly and sadly, calling for their mothers, as we passed.

While in England, I had a short "walking holiday" in the Cots-wolds, an area of rolling hills and charming towns in the southern part of the country. I was met at a bus station by Lois, the sturdy, middle-aged woman who had arranged my itinerary. ("I've always wanted to hike in America," she told me, "but all that hanging of foodstuff in trees and avoiding bears has put me rather off it, I dare say.")

For two and a half days, following the carefully written directions provided by Lois, I walked through the gray winter countryside. The farmers' fields are bordered by tall hedgerows, copses, and wooden fences complete with kissing gates. In the evenings, the sprinkle of lights from small villages consisting of perhaps twenty or thirty houses, a general store / post office / petrol station, a pub, and a church or two beckoned to me.

My lodgings were in simple homes or old barns converted to inns. I slept on mattresses that seemed to be filled with feathers and ate food—homemade jam and freshly baked bread, cheese made from the local supply of goats and cows, pot pies stuffed with vegetables grown in the allotments—that seemed to have been prepared by the gods. The weather was overall foggy rain, but I found the sheep were no less beguiling in their sodden woolen coats, and the scenery no less enchanting in its shroud than they would have been on a golden summer day.

* * *

Although my AT progress for the year had only been 125 miles, the hikes on other trails must count for something, even if just to remind me that everywhere there is magic, and everywhere there are angels. The world is really just a village after all. People like Tim and Melanie in Ireland, Lois and the Met officers in England, and on the Trail, Bill and Randy and the little hippie couple and the porcupine guys not only help make the journey easier; they make it infinitely more memorable. I never felt alone.

CHAPTER 8

2012 (150 MILES)

SMITH GAP ROAD, PENNSYLVANIA, TO WIND GAP, PENNSYLVANIA

JENKINS GAP, VIRGINIA, TO TRICO FIRE TOWER TRAIL, VIRGINIA

CLINGMANS DOME, TENNESSEE, TO NEWFOUND GAP, TENNESSEE

BEARWALLOW GAP, VIRGINIA, TO LONG MOUNTAIN WAYSIDE, VIRGINIA

LONG MOUNTAIN WAYSIDE, VIRGINIA, TO TYE RIVER, VIRGINIA

TYE RIVER, VIRGINIA, TO RIPRAP TRAIL, VIRGINIA

The eighth year of my hike would contain, like each year so far, joy and challenge. But it would also carry carelessness and loss, near misses and tragedy. Previous years had seen difficult hikes, to be sure, along with complications and hard times. But I would say, for the most part, I had sort of skipped blithely along, taking the smooth with the occasional rough, believing that all would be well if I just kept my head down and continued walking north. Taking life—and the people and things in it we love—for granted is not only dangerous but heartbreaking.

Tim and I flew to Yardley to visit his brother Tom and family over the January MLK holiday weekend. Tom's wife, Lynne, agreed to accompany me on a ten-mile AT hike from Smith Gap Road to Wind Gap (just south of the section I had done on my 2008 trip to Pennsylvania). Tim and Tom declined the invitation.

"No problemo," we told them. "You guys spend the day doing brotherly things, and we'll be home by dinnertime."

Lynne and I drove an hour or two west and parked at the Saylorsburg Road crossing at Wind Gap, our planned end point. We stood at the side of the road for a worryingly long time, hitchhiking thumbs aloft, before a very young man on his way to work at the nearby ski resort stopped in his small, beat-up car. I gave directions to Smith Gap as we putted along increasingly remote mountainous roads. Our driver began to worry about being late for work. Suddenly, he braked.

"Ah, here we are! I knew it was around here somewhere," he said proudly, pointing to an AT crossing sign.

I insisted our knight in beat-up armor take money for gas, and we waved goodbye as he sped off.

Several inches of snow covered the ground, but thankfully, no more was predicted. Though the sun was blindingly cheerful in a cloudless, bright-blue sky, the temperature remained in single digits all day, subzero with the wind chill factor.

We were dressed appropriately with hats and gloves and layers. Lynne had been raised on a farm in central Michigan and was no stranger to extreme weather. We would just have to walk briskly and take only very short rests in order to be safely back at the car by sundown.

The well-marked trail was rocky and sometimes slippery, but the views of farmland spread out below were beautiful. This was Lynne's first AT hike, and she was delighted. We occasionally stopped on a summit to snap photos and have a snack, but it was unpleasant to be still for more than a few minutes in the bitter cold. After several miles and a few hours, we came to a road crossing.

Smith Gap Road.

What?

This was where we were supposed to have started. Our knight, following my muddled directions, had dropped us off at the wrong road crossing. Instead of being halfway finished with a ten-mile hike, we were only a third of the way into a fifteen-mile trek to our car.

I couldn't apologize enough, but Lynne was gracious and willing to press on. The only other option was to try to get a ride from where we were, as there would be no more road crossings or side trails. We pulled out cell phones to tell Tim and Tom we would be late and discovered we had no service. Lynne suggested we turn off our phones to conserve the batteries in case we *really* needed them later.

We crunched on through the snowy heights, following one switch-back after another. The rocky trail was increasingly difficult to follow as the afternoon waned, sunlight diminished, and starlight took its place. I had two headlamps and gave one to Lynne, but the battery soon failed, and we were down to one beam of light to illuminate our progress from blaze to blaze. To stray off the trail and be lost in the woods with no shelter in these frigid temperatures would be a death sentence.

In contrast to our dismal situation, the landscape was stunningly beautiful. The moon was a huge yellow orb that seemed to take up the entire sky, and the trees were black skeletons that, paradoxically, seemed friendly as they rose from the crystal-white ground. We walked along, slowly and with steady encouragement to each other, until, laughing in relief, we reached the car.

It was near eight o'clock, and I immediately called Tim, concerned that he and Tom would be very worried about us.

"Oh, hey, there you are," he said. "When you gonna be here? Dinner's ready."

I chose to interpret his words as faith in my abilities rather than lack of concern. When we later regaled our husbands with our harrowing tale, I chose to minimize my role in getting us into this predicament in the first place. Lynne generously did not correct me.

✳ ✳ ✳

In late February, I was scheduled to attend the annual Special Agents Advisory Committee (SAAC) Conference, a forum in which representatives from each division bring agents' issues and concerns to the attention of the FBI director and upper management. Attendees are selected by their peers, and I was honored to have been chosen by the Memphis Division in a landslide of one vote to...well, I guess zero. I think the lone person who voted was the guy who had previously held the position and didn't want to do it anymore.

The conference was to be held at our training facility in Quantico, Virginia, which is within a couple of hours drive to several points along the AT. On a Friday evening, I flew into DC, rented a car, and drove to Front Royal, a historic old town beautifully situated in the Shenandoah Valley. I got a room, and Heather, who happened to be temporarily working in the DC area, joined me.

We hiked the first day of a surprisingly mild winter weekend from Jenkins Gap on Skyline Drive—an extension of the Blue Ridge Parkway—to Chester Gap at US Route 522. This relatively easy eight-mile section begins at 2,500 feet at Compton Peak and meanders down to one thousand feet. Heather and I, happy to once again be on the Trail and in each other's company, chatted the day away as the miles and hours slipped by. The woods were still and shadowy, the previous autumn's leaves dead and layered beneath the rime, sharing the black soil with the unborn grasses of the upcoming spring.

Next day we started at Chester Gap to hike the thirteen miles to Trico Fire Tower Trail where we had dropped a car. Our first several miles were a pleasant, uneventful ramble at low elevation with views of the Blue Ridge and the frequent company of deer and turkey. We stopped for lunch five miles in at the Jim and Molly Denton Shelter—named for a couple of trail maintainers whose work and love for the AT is well documented and is much appreciated by the weary hiker—but we could not linger to fully enjoy its nice lawn, tent pads, and picnic tables. We each faced two-hour drives to our respective destinations that evening, so we moved on.

The trail continues through woods and fields, crossing several streams and an old road or two. Heather, with her long legs, wandered ahead and out of my sight. In late afternoon, I passed an access trail to a shelter and briefly wondered if Heather might have nipped in there for a break, but I didn't stop to check. I hiked on another mile or two until I came to the Trico Fire Tower Trail, which would lead us a half mile to our car. This blue-blazed side trail was not well marked, and one could very easily clomp past it without even noting its existence.

Okay, a bit of a dilemma here.

Best-case scenario, Heather was ahead of me, had seen the blue-blazed trail, followed it to our car, and was propped up there, checking her watch and wondering where I was. Second-best, she was behind me, had stopped at that last shelter, and would now be along soon. Worst possibility, she had reached the intersection ahead of me, had not seen the blue-blazed trail and was now blithely skipping north along the white-blazed AT.

I sat there for several minutes, occasionally shouting out Heather's name as the shadows lengthened and pointlessly checking my cell phone for service. Then—mild epiphany—I decided to leave a sign. This would do no good if she were ahead of me, but I began to feel fairly certain she was behind me. I had been hiking pretty fast and felt sure I would have caught up with her had she still been ahead of me.

I arranged stones and sticks to form a large H directly on the trail where no one could miss it and fashioned an arrow pointing west at the trail intersection, like an island castaway spelling out SOS with driftwood. I don't get a lot of bright ideas, but this one was pretty damned good.

Trying the phone once again with no luck and with one final shout into the darkening woods, I hoisted my pack and stepped onto the access trail. A half mile and ten minutes later, I reached the car. No Heather.

Still no need to panic, but I was tired and frustrated. Heather probably was too, wherever the *fuck* she was.

I reached for the cell phone. Utter, blessed relief when I saw the bars. I heard the ringing, and Heather's voice said, "Hello?"

"Oh, my god. Where are you?"

"I'm not sure. I'm still on the AT. Did you already turn off?"

"Yes. Did you stop at that shelter?"

She had, so she had been somewhat behind me for the past few miles.

"It's all good. Just keep going, and you'll come to a trail crossing. I made a sign with sticks there on the path."

Silence.

"Oh…Well, I passed that. I guess I didn't think it was for me."

Who the hell did she think it was for? Hernando de Soto?

I shook my head in disappointment with myself. This was really my fault. We should not have separated, or at least, we should have had a designated meeting place and time.

"How long ago did you pass it?"

"Maybe a half-mile back."

She must have come across it within minutes of my turning off the AT.

"All right. Just turn around and walk south till you see that crossing. Follow the blue-blazed trail, and I'll walk in to meet you."

We were reunited within a half hour, and I felt chastened by the near miss; you don't always get second chances on the Trail. As I drove to Quantico, I thought of my carelessness not only on this hike but on the previous hike with Lynne. These woods and mountains are no place for sloppiness, and I needed to sharpen my game.

* * *

It had become a custom each year for my older sister, Patty, my mom, and myself to have a little vacation down on the Gulf of Mexico. Each May around Mother's Day, we packed the car with coolers, lawn chairs, beach towels, sunscreen, books, and groceries and drove south to a little oceanfront beach house in Gulf Shores. Here, for several days, we slept late, walked in the sand, read novels by day and played cards by night. We ate delicious greasy meals in tacky restaurants and watched the dolphins play in the waves and the pelicans fish for their dinner. It had been my foolish expectation that this annual tradition would go on indefinitely.

But in early March, Patty died unexpectedly. The world now seemed a little more out of kilter. Death, untimely, made me feel unbalanced. It's like a big stone in a pocket that forever pulls you sideways and makes it hard to stand up straight. All you can do is hope that whatever stones your loved one had to carry are tossed away now.

❋ ❋ ❋

We stumbled along through the ugly bitter March until it at last brought April. Hoping to make some sense out of the tangled year so far, I traveled to Gatlinburg to finally hike the elusive eight-mile stretch from Clingmans Dome to Newfound Gap.

Jen and Smokin' Goat accompanied me, and we got a room at our beloved "Balcony views!" and "Hot tubs!" hotel in Gatlinburg. Here we spent an evening of camaraderie with the raccoons (possibly the same family from our last visit?) playing in the trees along the riverbank.

Next morning we left the car at Newfound Gap. Hoisting light daypacks and wearing layers of clothing we would shed as the temperatures rose, we crossed busy US 441. Along paved and well-traveled Clingmans Dome Road, we turned to smile and lift our thumbs whenever a car passed, but we walked two or three miles before a minivan with a smiling couple and their very young daughter pulled over.

They drove us to the Clingmans Dome parking area from which we walked the half mile to the observation tower and the AT trailhead. Starting at 6,643 feet, the highest point on the AT, the exact spot where we had finished in 2007 (and where Denise Wolfe had stepped off the Trail and burst into tears), we hiked eight miles down to Newfound Gap at five thousand feet. After the descent of Clingmans, we ascended and descended Sugarland Mountain along switchbacks that zigzag through the woods, and we crossed muddy bogs on foot logs provided by diligent trail maintainers.

Spruce and fir covered the mountains, and the pungent scent reminded me of Christmases as a child when Daddy would chop down a tree. Early spring wildflowers, still tender and timid, and bramble bushes, not yet aggressive as they would be in late summer, lined the trail. I thought them sweet and shy and hoped that the wave of hikers soon to come through this place would be gentle.

By late afternoon, this long-delayed jaunt from Clingmans Dome to Newfound Gap was over, without misstep or mishap. Physically challenging, emotionally moving, and shared with two good friends, I had at last found closure with the Smokies and could close the book, literally and figuratively, on Georgia, Tennessee, and North Carolina.

* * *

I took off work for an entire week near the end of June to hike almost sixty miles from Bearwallow—or Bear*swallow*—Gap to Long Mountain Wayside, both points accessible from the Blue Ridge Parkway. The two Virginia towns marking either end of this hike are Buchanan and Buena Vista (charmingly pronounced Buck-anan and Boo-na Vista by the locals). I made the eight-hour drive from my house with the plan to be solo on the Trail for four days. Detailed plans had been laid and maps minutely studied, but even so, this was a long hike for me. I was nervously aware not only of my limitations but of the challenges of the Trail. I resolved to walk slowly, steadily, and above all, carefully.

The weather was fine, with a forecast for mild temperatures and occasional rain showers, when I stepped onto the twelve-inch-wide path at Bearwallow Gap. I immediately began a very steep ascent of Cove Mountain, followed by a five-mile descent to Jennings Creek. In those five miles, elevation drops from 2,700 to 1,100 feet, but strangely, it feels like you're always climbing. By the time I reached Jennings Creek, I wouldn't have been surprised to see smoke puffing from my boots.

After a nice footbath in the creek, I continued on for several more up-and-down miles and some ridgewalking. The sun was beginning to disappear behind the mountains when I reached Cornelius Creek Shelter, exhausted and still facing a few more miles to my planned campsite. A nice young couple, northbound thru-hikers, were finishing their dinner. They implored me to stay with them.

"It's getting dark," they said, "and there's plenty of room in the shelter."

"I better push on," I answered as I wearily dug out my headlamp. But the thought of walking even one more step and then having to set up my tent at some desolate site made me reconsider.

"Yes, thank you. I believe I will stay if you don't mind."

They seemed genuinely pleased. I suspect they were concerned about my clearly visible state of exhaustion and my advanced age (fifty-three!) and didn't want to worry about me stumbling along in the dark.

Hours passed peacefully in deep slumber. Then a terrifying, recurring nightmare visited me, and I woke, drenched with sweat, to see two anxious faces inches from my own.

"Oh, my god, are you okay? We heard you calling out in your sleep, and we were so worried."

"I'm sorry," I said, sitting up slowly in my sleeping bag, taking stock of reality. "This happens sometimes. I'm really sorry I scared you."

"It's okay. We just didn't know whether to try and wake you."

I reached for my water bottle and splashed some drops on my face. "I'm fine, really. Try to get some sleep. It won't happen again tonight."

After I assured them that I didn't need anything, they settled back into their sleeping bags, and I eventually drifted off to their soft rustlings and murmurings.

At first light, I heard them packing up their gear to move on. I did not rise but called out softly, "Thank you. I'm glad you were here."

They went on their way with what I suppose was another AT story to share with friends: "Hey, remember that crazy old lady with the nightmare?"

* * *

The next day brought me to Apple Orchard Mountain at 4,500 feet, through rhododendron tunnels as long as a city block, past stunning views of the James River Gorge, and finally down to the long wooden bridge crossing the river itself. I envied local teenagers their youth and daring as they clambered up the trestles and jumped into the cool, still waters below. I was content to soak my weary feet and rest my aching back and shoulders against the grassy riverbank.

The scene was marred only by posters that had been slipped into plastic sleeves and tacked onto posts and railings, regarding a thru-hiker who had been murdered on the AT the year before, apparently for his boots and pack. Authorities were still looking for his killer.

Violence is extremely rare on the Appalachian Trail, with only twelve documented cases of murder in roughly a hundred years. If you live in the US, you are much more likely to be murdered during a mass shooting or by a domestic partner or family member than by a stranger on the Trail. The murders on the AT have almost always been tragically senseless and random; the perpetrators drifters with long histories of drug abuse, criminal activity, and/or mental illness. Nature has no malice and—as dangerous as she can sometimes be—does not choose her victims. She has left those hateful traits to humankind.

As rare as murder is on the AT, it is important to remember this is serious hiking, and there are dangers just as there are on any trail. You can have an injury from a fall or suffer a medical emergency, such as a heart attack or stroke. This type of thing happens much more frequently than violence. Always let someone know your plan and expected time of return. There are phone apps now which will allow others to pinpoint your location and follow you remotely.

I went on through the Washington National Forest and found another poignant description of tragedy in the woods, a small stone marker engraved, "This is the exact spot Little Ottie Cline Powell's Body was found April 5, 1891, After Straying from Tower Hill School House Nov. 9, a distance of 7 miles. Age 4 years, 11 months."

These were dark reminders of the drama and grief these Appalachian Mountains can render even here in the gorgeous, sweeping Shenandoah Valley. The fields of yellow and purple wildflowers high as my waist stretched out ahead of me and to either side but always eventually sloped back into the shadowy woods. There is no happily ever after.

The days turned hot, and my pack was heavy under my narrow shoulders as I continued on. The long miles and inadequate diet were taking their toll, and exhaustion set in. But as I neared the end of this particular journey, tired and ready to be done—*Done I tell you! Done!*—a tiny bit of Trail Magic appeared exactly at my eye level.

Hanging from a twig on a short, scruffy tree near the edge of a meadow was manna—a snack-size Almond Joy, my favorite candy bar. It had to have been placed there recently; the wrapper was neither wet nor faded, and the chocolate shell was dark and not in the least melted. Whoever had hung it on the tree had done so carefully. The twig pierced the paper at the top without touching the candy within.

I stopped and looked around for whatever Trail Angel had left this little bit of magic. The meadow and surrounding woods did not give up their secret, and the only sound was of a small plane overhead. Nevertheless, I softly called out, "Thank you," and sat down to rest and savor not only the little treat but the knowledge that for every evil person on the Trail (or anywhere for that matter), there are countless good ones.

❄ ❄ ❄

The final night on the Trail, I pitched my tent at a cheerful site close to a sweet little babbling brook near Pedlar Lake. There was no room for other campers in the clearing, and I settled in for a solitary night.

After crawling into my sleeping bag, I realized the tent flap wasn't completely closed at the bottom. A piece of cloth was stuck in one of the zippers, creating a two- or three-inch gap. Following some frustrating attempts to make the twain meet, I decided, *Oh, well, the night is cool and pleasant and not particularly buggy. It's fine.*

Next morning I woke to find dew had seeped into the tent, and the floor near the opening was wet. I sat up and opened the flap. Easing on my camp shoes, I looked out into the still, quiet morning.

Not three feet in front of me, a rattlesnake was curled up on a flat rock, having himself a pleasant little sunbath. Had I noticed him through the zipper's gap when I was still lying down, we would have been at exactly eye level, separated only by air and species. He smiled at me, and I smiled back.

My tent has two side openings, and I found it prudent to ease out the opposite side from the snake, who appeared in no hurry to abandon his post. I carefully set about my morning routine—dressing, deflating pad, stuffing bag into sack—while keeping an eye on him. Eventually, my awkward human movements must have disrupted his serenity, and he slithered off.

I never again went to sleep without the tent flaps completely closed. But if you must because you're hot or stinky—or your partner is—leave the gap at the top of the tent, not the bottom. Snakes don't frighten me particularly, but I have no desire to sleep with one. I was grateful to my reptilian visitor for his chivalry and discretion.

* * *

Over Labor Day weekend, Melanie and Cade joined me on a three-day backpacking trip to tackle the twenty-two mile section from Long Mountain Wayside at US 60 to the Tye River at VA 56. This calls for some pretty serious hiking, but these young women were brimming with life and energy. Melanie, now having lived three years in Chattanooga with its abundance of rivers and mountains, had embraced the outdoor lifestyle. She had been on many day hikes, canoe trips, and kayak adventures, but this was to be her first overnight experience. She voiced no concerns whatsoever, only excitement and joy.

Late Friday afternoon, we left our car in a fairly large parking area where the AT crosses well-traveled VA 56 near the town of Montebello, Virginia. We planned to get a ride back to Long Mountain Wayside on US 60 near the Blue Ridge Parkway, hike for a few miles, and set up camp.

For nearly an hour, cars whizzed by as we sat near the side of the road with full packs and hopeful smiles. At last a pickup truck slowed as it passed us. We saw the glow of reverse lights, a joyous sight to hitchhikers, and scrambled to our feet as the truck backed up. A working-man type of guy leaned out the window.

"Hey!" he called out happily through a funk of smoke and sweat and beer. "Where y'all headed?"

While I explained our intentions and route, his passenger, a similarly relaxed fellow, chugged a Miller Lite.

"Well, I can take y'all as far as the Blue Ridge, but I ain't gettin' on that goddamned parkway. Them federal boys is just sitting up there on their asses waiting for me."

I saw no reason to mention I was a "federal girl."

"Joe," the driver said, "get out of the goddamned truck and load up those packs."

"Oh, no, that's okay," I hastily said, afraid Joe would fall flat on his face in the middle of the road. "We've got it. Come on, girls."

Melanie and Cade, who had said not a word during this exchange, threw our gear in the truck bed. We all climbed aboard, and the truck pulled out, slinging gravel. We hadn't gone far along the shaded two-lane highway when the window separating the cab from the bed slid open. Our chauffeur looked over his shoulder and called against the rushing wind, "Hey, sweetie, reach in that cooler there and hand me and Joe a couple of beers. Y'all, too—help yourselves."

Cade passed the beers through the window. *Dear lord, I hope she doesn't tell her mother about this part.*

The driver stopped the truck at the entrance to the BRP, and we disembarked. Wishing us well, he and Joe drove off into what was now nearly the sunset to continue their celebration of Friday and this three-day weekend.

We again pasted on our hitchhiking smiles, and just as my hopes were beginning to fade with the sun, a small old car that had seen better days pulled off the road. I explained to the driver, a pretty young woman with a shy expression, that we were trying to get several miles down the parkway to Hwy 60.

"Sure, we'll take you wherever you want to go. We just out driving around."

Her dark-haired, handsome passenger jumped out to help us with our packs. A baby girl grinned and cooed from an infant carrier strapped onto the back seat.

The car was cluttered with empty fast-food sacks, a box of diapers, and bright-yellow plastic bags from the Dollar Store. The young man opened the hatchback to reveal piles of clothes and personal belongings. He tried to position a pack or two on top. We finally all got squeezed in, baby behind the driver, Melanie in the middle, me with Cade on my lap. When Mom put the car in gear and moved forward, the infant realized these three loud and large (from her perspective) strangers were now a part of her life, and her pleasure at meeting new people quickly turned to screaming terror. You couldn't blame her; we were taking up all the space in her immediate world.

When we reached our destination, I tucked some folded bills into the console, and we extricated ourselves from the car to the child's great relief.

Exhilarated at finally being able to stretch our legs, we made fairly quick work of the steep climb to Bald Knob. A couple of miles farther brought us to Cow Camp Gap just as darkness surrounded us. I set up my tent while Cade and Melanie scouted for a good location to string up their hammocks. This was during the height of the hammock craze, and they were adamant this was the way to go. Hammocks weigh less and are less bulky than a tent–sleeping bag–sleeping pad combination, but they offer almost no protection from the elements. Nevertheless, it was very common in those days to see a group of thru-hikers hanging from a copse of trees like so many giant bagworms.

Next morning, with a long day ahead of us, we shook off the cool night and headed north to an immediate ascent of Cold Mountain. Despite the chilly name, this warmed us considerably, and we continued on to Hog Camp Gap to Tar Jacket Ridge to Salt Log Gap. We trekked across grassy, open knolls and through forests once home to giant chestnut trees, but now the domain of oak and hickory after blight all but wiped out the American chestnut in the early twentieth century. Switchback after switchback revealed the remains of once-sturdy stone walls denoting property lines and livestock boundaries, reminders of human presence and how quickly nature can regain her foothold when left to her own devices.

Cade's pace was somewhat faster than Melanie's and mine, and she often disappeared ahead of us in the bend of a switchback. In midafternoon, we heard a shriek and saw her running back toward us at full speed, eyes wide and hair flying.

"Bear, bear!"

When she reached us, she bent over and placed her hands on her knees, huffing and puffing.

"A huge bear," she gasped. "Just up ahead. He ran right out in front of me."

"It's okay," I said in a calm, soothing voice. "He's probably a mile away by now. You scared him more than he scared you. We're going to walk normally and talk normally and keep moving," I told the wide-eyed girls. They nodded and took each other's hand; I felt touched by their trust in me.

I took the lead as we moved on, Cade still sweaty and trembling. After only a hundred yards or so, we heard the high-pitched, excited yapping of a pack of dogs. Before we could even remark on this, several hounds were joyfully jumping on and sniffing at us. Sleek and well fed, with tracking collars around their necks, clearly they were chasing the bear that ran across Cade's path, and now we had thrown them off the scent. The hunters—no doubt down at the road crossing in their pickup trucks—would not be happy with us. Oh, well, we had equalized the hunt somewhat. Cade pointed in the opposite direction from where she had last seen the bear and told the dogs, "He went thataway."

The show over, we continued north through the deepening afternoon, meeting several southbound hikers we regaled with our tale of bear and dogs. Our destination for the evening was a shelter just south of the Priest. (Other mountains in this area include the Cardinal, the Little Priest, and the Friar. I have no explanation for this religious theme.) We reached it as the temperatures dropped and the winds picked up.

Two middle-aged section hikers occupied the shelter itself. They invited us to join them, but I set up my tent, and the girls strung up their hammocks, even though I was doubtful about the weather. Indeed, as the evening went on, thunder, lightning and lashing rain arrived with ferocious winds. I have a legitimate fear of a falling branch or tree crushing my little tent. The AT is strewn with trunks four and five feet in diameter that have been sucked out of the ground with their root systems pointing skyward like cypress knees. In fact, this very area we were in now had been the scene of serious destruction from Hurricane Camille in 1969.

We abandoned tent and hammocks and dashed to the shelter, where, in happy company with other hikers, we rode out the storm.

The next and final day was sunny. We packed up our wet gear and hiked down to the Tye River, the path littered with branches and uprooted trees. When we crossed the footbridge over Cripple Creek, the stream was fast and swollen. The trail morphed into old roadbeds, and soon the highway stretched out, black and ribbonlike, in front of us.

I, for one, was glad to be out of the woods. Cade and Melanie, elated with their accomplishment and seemingly not in the least tired, happily chattered as we walked across the gravel lot to our car. They seemed to have already forgotten the crazy hitchhikes, the bear encounter, and the very real danger of the storm. I was exhausted and weepy with the relief of having delivered them back to the acceptable risks of the normal world.

* * *

I had covered more than one hundred miles so far in 2012 and, with the April descent of Clingmans Dome, had left no section unhiked from Springer Mountain, Georgia, to the Tye River in the Shenandoah Valley. Now there were no gaps behind me, and as a bonus, I'd already hiked a few sections in Northern Virginia and in Pennsylvania, so I could skip those as I trekked ever northward.

Nevertheless, I wanted to get in one more substantial trip. I cleared my calendar for a four-day weekend in mid-October for a thirty-mile hike. Cecilia, to my delight, would be joining me for twenty miles from the Tye River to Rockfish Gap and I-64 and Skyline Drive. She would have to make her way home after that, but I would go on to hike another ten miles to Riprap Trail.

The October days were crisp and cool, the sky blue, and the air clean, perfect weather for hikers…and for hunters. On this trip, we often saw them or heard their gunfire. Several times, we saw trails of blood where a hunter had dragged or dressed his kill, or where possibly the fleeing injured prey had crossed the path. I worried about Cecilia in her black-and-gray hiking clothes. The white scarf she wore about her neck reminded me of nothing so much as the flicking tail of a Virginia deer.

The AT crosses private lands, recreation lands, game lands, as well as some national and state lands, where hunting is permitted. It is difficult to know exactly when and where you might not be safe from an errant gunshot or misdirected arrow. Deer season, bear season, and turkey season, among others, overlap, and the seasons are also categorized by choice of weapons. In autumn, I always try to wear a bit of bright orange—a toboggan or ball cap, even a vest. The hunters are used to seeing hikers, and I've never heard of any problems between the two subspecies. We're all just happy (or crazy) to be out here in the great outdoors.

We warily moved along on rocky switchbacks up to the peaks of Three Ridges at nearly four thousand feet. The descent took us across numerous rockslides, where we heaved ourselves over boulders and around huge uprooted trees. The going was slow, but we had each other to offer a hand, a boost, or a word of encouragement. Sometimes the mental support means as much or more as the physical.

After a sixteen-mile day, we made camp at Cedar Cliffs in chilly night air. Cecilia had brought a stove, and it was bliss to wake the next morning and sip coffee while we looked out over the valley. Each leaf of every tree, every bush, seemed in some state of vivid and dramatic color as it hung on for one dear moment more before ceding to the inevitable and dropping, spent and lifeless, to the ground.

Almost rendered speechless by the beauty, we moved quietly on for an easy five-mile hike paralleling and at times crisscrossing the northern end of the Blue Ridge Parkway. We climbed to the ridge of Humpback Mountain and walked the couple of miles to the mountain itself, our reverie often broken by the many day-hikers enjoying the foliage. Once, we came upon the somewhat jarring sight of a golf and ski resort fitted into the mountains, as if someone who was solving a giant jigsaw puzzle had tried to make the wrong piece work.

We descended across Humpback Rocks outcropping and yet again down to the Blue Ridge Parkway. Here, we had the pleasure of visiting a work-in-progress of a recreated pioneer farm. The buildings were not open, and there were no caretakers or guides about, but we peered into the windows of the outbuildings and sat on the porch of the cabin, easily imagining chickens pecking in the yard and the smell of Sunday beans simmering on the stove.

We moseyed on through Mill Creek Valley with its little falls and ponds and the creek itself. At Rockfish Gap, Cecilia said her goodbyes, and I went on to hike another day through Shenandoah National Park. Dozens of blue-blazed hiking trails wind their way through this park, many radiating out from the boundary of Skyline Drive.

The relative accessibility and popularity of this section belies the challenges. The ascents and descents of Bear Den Mountain, Calf Mountain, Wildcat Ridge, and Turk Mountain left me wobbly-legged and light-headed. Though renowned for her beauty, Shenandoah is not to be taken lightly. This final day was a not-so-gentle nudge; it was time to go home.

* * *

There would be no more hikes for me in 2012, and if nothing else, this year had shown us there might never be. January and February had found me careless and slipshod on the Trail, but March had shown us what true loss is. The spring had brought closure to me in the Smokies and a fleeting feeling of accomplishment, but the summer had again brought nightmares. The signs of tragedy on the Trail and the brushes with danger were reminders that this is a difficult path. As autumn waned and winter came on, I tallied up the year's gains: 150 miles and a lot of hard lessons.

CHAPTER 9

2013 (130 MILES)

SKYLINE DRIVE MILEPOST 59.5, VIRGINIA, TO BALD FACE MOUNTAIN, VIRGINIA

SKYLINE DRIVE MILEPOST 41.7, VIRGINIA, TO JENKINS GAP, VIRGINIA

SKYLINE DRIVE MILEPOST 41.7, VIRGINIA, TO SKYLINE DRIVE MILEPOST 59.5, VIRGINIA

TRICO FIRE TOWER TRAIL, VIRGINIA, TO HIGHWAY 605, VIRGINIA

HIGHWAY 605, VIRGINIA, TO BLUEMONT, VIRGINIA

RIPRAP TRAIL, VIRGINIA, TO HARPERS FERRY, WEST VIRGINIA

The Appalachian Trail meanders its long way through the state of Virginia from its southwestern corner at an almost perfect northeast heading. Just before it leaves the state altogether to cross into West Virginia, it passes through the mountainous countryside perilously near the sprawling southern and western suburbs of Washington, DC. In one of those fortuitous (with a little force of hand from me) right-place-at-the-right-time situations, I was to spend the first few months of 2013 at the FBI Academy in Quantico, near enough to the Trail for easy weekend accessibility.

In early January, I drove from Franklin to Northern Virginia, and within eight days of ringing in the New Year, I was standing on the snow-covered Appalachian Trail near Elkton. I had taken a little detour while on my way to Quantico, and now a pleasant nine-mile jaunt accessed from Skyline Drive milepost 59.5 awaited me. Bundled up for the northern winter, I walked up, over, and down Saddleback Mountain and crossed the South River Falls Trail before going up again to the crest of Bald Face Mountain. The ascent took me down to old pastureland abutting the drive and the end point of my hike. This was a chilly, challenging beginning of the hiking season and a positive start to this year. I reached my car before sundown with plenty of time to make it to Quantico for dinner before the cafeteria closed.

The National Academy is a prestigious twelve-week course for high-ranking law enforcement officials—men and women at the peak of their careers—from across the United States and a few from other countries. Held a few times a year, the course is a challenging combination of university-accredited classwork, physical regime, and the pressure of living away from home and work for months at a time in a dorm-like setting.

Each session is monitored by several FBI field agents, who mentor the attendees and facilitate the schedule. I may have had a hidden agenda when I volunteered for this assignment, but there's something to be said for multitasking.

* * *

After two weeks of learning the routine at Quantico and getting to know the students, staff, and my fellow counselors, I was ready to get out of the hamster tunnels of the academy and stretch my legs with a thirty-mile hike. My exact routes would be determined by Mother Nature and what sections of Skyline Drive were passable.

On this late January weekend, very cold but with no winter storms in the forecast, my goal was to hike north from Skyline Drive milepost 41.7 to milepost 12.4 near Front Royal, where Heather and I had begun in February 2012.

I made my headquarters at a little roadside motel just off Skyline Drive. A bell on the door jangled as I entered, and the proprietor looked up from the screen of an old desktop computer. He seemed a bit surprised to have a paying guest, not to mention a middle-aged hiker, in the dead of winter.

The shabby lobby was full of dusty magazines and plastic artificial flowers, and it seemed to double as a living room. Several cats of various colors and sizes were draped across the furniture. The host did not appear to be of advanced age but moved slowly as he went about the business of checking me in. Attached to an oxygen tank, he had the ashy, waxen look of a corpse. My room, carpeted in green shag, had the musty smell of mildew, as if the heavy curtains had never been open to sunlight. I quickly changed into my hiking gear, ready to be in the fresh air and out of this forlorn place.

* * *

The AT was snow-covered and beautifully serene. I climbed the cliffs of Stony Man and the peaks of the Pinnacle and admired the views of the Shenandoah Valley from Marys Rock. I often saw tracks of the shy and elusive bobcat but, regrettably, never met one. Silent deer and noisy chipmunks marked my progress. Once, a coyote stepped onto the trail not fifteen feet ahead of me. We both froze for an instant and locked eyes before she nonchalantly moved on into the opposite woods.

I crossed crystal streams on footlogs or slippery stones and meandered along switchbacks and ridges to Pass Mountain, Sugarloaf Mountain, and Hogback Mountain. I practiced differentiating the caws of the crow and the croaks of the raven. It was a time of comfortable loneliness.

There are radio towers and old fire roads, such as the Keyser Run Fire Road on this section of the Trail. *Exploring the Appalachian Trail*, by David Lillard and Gwyn Hicks, says the Keyser Run Fire Road appears on very old maps as Jinney Gray Road. This name, in its brevity and unusual spelling, struck me as beautiful. The name was eventually changed to Keyser Road because no record could be found to identify Jinney Gray, and so, as Lillard and Hicks poignantly remark, "Now, not even the old road recalls this forgotten person."

Each of these three-day hikes covered about ten miles, and each evening, I spent quietly reading at the bleak motel. Eighty hours passed without real conversation, only superficial exchanges with folks who gave me rides or the very occasional day-hiker I encountered in the woods. When I returned to Quantico and the routine of meetings, workouts, and cafeteria meals, I seemed slow to adjust—like a groundhog tentatively testing the wind when she emerges from her winter quarters.

＊ ＊ ＊

The second weekend of February, I drove north from Quantico on I-95 with the intention of hiking the twenty-mile section from Bald Face Mountain to Stony Man Mountain. This would be a fairly easy two days with a motel stay in between, and it would close the gap between the two January hikes.

Nature thought otherwise. Sections of Skyline Drive were closed off because of snow earlier in the week.

Okay, Plan B. Skyline Drive was passable to milepost 56.4 where the AT crosses. This was some five miles north of Bald Face Mountain, but I really did not want to skip it and have it hanging over my head. The only thing to do, I decided, was an in-and-out. I would hike five miles south on the AT until I reached the spot where my feet had trod before, slap the nearest blaze, turn around, and hike five miles north back to my car.

The day was very cold and the snow well over my boots in places. The terrain, with gentle ascents and descents, was not very difficult, but the woods seemed close and foreboding. I don't know why I felt this sense of impending tragedy, but in what may have been a case of self-fulfilling prophecy, I wandered off the Trail.

In the late afternoon, I realized I was walking in a sort of ditch that just didn't feel like the AT. I started looking for blazes. Whenever I thought I saw one, my heart would lift—and then sink again. *No, it's only a patch of snow on the tree trunk.* I told myself over and over, *I'll just go a little farther, and if I don't see a blaze, I'll turn around.*

The ditch petered out. I forced myself to remain calm. If I retraced my steps *exactly*, I would eventually reach the AT. But if I veered off in one wrong direction or another, I'd be in real trouble. I slowly and carefully backtracked, moving only when I was sure of my previous boot prints in the snow until I reconnected with the Trail.

The Appalachian Trail is extremely well marked and as well maintained as the caprices of nature will allow. But the key point to remember is that, while the AT itself is well marked, the wilderness surrounding it is not. If you stray from the Trail for whatever reason—to take a potty break, to snap a photo of an interesting flower, to attempt a shortcut—you will see very quickly that only a few feet can literally mean the difference between life and death. The vast majority of the Trail goes through extremely dense woods, where it is easy to become disoriented, and there are no signs out there pointing you back in the right direction.

In the summer of 2013, AT flip-flop hiker Geraldine "Inchworm" Largay went missing in Western Maine. She was a middle-aged woman from the Nashville area who was last seen at a shelter by several other hikers. Many people questioned how someone could get lost on the AT, but I have no trouble at all imagining how one can stray off the trail ten feet, then twenty feet, then to the point of no return. A logging company surveyor found Inchworm's remains two years later. The journal she continued writing even after losing her way indicates she died of starvation and exposure.

I moved cautiously along the Trail from one blaze to another, constantly aware of my surroundings. Dead winter in the central Appalachian Mountains is not the time and place to let your mind or body wander. I reached the safety of my car just at dusk and then, thankfully, the haven of an anonymous motel.

✳ ✳ ✳

During the night, temperatures remained low, but no new snow fell. The plows had done their solitary jobs, and Skyline Drive was open to traffic when I arrived at milepost 56.4 the next morning. This hike would be a long one—fifteen miles—to milepost 41.7. I got a ride from a dad and his teenage daughter who were out for the day working on a school science-class assignment, part of a large project involving a beetle detrimental to the pine trees in the forest. I felt grateful and humbled that people were, on their own time, trying to protect this beautiful pocket of nature.

The hike along the snowy AT took me through Big Meadows, now snow-covered and lonesome, but in the warmer months, it would be filled with holiday-makers from the nearby lodge and campground. At Tanners Ridge Cemetery, I stopped to read the inscriptions on the old headstones. These Appalachian Mountains were once home to scattered tanneries, a small industry that provided yet another way for people to eke out a living by hand and hard work.

This section of the Trail offers some of the best views anywhere along the AT. From the Franklin Cliffs you can see the Alleghenies to the west and Stony Man to the north. When you think the views cannot be more stunning, you reach the summit of Hawksbill and see a panorama of mountain ranges. I lingered as long as I could and then, with a grateful sigh, hoisted my pack and pulled myself away from the splendor that was the mountains to return to the everyday that was Quantico.

The very next weekend included the Presidents' Day holiday, but obligations with my NA students did not allow me to get away until Sunday. I drove to the Trico Fire Tower Trail where Heather and I had finished in 2012 and, from there, hiked sixteen miles to VA 605. This section includes Sky Meadows State Park and crosses busy US 50. Even so, in this dead of winter, I saw very few hikers. It's an amazing thing to be less than a hundred miles from our nation's hub, with its traffic jams and politics, and find solitude and crisp air, with only the bickering and scolding of the chipmunks and the squirrels. On this long, quiet day, I was accompanied only by the sounds of my breath and my footsteps on the frozen trail. This was enough.

The end of my Quantico assignment was quickly approaching, and I made one last trip to the AT in mid-March. My friend Bob, a retired agent now living in Woodbridge, Virginia, agreed to shuttle me to the trailhead. There is no greater gift to a section hiker than a friend who is willing to give up half of his Saturday to act as chauffeur. We met in chilly midmorning in the sweet little town of Bluemont. I left my car, and Bob took me to the trailhead at the AT crossing of VA 605.

He remarked that he and Amy, living as close as they did to the beautiful Shenandoah Valley with its scenic drives and nature parks, rarely found time to visit the area.

"It's a shame. There we are, seventy-five miles from all this, and so busy with work and stuff, we never take advantage of it."

Exactly.

This first day's hike was only about seven miles but held a surprise in store for me. Many times the AT presents hikers with an unexpected feature or an unforeseen situation. Official notices slipcased into plastic envelopes and nailed to a tree may advise of trail reroutes or you might see Park Service signs warning, for example, "Use caution. Frequent bear activity in this area." (When I stop to read those, I become uncomfortably aware of the smell of last night's pizza wafting out of my backpack, and I hurriedly move on.) But sometimes you come upon a feature or a section that is not shown on your maps nor indicated by signage.

That's why, on this cold March weekend, I believe I hiked the notorious Roller Coaster without even realizing it. I know—because these features are noted on the maps—I climbed Buzzard Hill and gazed out from Lookout Point within a tortuously up-and-down, up-and-down, two-mile stretch. Other hikers later told me that this was the Roller Coaster, a much-dreaded feature of the AT in Northern Virginia. It is not named on official maps; its nickname was attached over the years by exhausted hikers. It was probably a good thing I didn't know the Roller Coaster was part of the day's schedule. Anxiety and dread might have taken the fun out of it.

I followed the white blazes out of the woods and found myself walking along a narrow service road. The surrounding land was chain-link-fenced and peppered with "No Trespassing" and "U.S. Government Property" signs. The road was deserted. All was eerily quiet.

The AT took me alongside long, low, corrugated buildings with a huge number of antenna and cell towers. At one point, a discreet sign identified the facility as a "weather station." *Ha!* I was not fooled. As I trudged along, I invented scenarios of its possible functions as an experimental lab for captured aliens or a clandestine meeting locale for classified briefings.

I was anxious to get past this mysterious place—because I really, really had to pee. But the AT continued to hug the perimeters of "Camp X," and I was finally forced to tinkle in the snow-covered berm. I tried to be modest and discreet. There was no doubt in my mind the eyes of cameras and those of faceless government officials manning them were trained directly on me.

The AT eventually returned to the anonymity of the woods, where one's privacy can be expected and respected. In the late afternoon, I reached the paved road leading to the Blackburn Trail Center, where I spent the night in a warm clean bunkroom. I fell asleep with a smile on my face thinking of the day's events and surprises.

The next day I finished up this weekend with a leisurely seven-mile stroll to my car parked at VA 9 (Keys Gap) in Bluemont. The temperatures had risen, and now the path was slushy. The very earliest of the spring grasses bravely sought the still-weak rays of the sun and tiny, newly hatched toads hopped about with jubilance. Was there a finer place to be on a cool Saturday in March? I suppose in my life, there will eventually be many things I will regret doing, but hiking the AT certainly won't be one of them.

Two weeks later, after a rush of celebratory dinners and award ceremonies full of pomp and circumstance, our NA students graduated. They went their separate ways with promises to keep in touch, to visit, to post on the session's Facebook page. I believe it is some measure of how much I wanted to get home that I didn't even stop to hike when I drove back to Tennessee.

✳ ✳ ✳

The heat of summer arrived. Hummingbirds that stopped by our house on their seasonal migration north had come and gone, and I again felt the need for cool mountain air. Melanie had come home after her spring graduation and would begin graduate school at Appalachian State University in Boone, North Carolina, in the fall. Eager to learn more about the mountains she would call home for the next couple of years, she agreed to accompany me for a weeklong hike on the Trail.

I wanted to go back and finish any sections in Virginia that I had left undone. Harpers Ferry, West Virginia—the official halfway point on the AT—loomed ahead, and I wanted to walk into it with a feeling of closure. I needed to do about thirty miles from Riprap Trail to US 33 and a separate eight-mile section near the Blackburn Trail Center. With those done, we would be free to cruise the twelve miles from Keys Gap at VA 9 to Harpers Ferry with no stone unturned behind me.

We left Franklin on a hot Thursday morning in late June with full packs and the belief this would be a wonderful mother-daughter bonding experience—provided we didn't kill each other. We reached Skyline Drive with enough daylight left to do a quick day hike. Stowing tent, sleeping bags, and other unnecessary items in the car, we stepped on Riprap Trail to hike the five miles to Jones Run. As this section of the Trail meanders along and sometimes crosses the drive, we had no trouble getting a hitch.

Oh, it was good to be back in the woods! Melanie was cheerful and excited, and we fairly skipped along the trail. A couple of somewhat steep climbs, including the cliffs of Blackrock, brought no complaining or whining.

A light rain began to fall as we approached the end of our hike. Just as we reached the safety of our car, the rain ceased and a perfect rainbow appeared in the early evening sky. We drove along, literally following a route to the end of the rainbow. At the motel parking lot, we walked through the red, yellow, green, blue, and purple spectrum of misty drops until they disappeared. *What a good omen for our week.*

We were at the same Skyline Drive roadside motel I had patronized on some of my sojourns from Quantico. Despite its shabbiness, it had been comfortable enough and cheap, and I was interested to see if the zombie proprietor had survived the winter. I had no expectation that he did. But when we entered the lobby, there he was, still behind the counter, and I greeted him as an old friend.

❉ ❉ ❉

We rose early the next morning, Friday, packed up our gear, and checked out of what we had begun to fondly (the place had grown on me) call the Bates Motel. The day was hot and would get hotter.

We parked our car at the US 33 crossing of Skyline Drive and stood patiently waiting at the side of the road, our packs loaded for two days. Within a short time, an SUV towing a small camper pulled over. The driver, a cheerful, thirtyish fellow, called out, "Hop in the back! Front seat's full. Just push that stuff out of the way."

As we headed back down to our starting point at Skyline Drive milepost 84.1 (where we had finished the night before), our driver told us he was on his way to set up camp for the weekend at Loft Mountain Campground, where his wife and kids would join him later in the day. I don't know how many kids he had, but Melanie and I were crammed in among coolers, lawn chairs, and bulging bags of groceries.

The fellow listened intently and asked many questions as we told him of our plans. He seemed a little envious of our minimalism, and I can say I felt the same about him and his luxuries. A large bag of Doritos poking out of the top of a brown paper sack looked particularly inviting.

The Trail in this section is level and smooth, and aside from one aerobic challenge—the ascent of Big Flat Mountain—our hike was a leisurely saunter. We walked along a path carpeted with layers of soft, dead leaves and spongy moss. An overhead canopy of tall tree branches filtered the sun's rays and provided a cool tunnel filled with the rotting, but somehow pleasant, smell of musk. Deer were abundant and surprisingly untimid. One doe actually followed us for some distance, only a few feet behind, pausing in her tracks when we turned to look back at her. She must have had a fawn or two hidden in the underbrush and was gently encouraging us to move along.

We made very good time and reached our destination at eight miles in, a shady glen at Ivy Creek, well before dark. It was a luxury to have a few hours of daylight in which to relax and enjoy the evening. Melanie strung up her hammock, and I gathered wood to build a campfire—a rare treat because I am usually so late to camp and so tired from the hike, I almost never go to the trouble of a fire. But here we were with time and energy to spare, and the setting was picture perfect.

❊ ❊ ❊

The next day brought drizzle and a fourteen-mile hike. For the first couple of miles, we continued along easy terrain, skirting Skyline Drive, but the cumulative effect of many miles was catching up to Melanie. She began to complain that her boots were rubbing her feet painfully. The next ten miles grew increasingly strenuous. The ups and downs punished Melanie's toes, and she was often in tears. We stopped several times to apply fresh moleskin and Band-Aids to her blisters as we hiked up Flat Top Mountain, down to Powell Gap, up Little Roundtop Mountain, down to Smith Roach Gap, up Hightop Mountain, and finally down to US 33. We reached the car with great relief but also with misgivings about our ability to go on the next day.

We arrived, exhausted, at our motel in a little crossroads town that evening. Our clothes were wet and muddy, our gear damp. After we draped the tent and our sleeping bags over the furniture in our tacky little room, I headed to the laundromat. Three or four thru-hikers were going through the trash bin hoping to find discarded detergent. I huddled near-naked beneath my rain poncho and dejectedly watched our socks and shirts and pants tumble about in the machine.

When I returned, Melanie had taken a hot shower and was wrapped in a towel, looking defeated and scared. I handed her the clean, dry clothes and gently tended to her feet.

"You know, Melanie," I said as I cut squares of moleskin, "we don't have to hike the next section."

"Oh, Mom, I feel like I'm letting you down." Tears threatened to spill. "I liked the hike, but my feet hurt so bad, I just don't know if I can do it."

"Look," I said, holding her face in my hands and looking her straight in the eye. "The AT is really, really hard. There is absolutely no shame in stopping. You can try it another time maybe."

She took a deep breath and sat up straighter on the bed. But then, perhaps recalling the agony of each step, she crumbled again. "Oh, I just don't know."

"Well, we don't have to decide right now. It's late; we're tired and hungry. C'mon, let's go find some food."

❊ ❊ ❊

The next morning we felt a little more optimistic, and Melanie said she wanted to try to hike if I promised we would stop if it became too painful. Well, of course I promised! I'm not a drill sergeant, and as Bill Bryson famously said about the AT, this is not the Army.

We drove to Harpers Ferry, West Virginia, and parked the car on a quiet side street in the hilly, quaint downtown area. The Appalachian Trail Conservancy is housed in a modest, stone-faced building on the main street, and we entered it reverentially, as is appropriate for a shrine.

The Appalachian Trail Conservancy is the benevolent yet fiercely protective steward of the Appalachian Trail. Its responsibilities are awesome and many: to educate hikers and the public alike; to conduct and facilitate fundraisers; to solicit and enlist members and supporters; to coordinate with countless federal, state, and local entities, which have Trail interests; to publish its quarterly magazine and countless e-transmissions; to communicate and cooperate with private landowners, politicians, donors, maintenance groups and clubs, and volunteers. It also operates the little museum and gift shop at its Harpers Ferry headquarters, where no doubt the staff responds to countless thousands of questions (many of them probably pretty stupid if my experience is any example). The ATC does not serve as a referee or statistician or coach; it loves all its children equally from the fastest known hiker to complete the entire trail to the city-dweller who comes out on the weekends to walk a few miles.

We did not spend much time browsing because I wanted to get on the Trail, and I thought it would be more appropriate to enjoy the ATC memorabilia after we had, in fact, hiked there. To that end, I inquired about shuttle lifts, and the helpful clerk gave me a list of names and phone numbers. After calling several with no success and beginning to feel some stress, we reached a fellow who said he'd be glad to drive us down to VA 7 and could pick us up in about half an hour.

Our driver arrived in a panel van loaded with the tools and solvents of the painting profession. The long drive to VA 7 was slow and traffic-choked, and the fumes from the partially opened cans and used rags in the van were headache-inducing and probably dangerous. But beggars can't be choosers, as any AT or other long-distance hiker will tell you, and we were grateful for the ride.

Stepping onto the Trail in fresh air, with Melanie's feet carefully bandaged, gave us new life and energy. We trod slowly and carefully, but we had two days to hike the twenty-plus miles into Harpers Ferry, and so were not in a particular hurry. We had sunshine, each other, and the company of numerous northbound thru-hikers excited to reach the official—if not exactly accurate in terms of mileage—halfway point of the Appalachian Trail.

Two long, slow days and two balmy, star-filled nights later, we limped into the ATC building. We signed the trail register, bought a few souvenirs, and posed for photos. I was grateful I could do so with the knowledge that no step had been skipped, no blaze unseen, no mile unwalked from Springer Mountain, Georgia, to this little stone building on a peaceful small-town street in West Virginia. It had taken me nine years to arrive at this halfway point. I made a vow to myself and to Melanie that it would not take nine more years for me to hike the second half.

✳ ✳ ✳

This ended for me the 2013 hiking season, and I was fine with that. There would be "world enough and time" to walk another thousand miles in future years; I had decided to retire from the FBI. I had been eligible for a few years but had not, until now, felt I was quite ready. My eyesight wasn't getting any better, the technology was becoming difficult for me to follow, and my time at the National Academy had revealed many "senior moments" on my part compared to the robust and ambitious students.

Through the rest of this year, I transferred cases, contacts, and program management duties to younger colleagues. I cleaned out my desk and shredded paper that had piled up. I taught one last forty-hour crisis negotiations class and attended my last firearms training.

It was time to let go and start a new chapter. I would deeply miss my friends and coworkers, the daily routine, and the sense of purpose this career had given me. But as I did with my arrival at Harpers Ferry, I could look back with the knowledge that I had done it—not without misstep or with perfection—but with my heart always in it.

CHAPTER 10

2014 (230 MILES)

HARPERS FERRY, WEST VIRGINIA, TO DUNCANNON, PENNSYLVANIA

DUNCANNON, PENNSYLVANIA, TO PORT CLINTON, PENNSYLVANIA

FOX GAP, PENNSYLVANIA, TO CULVER LAKE, NEW JERSEY

was set to retire on January 31. Paperwork was finalized, announcements had been made, the venue for farewell luncheon booked. But the rest of the world continued turning, and on January 2, the Crisis Negotiations Unit (CNU) at headquarters called.

"Could you go to Algeria for a couple of weeks in early February?"

Sure, I said, unless you want someone younger and faster, reminding the unit supervisor of my planned retirement. *But*, I thought, *maybe this is the way it should end: one last adventure on the final leg of my career's journey.* I had often told younger agents to never turn down an assignment—to go on a TDY, to participate in a search warrant, to speak at a school, to accept a collateral duty—if at all possible. Yes, timing is rarely perfect, and there are always reasons to demur or delay, but it has been my experience that we rarely regret the things we do, only those we don't. I signed on for Algeria.

The North African sun, hot even in January and even in the late afternoon, beat down on our necks as we jogged on the Mediterranean beach outside our hotel each day after work. Concertina-wire-topped concrete fences stretching a hundred feet into the sea marked our boundaries. Guards armed with MP5s patrolled the inside perimeter, where broken glass and plastic bags littered the sand. I thought of the pristine cleanliness of the Appalachian Trail and the utter lack of restrictions one finds on it, except those imposed by nature.

The world is full of contrasts; otherwise, how would we appreciate or even recognize anything? Ugliness and beauty, freedom and constraints, busyness and sloth, pain and pleasure, plenitude and scarcity, family and strangers, preservation and destruction, civilization and wilderness, sickness and health, east and west, deserts and oceans—all of these contradictions would become apparent to me this year as I made the transition into this next phase of my life.

* * *

Denial is sometimes helpful, and I guess I had relied upon it in those last weeks leading up to retirement. I found the reality hard to face even as I drafted my farewell speech and made accommodation arrangements for visiting family and friends. On the morning of my retirement lunch—my last day in the office—I was reluctant to hand in my gear. My boss called me into his office.

"You want to go ahead and give me your property?" Rich asked gently.

"Now?" I asked. "I'll come back this afternoon after the party and turn everything in then."

Rich smiled softly and shook his head. "You won't want to do that." He paused. "It's like a Band-Aid—you just need to rip it off quickly."

He was right, of course. I laid my keys to a bureau car, my credentials, and badge on his desk. After a second more of hesitation, I unthreaded my holster from my belt and placed it, with the gun nestled safely inside, beside the other items. I shook Rich's hand and walked out of the office.

* * *

By June, I was three months into retirement, and I still hadn't added any more miles to my AT total. The days of popping over to Virginia for a long weekend were over. The remaining hikes would be in northern states hundreds of miles from home. Common sense mandated longer trips, and now I had the time. Even so, I did not want to camp in the cold, and I was tired of the stress and inefficiency of day hiking. AT adventures would have to wait until the warmer months.

But I did not spend this time (or most of it anyway) sitting around in sweatpants, drinking scotch, and binge-watching *The Office* on Netflix. I admit there were feelings of restlessness and the itch for travel and adventure. For almost thirty years, my schedule had been dictated by my job, and now those constraints had been removed. My friends and family seemed to understand this and were my willing accomplices.

I went to Florida with Jen in March. In April, Tim and I traveled to Gulf Shores for a vacation with Teresa and her husband. For our twenty-fifth wedding anniversary in May, Melanie treated Tim and me to a weekend raft trip on the Ocoee. All of these getaways were welcome diversions (although the latter one was a bit more hair-raising than necessary for two people who were now eligible for discounts at the movies), and I was grateful.

Melanie was spending the early part of the summer in Whitesburg, Kentucky, the seat of Letcher County, as an intern with Appalshop. This is a nonprofit organization—an education center, basically—focusing on the media and arts of southern Appalachia. Tim and I drove over to attend Seedtime on the Cumberland, an annual musical and cultural festival, and to spend a long weekend with—what seemed unbelievable—our now-adult daughter.

Honeysuckle bushes laden with fragrant blooms lined the winding mountain roads leading to the little town of Whitesburg. Rising above the lush greenness of the deep woods are once proud mountains now scarred by wide swathes of roiled dirt. Heavy earthmoving and coal-extraction equipment dot large sections of ridges and banks where summits once loomed. Mountaintop removal, or strip-mining, is heavily restricted in Tennessee and North Carolina, and my journey on the AT, which does not pass through Kentucky, had not exposed me to this tragic reality.

In contrast, the festival's atmosphere is full of promise and excitement: a child might win a teddy bear, or a teenager might fall in love. Vendors selling everything from homemade candles to organic eggs line the banks of the river. Craftspeople demonstrate quilting, basket weaving, and furniture making. The air is filled with the sounds of fiddlers scraping and guitars tuning. The nasal voices of bluegrass singers compete with the laughter of children, sometimes punctuated by a baby's cry or a dog's bark. The aroma is like that of any county fair—buttery corn popping, sugary candy burning, sliced potatoes frying—except underneath it all is the slightly rank smell of sluggish catfish and swollen bullfrogs making their slow way on the Cumberland River.

In the evenings, we square-danced to a trio of musicians and a word-perfect dance-caller until we collapsed, laughing and exhausted, on blanketed hay bales. Strings of electric bulbs illuminated the canvas walls of the tent while, outside, the silent disfigured mountains stood quietly by.

* * *

The year 2014 was exactly half over when next I hiked the AT. Melanie—outfitted with a new backpack, a decent sleeping bag, and properly fitted boots—eagerly accompanied me on an ambitious thirteen-day backpacking trip of some 125 miles from Harpers Ferry, West Virginia, to Duncannon, Pennsylvania.

We drove the eleven hours from Nashville to Duncannon, where we left our car. Our friend Bob—the retired agent living in Woodbridge, Virginia—graciously shuttled us from there to the trailhead in Harpers Ferry. Our goal, on this sweltering morning of July 6, was to reach the Crampton Gap Shelter, some eleven miles north, by nightfall.

We quickly left West Virginia behind as we crossed the Potomac River into Maryland on the Goodloe Byron footbridge (named for a Maryland congressman who was chief sponsor of what is widely known as the "Appalachian Trail Bill" to preserve and enhance the AT). I always think of West Virginia and Maryland, encompassing together only about sixty miles of the AT, as bashful young girls at a party who shyly watch from the sidelines as the more popular and brazen young women, the other twelve states through which the AT passes, chatter and dance.

Starting at scarcely two hundred feet above sea level, we fairly flew along for several miles on a towpath beside a canal once used to transport freight and livestock from the eastern US through the Appalachians to the Ohio River Valley. Melanie remarked that she could walk forever on trails like these.

Well, keep that happy thought, my child. Hard times will come again.

Sure enough, an abrupt, steep, one-thousand-foot climb to Weverton Cliffs awaited us as the Trail turned away from the towpath. Our pace slowed, and we stopped frequently to sip water and catch our breath. Stomach-churning drops to treetops below edge the narrow path, and I turned my eyes beyond to the Potomac River.

The Trail again levels out, and we hiked quietly and peacefully through lush green tunnels until we reached Crampton Gap. There, a rather odd-looking monument known as the War Correspondents Memorial Arch honors news correspondents and artists of the Civil War. It stands on the grounds of what was once an elegant estate. The stone foundation and other remnants of the estate's original buildings are preserved as part of Gathland State Park. As always, we welcomed the break from the woods and the opportunity to take in a little human culture, no matter how obscure.

We continued north into the woods for scarcely a half mile and reached the blue-blazed trail leading down to the Crampton Gap Shelter. In our eagerness to reach our destination, we fairly tumbled down the steep path to the little clearing that teemed with humanity—a large Trail Family who were about halfway through their four- to six-month odyssey.

AT thru-hikers, as a body, are an amorphous, ever-shifting population. Each year, about two thousand dreamers will step on the Trail at either Springer Mountain, Georgia, or Mount Katahdin, Maine, to begin their 2,200-mile walk. Physical strength, superior knowledge, and technical skills do not necessarily decide who will complete this journey. Friendships form, but no alpha dog emerges to guide the pack. The weakest are not culled from the herd.

Shifting units of six to ten hikers come together to form what are called Trail Families. They seem to consist entirely of brothers and sisters with no parents. Although they depend on each other for companionship and fun, each person is self-sufficient. These do not appear to be parasitic relationships; those few that are will not last long. Of course, one helps the other out when needed, but that assistance will be reciprocated. Equality and respect define the familial bonds.

Family members may switch allegiance from time to time as events demand—someone gets sick and has to go off the Trail, someone lags behind or bounds ahead, someone falls in love—but rancor and pettiness are very rarely seen. These families often form connections that will last long after the hike is finished.

Because my time on the Trail had stretched out over nine years, I had never been with any one group long enough to join a family or earn a name. But now, it would be over the course of this two-week adventure with Melanie that I finally was christened.

I had sporadically been known as No Sticks—over these nine years and one thousand miles—because I traveled without the benefit of the trekking poles that almost one hundred percent of rough-terrain hikers use. They use them for good reason, I had learned. Finally, for this 2014 trip, I succumbed to good advice and carried a set of Black Diamonds, a gift from Tim.

What a gift! My pace increased dramatically, I fell much less frequently, and fear of water crossings became a thing of the past. But because the poles were not yet an integral part of my hiking body, like my pack and boots, I often forgot about them. Many times during this two-week trek, I would be happily marching on, and then a rock scramble or a rushing creek would cause me to stop short and exclaim, "Shit, I left my sticks at the shelter!" Or at the diner in town. Or on that nice ledge where we stopped for lunch. *Dammit!*

Happily, each time this happened, my carelessness was overcome by a hiker hurrying up behind me brandishing the Black Diamonds.

"There you are!" He or she would proudly grin. "Been trying to catch up with you. You left your sticks at the shelter." Or the diner. Or on the ledge.

So I became known as Sticks. A trail name implies acceptance and affection, and even though, as a section hiker, I would never be a member of an immediate Trail Family, I could be content as a forgetful old aunt—nonessential but tolerated and even loved.

* * *

Melanie and I slept well and woke early to begin our second day, still fresh and excited. Our goal was twelve to seventeen miles a day, with stops in towns every three to four days for resupply and reassessment. We recognized the need for flexibility and carved our plans with stubby pencil rather than in stone.

We left the shelter, ahead of some of our new friends and behind others, and climbed out of the gap. We ridgewalked for several miles at two hundred feet and, aside from the steep scramble up to White Rocks and back down again, continued at that elevation for the rest of the day and for the next couple of days. Our rhythm was compatible and our pace fairly consistent. There were many times, if the narrow path allowed, we walked shoulder to shoulder and sometimes even hand in hand, my mind still even as our bodies continuously pressed forward.

We reached Pen Mar Park (Pennsylvania-Maryland state line) on Day Three. Picnicking families filled the park. Children laughed and yelled as they tumbled about on the playground. Sweat-drenched and dirty but proud of ourselves, we eased off packs and made ourselves at home near the snack bar. There is nothing that satisfies a hungry, thirsty hiker like a greasy grilled cheese sandwich, a bag of salty chips, and an ice-cold fountain drink.

An impeccably groomed middle-aged woman approached Melanie and I as we enjoyed our lunch under a shade tree. She appeared to have stepped from an advertisement for J.Crew, wearing crisp white shorts, a navy-blue sleeveless blouse, and a jaunty polka-dot neckerchief. Her espadrille sandals revealed a perfect red-nailed pedicure. I hoped the funk surrounding me would not reach her nose.

The woman smiled as her bright-blue eyes darted from our packs to our boots to our black-rimmed fingernails. "We saw you walk in from the woods. Are you hiking the AT?"

"We are. I'm Sticks, and this is my daughter, Melanie. We're section hikers out here for a couple of weeks." I wiped my mouth with a paper napkin and wondered just how bad my hair, pulled back from my face with a sweat-stained bandana, actually looked. The woman seemed in no hurry to get back to her family and picnic.

We answered the usual questions. "Have you seen any bears? Do you get scared? Where do you sleep? How much does your pack weigh?"

"Well, mine's about thirty-five pounds, Melanie's a little less."

"Have you read a book called *Wild*?" she asked. "About a woman hiking the AT alone?"

"I just read it," I answered. "It's very good, but I believe the author, Cheryl Strayed, hiked the Pacific Crest Trail."

"Oh, yes, I believe you're right." She paused. Then, looking past the pavilion to the green mountains and blue skies, she said, "I've always wanted to take a long hike through the woods, enjoy nature. Just get away, you know?"

I nodded, in complete understanding of this woman who was

about my age, maybe a year or two older. "Yes, it's wonderful." I hesitated and then added gently, "Why don't you? I mean, you can do it. If I can do it, anybody can."

She turned her gaze back to us with sort of a rueful smile. "Yes, well. Maybe someday." She suddenly stood up straighter and briskly shook her head. "Well, I'll let you get back to your lunch. I've loved talking to you. I hope you both have a wonderful adventure, and I'll think of you."

We watched her walk away, tall and thin in her perfect outfit. I felt grateful for her apparent admiration of us, but also a bit saddened. I hoped someday she *would* just do it.

* * *

We stepped back into the woods, leaving behind vending machines and flush toilets and—according to a small sign just off the Trail—crossed the Mason-Dixon Line. Abundant wildflowers and small streams accentuated the idyllic nature of this lush, green walk, but increasingly frequent boulder scrambles reminded us we had reached Pennsylvania and her infamous rocks.

For the next ten or so days, stopping a couple of times in towns for resupply, Melanie and I simply walked. We enjoyed typical July weather—hot and buggy—most of the time, but afternoon rain showers were not uncommon. Our gear held up well, and we developed a satisfying routine. We hiked ten to fifteen miles a day and tried to make camp before sunset. At Melanie's insistence, we had brought along a stove and thus ate fairly heartily and healthily. Oatmeal and coffee started the day; prepackaged rice or pasta dishes finished it. We almost always slept well and peacefully. Occasionally, the howl of a coyote would wake one or the other of us, but that was no cause for alarm, only a reminder of the world outside our snug little tent.

Once, in the deep woods far from any road, we were startled by a full-grown doe thrashing about in the undergrowth just to the side of the Trail. Our footsteps had apparently frightened her. She bravely tried to find footing and rise but could gain no purchase. I saw no sign of blood or outward physical damage, but her long, lovely neck was clearly broken. Her head hung off to the side at nearly ninety degrees to her body. Her eyes were wild and huge.

Melanie and I were upset, but there was nothing we could do to comfort the poor thing. Our presence only made the situation worse as she struggled to get away.

"Let's just move on, honey," I said. We walked on and shortly overtook a small group of visibly distressed young thru-hikers.

"Did you see that deer?" one girl asked tearfully. "It's so terrible."

They told us they had called 911 on a cell phone, but the police said there was nothing they could do.

"No," I said to these sweet, concerned kids. "I believe she must have been hit by a car and ran, maybe for miles, up here into the woods."

"But we can't just leave her!"

"I'm afraid that's all we can do," I continued gently. "It was just her bad luck to finally falter right here at the Trail. Every time someone passes, she is going to try and get up."

We all finally walked on as a group for a while, each of us saddened and shaken. The thru-hikers eventually pulled ahead of us, but Melanie and I stayed close together for the rest of the day, the image of the broken deer, as we came to call her, always on our minds.

❋ ❋ ❋

This two-week Pennsylvania hike took us through local and state parks and alongside long-deserted iron forges and charcoal pits. Views from cliffs gave way to fern-tossed swamps. We crossed roads, paved and unpaved, and forded small streams when no footlogs or bridges were present. We scrambled across boulders and skimmed across meadows. Each morning and again each evening, the sun danced a pas de deux with the moon and stars. Our watches became useless things, as time measured by hours and minutes no longer mattered; dawn and dusk dictated our progress.

We camped one night at Caledonia State Park where the fee of twenty dollars or so included access to the bathhouse. By this time, having been on Trail several days, both of us were badly in need of showers, and I had no hesitation in forking over the money.

We checked in at the office, a typical little wooden booth, and were given our tent site assignment. I asked the attendant if she or the bathhouse happened to have any soap or shampoo. "Nope, sorry, no such luxury."

One of the park rangers, a young, eager chap, poked his head into the booth as I made this inquiry.

"Let me see if I can find something," he said, taking in our trail-worn appearance and no doubt getting a whiff of our ripe odor.

We hoisted our packs once again to walk the quarter mile or so to our tent site. Just as we arrived, the friendly park ranger pulled away in a golf cart with a wave and a smile. On a corner of the cement picnic table, he had left several small packets of shampoo and a couple of tiny, paper-wrapped soap bars. Yet again, we were reminded of how easily gratitude comes to us on the Trail.

In the bathhouse, the absence of shower curtains and the presence of spiders in no way detracted from the joy of the hot water. I reminded Melanie to check for ticks. We combed our long, tangled hair, finally free of sweat and dirt and bug spray. Dressed in clean underwear under our hiking shorts and soft cotton T-shirts, we returned to our campsite—to find a cheerful wood fire ablaze in the stone campfire ring and small logs stacked neatly nearby. I could only attribute this little miracle to the hospitable park ranger. Our hearts were warmed, as well as our hands and feet as we stretched them toward the flames.

After the evening meal and a pleasant hour or two of stargazing, we retired to our tent. Snuggled in my sleeping bag, clean and drowsy, with my daughter murmuring softly next to me, I was utterly content.

Then came the faint but unmistakable odor of skunk.

I heard the soft squeaks of small animal communication and the rustling of dry leaves. (When you sleep on the ground at eye, nose, and ear level with the little forest creatures, their emanations are much closer and clearer than when you tower five or six feet over them.) I flipped on my headlamp and, as quietly as possible, unzipped the tent flaps.

"Melanie," I whispered. "Sit up and look at this." Two skunks, as large as full-grown house cats, nosed about under the picnic table ten or twelve feet from our tent. They briefly stopped their snuffling to glance at our faces framed in the tent opening, and for an instant, their eyes were glowing pinpoints. I quickly turned off my headlamp, and the skunks resumed their search for a snack. We watched them for several minutes. They seemed unconcerned by our presence and our curiosity. I wanted to keep it that way.

"Okay," I whispered again. "Let's just lie back down and not bother them." I could imagine hiking for several more days with a skunk-sprayed tent in my pack. The prospect was not pleasant.

We drifted off to sleep, and the night, still and starry, brought us no more visitors. When we woke the next morning, the skunks were gone. They had graciously left us with no reminder of their nocturnal wanderings.

* * *

We continued on the eighteen-inch-wide path that was our temporary home. Just north of Shippensburg Road in Arendtsville, we crossed a rocky dirt lane marked "Dead Woman Hollow Road." I took a picture of the sign. Oh, what stories and mysteries these mountains hold!

Just as oddly, we passed what was once a prisoner-of-war camp for enemy soldiers captured during World War II. A small plaque just off the Trail marks the site. A few low stone fences and the crumbling foundations of what may have been a barn or barracks are all that remain.

This section of the AT seems to have an abundance of interesting social history features. Pine Grove Furnace State Park, where we camped for the night, preserves the home of the furnace ironmaster, which was also a stop on the Underground Railroad for enslaved people escaping from the bonds of inhumanity in the South.

It now houses a small museum dedicated to the AT, its founders, and pioneers. Memorabilia of some of its noteworthy hikers—including a pair of sneakers Emma "Grandma" Gatewood wore in 1955 when, at age sixty-seven, she became the first woman to hike the Appalachian Trail solo—are on display. We wandered through this little treasure house, remarking on the hardiness of our forefathers and foremothers whose gear and clothing now seem so heavy and inadequate.

Next to this sturdy stone building is the park store, famous on the AT as the home of the half-gallon challenge. A thru-hiker can plow into a half-gallon of ice cream—choice of flavors—and, if he or she finishes it, enjoys the dubious honor of receiving a wooden spoon stamped "Member of the Half Gallon Club." I purchased a carton, and Melanie and I dug in.

Steppenwolf, a thru-hiker in his late twenties, joined us on the store's porch. Our paths had crossed a few times over the past several days, and I had noticed he tended to keep to himself, saying little, when he found himself with others in the evening camps.

Now he nibbled on some dirty, untrimmed carrots while Melanie and I stuffed our faces with mint chocolate chip. I—in retrospect insensitively—asked Steppenwolf why he wasn't taking on the half-gallon challenge. He grinned shyly and—without really answering the question—told us the store proprietress had given him some produce from her garden. My eyes met Melanie's. We took a few more bites, then put down our spoons.

"Well, I am stuffed," Melanie declared.

"Oh, my god, so am I. I can't move."

The carton of ice cream, just beginning to melt and soften, was still well over halfway filled.

"Steppenwolf, will you take this? Please. I hate to see it go to waste."

He demurred, "Oh, no." Then, "Are you sure you don't want it?"

"No, no, can't eat another bite. Take it."

"Well, gosh, thanks. I mean, yeah, that would be great."

I pushed the carton toward him as we sat with our backs to the porch wall, packs at our feet, and trekking poles propped against the railing in the hot afternoon sun. Melanie went inside the store to get a spoon for our friend and fellow traveler. I closed my eyes and counted all our blessings.

* * *

On Piney Mountain, shortly after passing a sign marking the geographical halfway point of the AT, we crossed a footbridge over Mountain Creek. Rodeo (a thru-hiker with whom we'd crossed paths several times on this journey) and some of her Trail Family lounged on the banks in happy celebration of their having journeyed 1,100 miles thus far. Melanie and I declined the invitation to rest with them. We were sure they would leapfrog us again as we all made our way to Boiling Springs.

Now in our tenth day on the Trail, we hiked through the last of the Blue Ridge mountain chain. The elevation is low, and the Trail was often boggy even in this hot summer month. Creeks (I noticed this is about the point where what we Southerners call creeks start to be referred to by Northerners as brooks) and streams intersect and diverge into undefined marshes. Hardworking trail maintainers have built plank walkways over the swampiest sections, as much to protect the delicate plants and wildlife as the boots and socks of the hikers.

Rocky Ridge was our high point for the day, 1,150 feet, after which we cruised for six or seven more miles into Boiling Springs. There were some boulder squeezes, but mostly we hiked on fern-lined trail through sun-dappled, young-growth forest. We neared town and left the woods to hike alongside and through farm fields. Occasionally, we saw John Deere–capped men on their tractors, who always smiled and waved. We were respectful and mindful that on this section, we were often treading on private lands.

The good people of Boiling Springs have seen fit to provide a sort of camp field, complete with Porta Potty, for the waves of hikers that pass through this charming town. We arrived at this site, a flat, treeless half acre or so bordered by hayfields and train tracks, well before dark.

Several thru-hikers had already made a liquor run and built a large communal campfire. The halfway-point celebration was in full swing. Melanie and I set up our tent, freshened up as best we could, and walked into town for a much-anticipated dinner in a good restaurant.

The crown jewel of the quaint town of Boiling Springs is Children's Lake, which reflects the surrounding stone architecture, much as the pool at the National Mall in Washington, DC, reflects the Lincoln Memorial and the Washington Monument. Ducks and geese paddle about on the surface, and families stroll along the surrounding path.

Fly-fishers cast their rods into the brook that empties into the lake. I felt we had stumbled into a movie set of idyllic small-town America.

After a hearty spaghetti dinner, sated and sleepy-eyed, we returned to what I had begun to refer to as the hobo camp. We joined the thru-hikers in their happy talk around the campfire, but after a few minutes I felt the difference thirty years in age can make. I left the young folks to their beer and smoke, and with no regrets or envy, made my way to my tent and peaceful slumber.

The next morning I woke early. The camp was silent. As I peered out into the dawn, Melanie still sweetly asleep, I saw Graybeard—a wiry, taciturn man in his late sixties—emerge from his tent, stretch, and splash water on his face. A mist had stolen in during the night, adding to the nostalgic picture. I heard the distant whistle of an approaching freight train, and I would not have been surprised to see the ghost of Woody Guthrie walk down the tracks with a guitar on his back and a dog at his heels. I figured this was the closest I'd ever get to the romantic notion of riding the rails and drinking soup from a tin cup in a coal yard.

We left this blissful spot in late morning. Walking north out of town, we hadn't gone more than a mile or two when Rodeo and Blackjack came up behind us.

"Hey, Sticks! You left these back at that visitor center."

Blackjack handed me my trekking poles. After words of thanks, Melanie and I wished these wonderful people the best on their next thousand miles. They went on ahead, and we never saw them again.

✻ ✻ ✻

Our walk continued north through fields and copses. In this section, AT blazes are on wooden posts as often as they are on the trunks of trees. We climbed stiles over electrified fences and clambered over crumbling stone walls. We had a sense of an artificial hike—a temporary suspension of the real thing—as if we were just marking time and distance until we would reenter the deep woods. We passed very close to neighborhoods. On one occasion, we stopped to greet a small herd of goats corralled in a pen so close to the Trail we could have touched them.

In one section, the AT crosses (on overpasses, thank you) the Pennsylvania Turnpike, US 11, and I-81, all within just a couple of miles. The trucks rushing below often gave us friendly honks, which we replied to with a wave.

The next morning, Friday, July 18, we were tired, dirty, and hot as we broke camp at Darlington Shelter for our last day on the Trail. Thirteen miles remained between us and our car at Duncannon. We walked north, often on elevated plank paths through marshland. The woods became denser and the farm fields less frequent as we began our ascent out of the Cumberland Valley.

The Trail became rockier, which was to be expected as we were well into Pennsylvania now. We climbed Cove Mountain to the summit at 1,100 feet and stopped for lunch a couple of miles farther on at the beautiful and sturdy Cove Mountain Shelter. At Hawk Rock, we paused to admire the view of the Susquehanna River far below and point out to each other the collection of dots that was our destination, the town of Duncannon. We trod carefully on the steep, rocky descent, and our pace was slow in the hot afternoon. Finally, we emerged from the woods into the outskirts of Duncannon—and immediately lost our way.

A bridge across the creek that marks the town's southern boundary was under repair, and the white blazes seemed to have disappeared among detour signs and heavy construction equipment. After a couple of wrong turns down residential streets studded with vacant houses and abandoned cars, we wound up back at the washed-out bridge and found three bandana-clad thru-hikers there we recognized. We had leapfrogged with John Boy, Meerkat, and Popsicle over the past few days, and now they seemed to sag under their heavy packs in the dusty town heat.

"Hey, Sticks. What's the word here?"

I explained our dead-ended attempt, and we all agreed to try another approach. After a block or two in the opposite direction from the one Melanie and I had taken, we found blazes on telephone poles. We plodded on through a neighborhood of small, clapboard houses, many with chain-link fences around their tiny front yards. We passed a small brick church with one of those humorous signs American

Protestant congregations are so fond of. This one said something like, "We'll bring the pie, you bring the piety."

I turned to Meerkat, next to me. "What does that even mean?" I asked.

Meerkat shrugged her thin shoulders under the thick straps of her pack, too tired to answer or even care.

Just past the church, a young woman sat on her front porch, smoking a cigarette and chatting on a cell phone. A large dog, maybe a German shepherd mix, rested in the shade of the porch and watched our approach with his head on his front paws. At this point, because of the width of our packs and the narrowness of the sidewalk, the five of us were more or less in single file.

When I was directly in front of the house, the dog suddenly lunged at me. My mouth opened, but before I could even make a noise, this charging, snarling ball of fur and fangs had flown across the few yards from the porch to the sidewalk and sunk his teeth into my right thigh.

I staggered backward a few feet. The dog let go but did not back off and now continued to growl at me, all quivering restraint and raised hackles. This happened so quickly that the other hikers were not sure what was going on and stood ahead of and behind me in shocked silence. The woman on the porch leapt across the tiny yard and yanked the dog back by its collar. She was still holding her cell phone and screamed into it, "Hang on! Shit! My dog just attacked some hiker!"

The dog continued to buck and lunge, whining now, as the woman hauled him up on the porch. She momentarily ceased her telephone conversation. Holding the phone against her chest and breathing heavily, she said to me, "Oh, my god, I'm so sorry. He's never acted like that before."

My concerned friends and daughter clustered around me. "It's okay," I said. I was not truly injured, and we walked on. My hiking shorts, made of thin, durable nylon, reached to just above my knee, and the dog's bite had not pierced the material. The skin was not broken, but a bruise was quickly rising around two distinct teeth indentations. To this day, the marks remain as faint discolorations on my midthigh. I still don't know what upset Cujo, but the irony is not lost on me that I had shared the Appalachian Trail with bears, rattlesnakes, and a variety of other wildlife only to be attacked by a domestic dog on a city street.

We walked through the sullen town of Duncannon and made a stop at Doyles, a hostel widely known among thru-hikers, to donate what was left of our food supply to the hiker's box. Although somewhat past its prime now and a little rundown, Doyles, located on the main street, is a two-story wooden structure with a balcony, often draped with sleeping bags and tents, running along the second level and is still a must-stop for many hikers. This is probably in large part due to the spacious saloon housed on the first floor.

Hostels along the Appalachian Trail are privately owned establishments catering to long-distance hikers who are usually on strict budgets. They range from large, rambling hotel-like structures (as is the case with Doyles) to clusters of small cabins. Sleeping arrangements vary widely from dormitory-style to perhaps a small private bedroom (although almost never a private bathroom) and are priced accordingly. Services and amenities also vary but will usually include a ride to and from the trailhead and a grocery store, shower room, and do-it-yourself laundry facilities.

Hostels will also provide what is known as hiker boxes. These are bins which basically contain discards and leftovers from Trail life: old clothes, half-full fuel cans, slightly bent trekking poles or worn-out sleeping pads, dehydrated food packages. The items have been left behind by hikers who no longer need or want them, and they are free for the taking. In hiker towns, you might also see hiker boxes in front of the post office or other public building. It is really a lovely tradition.

I did not stay in hostels until I reached the New England states, where there is little choice. Because my budget was not as restrictive as the average thru-hiker, I could afford to stay in a motel room with my own bathroom. I also had a preconceived notion—born from reading too many tales of European backpackers—that hostels are not very clean, and the occupants and proprietors are rather shady, as if they were all sitting around in shalwars and smoking hashish. Fortunately, travel does open one's narrow mind, and in fact, every hostel I came across was clean and safe, and the managers were friendly and professional.

Melanie and I crossed the Clarks Ferry Bridge over the Susquehanna and faced the roar of traffic on PA 14, reaching our car with near delirious relief. Shoving our packs in the back of the Blazer and turning on the air-conditioner full blast, we hurriedly hit the open highway, eager to get home to Tim and Tennessee. As it was, I felt I had overstayed my welcome in Duncannon.

* * *

In September, Tim and I traveled to Pennsylvania for a few days' visit with his brother and family. Tom had just been diagnosed with cancer, and now he and Lynne were living in the new normal of doctors' appointments and medical treatments. We attended a memorial service honoring the victims of 9/11 as the northeastern mountains were just beginning to show their fall colors. Tim returned to Tennessee for work, and I stayed on for a seventy-mile solo hike.

Tom drove me to the town of Duncannon and dropped me off on the side of busy PA 147. I paused to watch the tractor-trailer rigs rushing by and then stepped on the Trail, which would be home for the next six days. The world, with its cruel cancer and evil terrorism, was left behind as I began an immediate ascent of Peters Mountain, my pack heavy with camping gear and several days' worth of food.

The Trail is steep here, but rock stairways, switchbacks, and lovely views alleviate the difficulty, and before long, I settled into several miles of pleasant ridgewalking at one thousand feet. I frequently had views of the wide Susquehanna, sometimes to the east, sometimes to the west. At each clearing or rock outcropping, I stopped and admired the little hamlets nestled along the river far below. About ten miles in, near sunset, I reached my first destination, Peters Mountain Shelter. This solitary day turned into a solitary evening, but sleep came easily in my exhaustion, and I was grateful for oblivion.

After a comfortable night on the shelter floor, snug in my sleeping bag and cushioned by my sleeping pad, I continued north on the rocky trail. The next shelter was twenty miles away at Rausch Gap, a pretty far distance for my old legs, so I would tent-camp for the night. A solitary and pleasantly warm day took me across several streams, through deep woods, and over boulders. About ten miles in, along the ridgewalk of Stony Mountain, I noticed at the side of the trail a small clearing, brush broken and trampled as if a deer had nested here—or a fellow hiker had pitched a tent. Here I made my home for the night and reflected that the farther one retreats into nature, the smaller one's needs become.

The following day, along a section where the AT morphs into what was once a stagecoach road, I passed by cemeteries, building foundation ruins, unidentifiable bits of rusty metal, copper-colored streams, and other reminders of the coal industry that thrived in this part of Pennsylvania in the late 1800s. I reached Rausch Gap easily before dark and laid out bag and pad in the shelter. As I waited for sleep to come, on this quiet and lonely night, it occurred to me that solitude is a wonderful condition when you know it's transitory. *But I wouldn't want to be alone forever; without each other to encourage and tease, any one of us would just be an old shell like these deserted towns.*

By lunchtime the next day, the fourth of this sojourn, I had climbed Second Mountain and began the descent into Swatara Gap. I crossed paths with other hikers, who told me the bridge across Swatara Creek was out and the Trail had been rerouted.

At PA 443, handwritten notices slipped into plastic sleeves gave information about an alternate route. I followed the detour across a low, swampy portion of the creek and back onto the white-blazed AT without too much hardship. One intrepid southbounder told me he simply swam the creek. *I have enough trouble*, I thought, *without adding drowning to the list of things that could go wrong.*

I climbed a thousand feet from the gap to the summit of Blue Mountain and walked along the ridge for several miles. The day continued fine, and I admired the patchwork-quilt views of Pennsylvania farms spread out below me. By nightfall, I reached the William Penn Shelter, another fancy lodge by AT standards. This was a long day for me—fourteen miles—but there were a few other hikers here, and it was nice to smile at other humans and hear their laughter even though I felt too tired and even shy to join in their conversation.

My food supply was getting low, so I rose early the next morning and hiked a couple of easy miles to PA 645 and hitched a ride into the nearby town of Pine Grove. Here, I resupplied my junk-food staples—Pringles, candy bars, peanuts, Pop-Tarts—and was soon back on the Trail. I hiked six more meandering miles on a sometimes rocky trail to Hertlein Campsite before nightfall, continuing in an almost trancelike state. My brief interactions with the townsfolk had found my voice rusty and unused, my eyes wide at the sight of traffic and storefronts.

An average AT hiker will burn five to six thousand calories in a full day of hiking. This is not the time for dieting: my advice is to eat whatever you want whenever you can get it. Optimally, you want foods high in protein and carbohydrates, but salt and fat are necessary too. The body signals what it needs, and hikers will find themselves craving certain things like ice cream and meat. Most hikers will carry a little stove, but I find the extra weight unnecessary, although a cup of hot coffee in the morning is always welcome. Dehydrated meals are widely available at outfitters or online but can be expensive and cumbersome to pack. Staples include tuna, dried fruit, nuts and raisins, energy or candy bars, peanut butter, mini bagels, jerky, hard cheeses, and cheap, dense pastries like honeybuns.

Thru-hikers walk themselves into a state known as "hiker hunger," where, after being on the trail for weeks and weeks, their appetites become insatiable. Because I didn't usually hike for more than a week or two at a time—at least during my first several years on the Trail—this did not happen to me. Actually, for me, the opposite was true. I often had no or little appetite because of exhaustion. The expression "too tired to eat" is hard for most of us to grasp, but this was in fact sometimes the case with me. I learned to force myself to eat, even if just half a candy bar or a cracker or two, at routine intervals. If not, energy is completely sapped and progress is difficult.

The next day brought humid air and gathering storm clouds. My goal was Eagles Nest Shelter eleven miles away. Beginning easily enough, I hiked past where Fort Dietrich Snyder once stood, one of several forts that popped up like mushrooms on the Blue Ridge Mountains during the French and Indian War. There is really no sign of humanity—of any skin color—here now, only a stone monument and a few low stone foundations obscured by thick blueberry bushes.

The Trail steadily became rockier as the day progressed. Rain spat on and off, adding another element of treachery, and I was grateful for my trekking poles. The first hint of autumn chilled the air. An occasional swirl of wind reminded the beeches it was time to begin letting go of their leaves. Grouse—who must have felt unsettled by the change in the weather and wary of predators preparing for winter— flew up at my feet and flapped their wings noisily.

This section is ridgewalking at 1,500 feet with almost no change in elevation, but the rocks under my feet were merciless, and my pace was slow. I amused myself by looking for the little teaberry bushes, whose fragrant leaves look like tiny mittens. Crushing one between my fingers, I was reminded of the smell of my grandmother's chewing gum.

Just when my feet felt as if they couldn't take another rock, I reached the decent-sized Eagles Nest Shelter. These had been difficult and lonely yet satisfying days. I was grateful to be almost at hike's end, and I was eager to return to the outside world—even with its mean imperfections—for the coming of autumn, leaving to the grouse and the mice the abandoned coal mines and creaking shelters that soon would be covered in fallen leaves and then by soft, silent snow.

* * *

In late September, Tim and I headed west instead of east for a change. Whisked away from our land of humidity and forested mountains, we landed in Arizona with its dry heat and treeless deserts. To hike in this climate requires light and breathable clothes, sunglasses, plenty of sunscreen, and lots and lots of water. To golf requires the same. Unsurprisingly, on our first day, I opted for the former, and Tim opted for the latter.

Camelback, just outside of Scottsdale, rises 2,700 feet from a valley that sits at 1,300-feet elevation. Even in late September, daily temperatures can easily reach over one hundred degrees, and shade on this mountain is almost nonexistent. The trail is rocky sand, and the vegetation consists of cacti and desert grasses.

The hike up and down on either trail, Cholla or Echo, or on a combination of both, is only a little over three miles, but it is strenuous.

The ascent set calves and quads burning, and the descent reminded me that knees may not last forever. But the views of the desert as it laps at the city's edge are amazing, and I found the unfamiliar terrain fascinating. This is an easily accessible, nonremote hike, and I was glad to be in the company of numerous other hikers of all fitness levels.

Tim and I were reunited at day's end, each pleased with our respective choices of entertainment, and now happy to be together for the next phase of this particular journey.

* * *

There are three ways to get to the bottom of the Grand Canyon—where we had reservations to spend a night at Phantom Ranch—by foot, by raft, or my mule. (Tim wouldn't even discuss the first option, and I wouldn't consider the second). We checked in with the mule outfitters at the lodge in Grand Canyon National Park, where we were weighed and given final instructions. The guides looked us over and chatted us up to determine our riding experience (not much). I was assigned Pauline, a petite, sweet-faced thing, and Tim was given Josey, a huge, lumbering but deceptively agile beast. I was just thankful to not get one named Thunderbolt.

The Bright Angel Trail, winding its way down switchback after switchback, is a feat of amazing ingenuity. Native populations improved on existing animal paths, and modern trail maintainers have honored the authenticity and ruggedness. There are no guardrails here, no warning signs, no guide ropes or rebar to hang onto. The only thing between you and a free fall into the abyss is the sure-footedness of your mule. There are no trees or other obstacles to block your view or hinder your imagination about what a body tumbling down thousands of feet of rock would look like when it finally reached bottom. Rounding switchbacks, Pauline's head and neck soared out over the vast emptiness as she stepped delicately over rocks to complete a forty-five to ninety-degree turn.

In spite of the stomach-heaving vertigo, it was a luxury to not carry a pack and to let someone else do the walking. In late afternoon, we crossed the suspension bridge over the Colorado River and arrived at the ranch. With great relief, we dismounted and set foot on the floor of the Grand Canyon. My legs and back weren't sore, but I can't say the same for my ass. (I mean my butt, not my mule. I have no idea how she felt.)

The next morning, as we trekked back up to the rim, I felt grateful for the change in perspective this week had given us. To see an arid, dusty trail from the back of an animal rather than a spongy green path under my boots and have the big western sky over my head instead of a dense tree canopy reminded me that a change of scenery is always good for the soul. I looked back at Tim, sitting tall in the saddle, and thought of the miles behind us and those yet to come.

✿ ✿ ✿

Autumn wound down and winter prepared its arrival. Frontier Airlines introduced a cheap direct flight from Nashville to Trenton, New Jersey. *What the hell? I'm retired.* I seemed to say this quite often in those days. *I'll just hop on up there, visit Tom and Lynne, and ask them to drive me to and from the trailhead.*

Lynne picked me up at Trenton Airport on November 12, a damp, chilly Wednesday, and I spent the night in Yardley in a warm, comfortable bed. Ever-obliging Tom, whose cancer was being held at least temporarily at bay, took me to Fox Gap on Thursday morning. I would not be camping in the cold northeastern November weather, and my pack, with no tent or sleeping gear, was relatively light. I planned to hike only about twenty-six miles from Fox Gap through Delaware Water Gap to US Highway 206. This section is contiguously north of the short Pennsylvania hikes I had done in 2008 and 2012, and would carry me through towns, or at least road crossings, where I could find lodging.

I stepped on the Trail in a misty, cold fog, knowing only seven miles of hiking lay ahead of me this day. But a long day it seemed. Pennsylvania lived up to her rocky reputation, and my pace was slow in the quiet woods. Midweek and mid-November is not a time of crowded trails, and I saw very few other hikers. For the first several miles, I followed the blazes along the ridge to the summit of Mount

Minsi. Low clouds obscured any view I may have had of the Delaware River below. I picked my way over the rocks, reliant on my poles, and down the 1,100-foot descent to Delaware Water Gap.

My chosen motel for the evening was a disappointment. Broken-slatted blinds hung from dirty windows along the hallways, and leggy potted plants, some with browned leaves and crumbling tendrils, decorated the lobby. The damp, foggy day that had provided little opportunity to interact with other hikers left me feeling lonely, and my doleful lodgings increased my loneliness. How long ago it seemed since I had touched down in Trenton on Wednesday.

Friday morning brought no break in the weather. A dampness crept through my winter clothes and seemed to touch my bones. I left the broad Delaware River and, with it, Pennsylvania. I had arrived in New Jersey.

Still feeling lonely and introspective, I hiked slowly out of the gap. The Trail crosses Dunnfield Creek on a wooden bridge and follows it for half a mile or so before turning onto an old logging road. I climbed a thousand feet over three-and-a-half miles and reached Sunfish Pond by early afternoon.

The clouds lifted a bit, as did my mood. It's always an interesting part of an AT hiker's day to see a large body of still water in the mountains. It seems unnatural, accustomed as we are to rushing streams and rocky springs. Sunfish Pond teems silently with aquatic life. Turtles rest on logs near the shoreline, and waterfowl grace-fully rise from the surface. Beaver handiwork is apparent; trees four to six inches in diameter are chewed to pencil points. I sat there for a long time, resting against a dying hemlock, to eat my lunch and watch for beaver. None showed themselves, but my spirit felt recharged by my quiet commune with nature. I moved on with a new lightness and joy.

Dark comes early to the Appalachian Mountains in November, and I hurried on through the cold, wet afternoon. On Mount Mohi-can, I met a group of elderly bird watchers who had walked in from a side trail. In their raincoats and wide-brimmed hats, with binoculars slung around necks and camera tripods in place atop the rocky summit, they seemed as happy and free as the raptors soaring overhead. They pressed snacks on me, this solitary wanderer who had stumbled into their midst, and wished me well.

I ended the day's eleven-mile hike at the Mohican Outdoor Center, a modern, sprawling facility operated by the Appalachian Mountain Club within the Delaware Water Gap National Recreation Area about a half mile off the AT. I had a little bunkroom to myself, this being off-season, and I was grateful for a warm, dry place to rest my tired body and soul.

The final day—Saturday—of this section hike dictated I get an early start. I had eighteen tough miles ahead to reach Culver Lake by nightfall. Lynne was to pick me up there, and I did not want to worry her or cause her to be out too late.

I would not be deterred—Did I have a choice?—by the weather. The temperatures stubbornly remained in the midthirties, and rain occasionally turned sleety. The damp mist obscured any views of the farmland below. I hiked along the Kittatinny Ridge for several miles on smooth, easy trail. The Pennsylvania rocks were now miles behind me. Or so I thought.

I crossed Flatbrookville Road at seven miles in after only a couple of hours of walking. There would not be another road crossing until I reached hike's end, still eleven miles north. This remoteness would guarantee another mostly solitary day. The smooth trail that I had flown along in the morning now turned rocky, and my pace once again slowed.

Navigating the slabs, cliffs, stones, and pebbles, I crossed over Rattlesnake Mountain and Bird Mountain, seeing none of the former but many of the latter. Checking my watch often and seldom stopping for breaks, I tried to keep a two-miles-per-hour pace. Just as what was already a dark afternoon turned even darker. I scrambled down a rocky hill to the road crossing of Highway 206.

From where the AT crosses the road, I could see a cluster of lighted buildings to the west. I followed the road along Culver Lake and found one of the buildings to be an inviting-looking local restaurant. I dumped my pack and poles on the wide front porch and called Lynne, who said she'd be there in an hour or so.

I went into the restaurant and checked my reflection in the bathroom mirror. My damp hair was flattened from a toboggan, and I tried to fluff it up. My cheeks were pink and wind-burned, the skin still cold to the touch.

The bar in the warm, club-like atmosphere of the restaurant was crowded, but I edged in and took a seat. The congenial bartender noticed my hiking attire and engaged me in conversation about the Trail. Several barstool occupants listened in and expressed their astonishment that I had just solo-hiked these remote trails for three days in the bleak weather. The admiration was some vindication for these lonesome, difficult days, and I was happy to bask in the feeling of accomplishment as I patiently waited for Lynne to join me.

* * *

Two hundred and thirty miles on the Appalachian Trail, my largest one-year total so far, did not eclipse the milestones of my retirement and our twenty-fifth wedding anniversary. The events of the year, on and off the Trail, reminded me that balance is beauty and that serenity is found on the very thin line between chaos and stasis. On our annual holiday card, Tim and I sent a photo of us on our mules with the caption "Happy Trails." I never meant it more, on this, my tenth year on the AT.

CHAPTER 11

2015 (270 MILES)

PORT CLINTON, PENNSYLVANIA, TO LITTLE GAP, PENNSYLVANIA

CULVER LAKE, PENNSYLVANIA, TO CLARENCE FAHNESTOCK STATE PARK, NEW YORK

CLARENCE FAHNESTOCK STATE PARK, NEW YORK, TO

CORNWALL BRIDGE, CONNECTICUT

WALLINGFORD GULF ROAD, VERMONT, TO CLARENDON GORGE, VERMONT

CORNWALL BRIDGE, CONNECTICUT, TO GREAT BARRINGTON, MASSACHUSETTS

Middle Tennessee's winters are dreary and damp and rarely offer any redeeming qualities, such as a lovely blanket of pristine snow. The skies are usually gray, and precipitation falls as sleet or simply very cold rain. The winter of 2015 was no different, and in March we received a different kind of icy blow. My younger sister, Lynne, who had been ill with various infirmities for years, had been admitted to the hospital.

During the first week of March, I drove back and forth to North Alabama for visits and grim news from the doctors. On March 9, at the age of fifty-four, Lynne passed away. She had four children and six grandchildren, including one-week-old Olivia. My mother had now outlived her husband and three of her four children.

I can offer no justification or explanation for the ways of the world. I will leave that to the philosophers, theologians, and sages. I can search for meaning in nature, but that doesn't mean I will find it. But I do know that this is where I can seek comfort in the recognition that winter turns to spring and that new birth offers some possibility of hope.

* * *

The miserable month dragged on and turned into the somewhat more hopeful month of April. Forsythia came and went followed by the daffodils and the tulips, and now the dogwoods bloomed. I longed for the solace of the mountains and the consolation of friends. Solo-hiking the fifty miles in Pennsylvania from Port Clinton to Little Gap that I had skipped earlier, followed by a high school girls' reunion (coincidentally in Boone this year), would give me this chance. I packed my gear, loaded the car, and motored east.

Sweet Al, a dear friend and my partner in Iraq, had retired from the FBI and assured me he had nothing in the world to do but work out, go to happy hour, and shuttle me to trailheads. In mid-April, he drove west from his home in Cherry Hill and met me at Little Gap, where Lynne and I had begun our freezing 2012 adventure. We left my car there and returned to Port Clinton, where I had finished solo in 2014. I was about to reach a milestone. Completing this unfinished section of Pennsylvania would mean seven states behind me and seven states ahead.

Al clucked around me as I tightened my bootlaces and strapped on my pack at the trailhead. He gave me a big hug as passing drivers slowed and craned their necks at this sight of a stocky, black guy and a small, white woman embracing at the side of the road.

"You be careful now. If you go missing, they're going to come looking for me first," Al said, not entirely joking. "And you know they gonna lean hard."

My boots tramped across the Schuylkill River Bridge on a perfect spring day. Very soon, even on rocky and steep trail, I was in the deep woods on the Blue Ridge Mountains at 1,300 feet.

I reached Windsor Furnace, where I had planned to spend the first night, but the weather was so fine, and I felt so strong that I kept on walking. Four more miles—the first two quite steep and strenuous—took me past Pulpit Rock with its gorgeous farmland views. Near the Pinnacle, a jutting cliff face, I found a flat spot to set up my tent and called it a day.

Next morning I woke refreshed. *Well, that was a successful first day. Weather fine. Trail not too difficult. A good pace that put me ahead of schedule. Let us see what the next few days bring.*

The descent from the Pinnacle to Pine Swamp Road is gentle, but the Trail turns rocky as it follows old logging roads hugging the side of Hawk Mountain. My initial plan called for me to stay Night Two at the Eckville Shelter near Hawk Mountain Sanctuary, which is devoted to the protection and observation of raptor birds. But I had made such good time on Day One that again, I pushed on, feeling self-impressed and a little smug with my uncharacteristically quick pace.

The ascent out of Pine Swamp is not so gentle. In fact, it is a bitch. Stretches of tumbled boulders test quads and glutes as you pull yourself up and over them. Again and again.

After a thirteen-mile day, I had had enough. I made camp before sunset, but I was again pleased with my progress. *Halfway done and the weather holding fair, steady on course.*

Day Three began with more rocky trail but still perfect weather.

This section includes The Cliffs, Bear Rocks, and Bake Oven Knob and is popular with locals and day-hikers. The views and bird-watching opportunities are spectacular, and it is fairly accessible from PA 309 and Bake Oven Knob Road. However, *popular* and *accessible* don't mean easy. The AT makes you work before she hands out the rewards.

Rocks, rocks, rocks. Each step must be carefully measured as your poles find placement on the stone-strewn path. The steady pace I had kept for the first couple of days now slowed considerably, and the thirteen miles I had planned now seemed improbable. I took only a few rest stops to eat a bite or two, chug water, and pop an Advil. I kept my eyes on my boots or the next blaze. A fall onto the jagged rocks on either side of the razor-thin knife edge that characterizes The Cliffs would certainly mean severe injury. I nodded grimly to the occasional passing hiker. This is not the time or place for idle chitchat. The AT leaves The Cliffs, but within another mile—my heart still in my throat—I reached the intimidating Bear Rocks.

Fortunately—grateful shout-out to the Trail planners—the AT doesn't pass directly over the knife edge of Bear Rocks but along the jagged base. A couple more rocky miles brought me to Bake Oven Knob—huge, sloping slabs of rock that rise out of the woods like humpback whales in the ocean. I am not ashamed to admit I traversed this landmark largely on my hands and knees. My progress was that of a barnacle on one of those metaphorical whales. Eventually this, too, passed, and I limped along the still-rocky trail for a few more miles, my hips and shoulders screaming in protest.

Near Ashfield Road, just before sunset, I found a decent campsite and collapsed. *Dear lord, what a day. That was really hard. But I did it.* And I had only ten miles to go on the final day. It couldn't possibly be any tougher.

* * *

Day Four dawned sunny and cool. My first few miles followed the ridge through pleasant woods before beginning the descent into the Lehigh River Valley. I only had five more miles to reach my car at Little Gap. It was a beautiful day, the Trail was somewhat less rocky, and I began to feel a bit more optimistic. Then I walked out of the woods into a dull and depressing landscape.

The mountainsides rising out of Lehigh Gap are scarred by decades of zinc mining. The descent into the river valley is perhaps the ugliest mile of the AT. I wondered how even the stunted trees and dusty clumps of grasses could grow in this stony, dusty soil. On either side of the gorge, the barren, copper-colored land slinks back from the river as if in shame.

Hurrying along as quickly as possible, anxious to put this miserable section behind me, I crossed a highway and the river bridge. Rocks become boulders on the north side of the river, and I reached the base of a huge hill of jagged detritus that looked like the aftermath of an implosion.

What the hell? was my first thought. *Could this possibly be the AT?* Well, yes, there were clearly white blazes painted here and there on the slabs. *Okay, I just have to go blaze to blaze. I got this.*

Throwing my sticks up onto each ascending rock, I climbed with hands and feet. Crevice by crevice, I slowly pulled myself up, heart hammering. A glance behind and below revealed only vicious points of torture. In a parking lot near the river, two police cars parked driver side to driver side were the size of matchboxes.

I could not, would not, believe this was the Appalachian Trail. Why, little kids hike the AT! Old people! If Grandma Gatewood hiked this section, I'll kiss your ass on the courthouse square. It occurred to me some local pranksters may have painted the blazes on the rocks as a cruel joke, and I had wandered off the true Trail.

One-handedly, I tossed my sticks up to the next ledge. The fingertips of both hands found a hold above my head and with a huge lunge from my quads, I propelled myself up. My feet found toeholds and then…I was stuck, splayed out like Wile E. Coyote against a cliff.

Obviously, I had not thought things through. I saw no escape route, no real possibilities for fingerholds or toeholds in any direction, but I was more pissed off than scared. *How ridiculous. What an ignominious way to die—stuck like the husk of a housefly on a rusty old screen door.*

I assessed the situation. On the plus side, the temperature was perfect, the sky cloudless. Several hours of daylight remained. Although I had seen few hikers this day, surely someone would come along. Again, I glanced at the police cars far below. Hopefully, the officers had noticed me glued to the mountain like a gecko. Maybe they would send up a rescue party eventually or—worst-case scenario—at least know where to begin the search for my broken body.

Minutes ticked by. I began to worry about muscle cramps. But then from the other side of the crest I heard voices—young, laughing, male. I briefly rested my forehead against the rock and breathed a little more easily. I could shout for help if need be. Then the unmistakable odor of marijuana wafted down from the summit. My potential saviors were apparently enjoying a bowl.

Several inches above and to the left of my hand's reach, a crumbling ledge jutted out an inch or two. I considered where to place my other three limbs if my left hand could reach this outcropping. *If.* I took a deep breath and jumped.

For a sickening instant, I was airborne across the traverse, the weight of my pack threatening to pitch me backward. Then, *contact*! Mother Earth and I were reunited.

Pretty dang proud of myself, I scrambled to the top of the rock pile. Two long-haired Doobie Brothers, packless and poleless, sat smoking and enjoying the view to the northwest. They turned as I came up behind them.

"Hey, how's it going?" I was cool and nonchalant now that I was safe.

"It's all good. You hiking the AT?"

"Yeah, this last climb was a bitch. Y'all get here from southbound AT?"

"Naw, we come up here all the time. There's a bypass trail that goes around the rocks and comes up here from the east."

Great. Now you tell me. Oh well, it was probably good I had not known about that bypass. I would have been tempted to take it, and this was far too late in the game. I was in way too deep to begin cheating now.

"Okay, guys, I'm pushing on."

"Cool. Good luck," one Doobie said.

To my great relief, the other added, "Next few miles north are a piece of cake."

And they were.

* * *

The shock of Lehigh stayed with me for the next few days at the girlfriend getaway. I seemed to be dazed one moment and hysterical the next. It's probably not accurate to say I had looked into the face of death and laughed. My guess is that it was the other way around.

My quarterly *A.T. Journeys*, the official magazine of the ATC, was waiting when I returned to Franklin. Quite coincidentally, the cover featured a photo of a young hiker at Lehigh Gap. The shot, taken from above, was a close-up of her laughing, pretty face as she raised her sticks in joy and triumph, the jagged rocks in the background. I just wanted to smack her.

* * *

Memories are fickle things. The pain of traumatic events (childbirth comes to mind) can be delegated to an old drawer in the brain, and we, consciously or unconsciously, slam it shut. Over the next couple of months, I sometimes got a whiff of the memory of Lehigh and shuddered involuntarily. For once, I was in no particular hurry to get back on the AT.

I traveled to Alberta, Canada, where my daughter and some of her Appalachian State colleagues had been invited to speak at the Thinking Mountains 2015 conference at Jasper National Park. Working around her academic commitments, Melanie and I took in some touristy half-day hikes and excursions. I have a not-unhealthy fear of grizzly bears (thankfully, not found on the AT) and did not wish to stray too far off the beaten path. We did, in fact, see one of these solitary *Ursus arctos horribilis* as it prowled near the Columbia Ice-field glaciers. Luckily, we were inside a bus at the time, and he was outside of it.

We saw plenty of other wildlife, though, as we hiked various snow-covered trails. Eagles, elk, and bighorn sheep are as common in Jasper as white-tailed deer and wild turkey are in Georgia. We were told caribou live in the very deep woods but are rarely seen by tourists. I am happy to just imagine them, nosing and pawing at the white ground, innocent and unmolested.

Most impressive of all are the Alpine hikers, bundled up in tobog-gans and gloves, with skis and ice axes strapped to their packs. They are a different breed from the AT hiker, and I admired them for the skillsets required to hike in this terrain and these conditions. This does not mean I had any wish to try this myself; I was content, as with the grizzly, to marvel from the side.

❋ ❋ ❋

In mid-May I rented a lakeside cabin for a few days for just my mom and me—the only two left of our immediate family—at Joe Wheeler State Park in North Alabama. We ate our meals at the lodge or in the tiny nearby town of Rogersville. We read our books and dozed in the afternoon sun on our little porch overlooking the water. In the evenings, we played Scrabble and passed the night in deep and sound sleep. Still early in the season, the lake was nearly deserted—motor-boats, wave runners, and water skis still in storage.

Each morning for three days, I ran the four-mile loop trail through the park and never encountered another human being. The trail, car-peted and fragrant with Alabama pine needles, shyly welcomed me. "What a treat to have a visitor," it seemed to say, like a lonely old woman at a nursing home, eager to share her treasures.

Small animals and birds, unafraid, scolded and chirped. I ran past a sleeping porcupine curled up in a tree. She didn't stir. The lake lapped at the muddy shoreline, where mallards fished for their breakfast. Great blue herons dipped their wings in greeting as they rose heavily from the water's surface. Occasionally, shiny black snakes slithered harmlessly across the trail. Turtles and frogs stopped in their tracks as if to politely motion that I go first like a pickup-truck driver might do at a rural four-way stop sign.

This weekend reminded me that we do not need to go far or high or wide or deep to find solace in nature. The common chipmunk is no less a masterpiece than an African lion. A run through an Alabama state park is no less an experience than a weekend on the Appalachian Trail. It seemed to me that nature just *is*, and I can find that lack of pretension and that incomprehensible contradiction of simplicity and complexity everywhere I look if only I remember to.

＊ ＊ ＊

The year passed its halfway point, and I prepared for a solo one-hundred-mile hike in mid-July. This was to be a nine-day trek over the Kittatinny Ridge in New Jersey and New York. Al once again graciously helped me out with the shuttle issue, dropping my car at Clarence Fahnestock State Park and taking me back to my start at Culver Lake.

I began my solitary adventure under a hot July sun. I climbed steeply for several hundred feet and reached a viewpoint where I could admire the lake far below. By midafternoon, I crossed the summit of Sunrise Mountain, where the AT emerges from the woods to cross a little park complete with picnic pavilion and parking lot. After this short-lived brush with pavement, I reentered the woods for the remainder of the day.

After a pleasant eight-mile day, I was tired but still fresh, relatively clean, and had ample food supply. I bedded down in the nice Mashipacong Shelter, situated very near the Trail, with several thru-hikers. The register notes indicated numerous bear visits, but we were not disturbed.

The Trail maintainers in New Jersey, reacting to a resurgence of the bear population in the state, have seen fit to supply metal boxes at all its AT shelters. This eliminates the need to hang your pack or food bag from a tree.

Campsites in the Great Smoky Mountains National Park have prefixed rope systems affixed to tall poles for campers to hang packs. These are efficient and easy to use but unfortunately rarely, if ever, seen outside this park.

To hang a food bag or pack, you must tie a rock to one end of a rope and throw it over a tree limb. Using that as a pully system, you tie the other end to your pack and hoist it up. The key is that you have to find a branch low enough you can throw the rope over and also a reasonable distance from other trees. In the dense woods of Appalachia, this is often difficult to accomplish. I have found that very few people have mastered the time-honored practice of hanging food from trees. I have often giggled at these efforts (mine included) and thought, *Why, any self-respecting bear in a tristate area would have that thing down before you could say "jelly doughnut."*

The next day I continued along the Kittatinny Ridge through deep woods interspersed with ledge views of farms below. Hiking steadily, I reached High Point State Park, which boasts the highest elevation (eighteen hundred feet) in New Jersey, by midday. Here, a 220-foot tall granite obelisk erected in 1930 pays homage to war veterans. Accessible by car, the park is a popular, picturesque tourist destination. Fresh-smelling and cleanly dressed day-trippers stood in line at the base of the Veterans Monument to climb some 250 steps to the uppermost viewing platform. I opted instead for a Diet Coke and a bag of Fritos from the vending machines.

After this refreshing break, I descended to five hundred feet through swamps and marsh to County Road 519 in the Great Appalachian Valley. This lowland is a break from woods, rocks, mountains, and switchbacks. Skirting fertile farmlands and county roads, I walked over what seemed like miles of planks and slippery, recycled railroad ties provided by the Trail maintainers. Long-legged herons and deep-throated bullfrogs generously share their territory. Cattails and tall marsh grasses gracefully wave hello. It is a magical interlude.

It was almost evening when I reached NJ 94, a paved road leading into two small towns, Vernon in one direction and McAfee in the other. I had hiked nearly eighteen miles that day and had slipped into the near-zombie state long-distance hikers often succumb to, born from too much solitude and the singular purpose of putting one foot in front of the other for mile after mile and hour after hour.

Crossing a flower-filled meadow, I saw a roadside farm stand. I entered and was instantly overwhelmed by what seemed like large numbers of locals and hikers milling about, laughing and talking loudly in the small space. In reality, there were probably only six or eight people, but the proximity to humans now felt odd and stifling.

Baskets of peaches, plums, and apples overflowed in juicy, riotous colors. Vegetables in piles and pyramids tumbled over one another as onions, potatoes, and bell peppers tried to escape their human-made configurations. Pots of marigolds blazed proudly alongside stalks of disdainful sunflowers arranged in tall, cylindrical buckets.

I stood in front of a waist-high deli case and stared at the options, unable to make a decision. Cheeses in small cubes and full wheels and eight-inch logs jostled pint-size containers of cut-up watermelon and cantaloupe. Berries in shades from sky blue to deep purple to bright red patiently waited in their green cardboard boxes. Cellophane-wrapped ham, turkey, tuna, and chicken-salad sandwiches, thick with lettuce and tomatoes, stood on their designated shelf.

I finally bought a cold drink and a sandwich and wandered outside to the porch. Blue Suit, a fortyish, solo thru-hiker, lounged in the shade of the stand.

"You staying around here tonight?" he asked.

"Nah, I think I can finish the Stairway by dark. Camp up on the mountain."

"I don't know. They say it's pretty tough."

That gave me the impetus I needed to get my ass moving. I hurriedly finished my sandwich and refilled my water bottles from a spigot in the yard. As I loaded my pack, anxiously glancing up at the mountain awaiting me across the road, the counter girl stepped outside.

"Here's something for you," she said, handing me a grease-stained paper sack containing several cinnamon-and-sugar-flecked doughnuts.

"Oh, really?" I said, grinning with delight.

"Take 'em. We're closing, would just throw them out."

I thanked her and she wished me well. I shouldered my pack, clutched my sticks, and turned resolutely to tackle the Stairway to Heaven.

After half a mile of gradual slope, I said hello to the Stairway, a six-hundred-foot ascent of rock steps, with a few switchbacks thrown in. These are not baby steps, my friend. Lift your right leg up eighteen to twenty vertical inches, then with effort bring your left foot to meet it. Rest a beat. Do it again. Several day-hikers sidestepped carefully past me on their descent. More than one was in tears.

After an agonizing hour or so, I reached the top and was met with…well…heaven. A charming little glen lay just to the left of the Trail and caught the last of the sun's rays through the tall trees. There may have even been a little babbling brook, but perhaps I am embellishing. In any event, it was positively Eden-like.

A tidy, one-person tent hugged a little corner of the grassy knoll.

"Greetings," I softly called in that direction.

A middle-age, clean-shaven man poked his head out of the tent opening.

"Well, hey," I said. "I'm Sticks."

He nodded but made no move to emerge or otherwise acknowledge my presence.

"You northbound?" I asked.

Another nod.

"That was some climb, huh?"

Shrug.

"Okay, well, I'm about done in. Mind if I pitch my tent here?"

His eyes scanned the area. "There's not really room here."

What? A clear, flat space in the little glen was obviously available. I had already started to remove my pack.

"Oh. Okay," I said after a beat. "I'll just go up the Trail a ways."

I refastened my pack straps and walked north into the woods. Though irritated, I did have to accede that this fellow was there first, and perhaps he wanted some solitude. He had staked out his home-stead, and I, wanting to follow the rules of camping etiquette, should be gracious about it.

After a quarter mile or so. I pitched my tent in a reasonably flat, clear space. The sun disappeared in the west, and the day's tribula-tions slipped away. The doughnuts, crispy and sweet, melted in my mouth. I ate three and considered the remainder. I could save them for breakfast, but they wouldn't be as tasty after ten or twelve hours. I sighed, strapped on my headlamp, and plodded back down the Trail.

"Knock, knock," I said as I approached Surly Dude's tent.

"Yeah?"

"Hey, it's Sticks. Got something for you."

The tent flap opened and out came the head.

"Here." I thrust the paper bag at him. "The girl at the farm stand gave me these. I'm full, and they won't be as good tomorrow."

He peered inside the bag and then looked back up at me, a genuine smile spreading across his face.

"Wow, these look amazing. That's really nice of you."

"No problem." I turned to walk away. "Take care."

"Bye," he called after me. "Thanks so much. Good luck! Be safe, Sticks."

* * *

The next day brought blazing heat and extreme thirst. I drank spar-ingly of my treated water and longed for an ice-cold Coke. I could visualize the familiar silver can with red curlicue script, beads of con-densation dripping down the sides. I daydreamed of rolling the cold can along my hot forehead before popping the flip top to hear the reassuring hiss of fresh carbonation. *Lordy.*

I trudged through deep woods along the sometimes rocky ridge-line of the last few miles of the New Jersey AT. Several lonely country roads cross this section, and it occurred to me that some kind local soul might leave a little Trail Magic in the form of liquid refreshment.

I stopped to chat with Blue Suit, who was replenishing his water bottles at an almost dried-up spring.

"Hey, Sticks. Was that you camped this morning at the summit? I did the Stairway really early and passed you."

I asked about Surly Dude, but Blue Suit said mine was the only tent he'd seen. Apparently S. D. broke camp early and was ahead of us.

I trudged on, and irrational thoughts entered my sunstroked head. *How much trouble would it be for these locals to place some cold drinks, a gallon of ice water, at a roadside? If I lived here, every day I would leave some Trail Magic for these hot, thirsty hikers.* I grew irate and indignant. In hindsight, of course, this was ridiculous. It is hardly anyone else's responsibility to provide me with nourishment. Nevertheless, my resentment built until I was mentally cursing the Trail, the weather, and the entire populace of New Jersey.

The woods opened up, and I heard the sound of a car engine. I stopped short at a blacktopped, two-lane road threading its way through the mountains. Could that be a Styrofoam cooler on the low stone wall just this side of the road? *Don't get your hopes up. Probably empty—could have been there for days.* I lifted the lid.

Bobbing around in several inches of water, a few slivers of ice not yet melted, were two cans of Coke. *Holy mother of god.* Not only was my feverish desire to quench my thirst answered, there was not even a moral dilemma; I could take one can without guilt and leave one for Blue Suit. I wondered if Surly Dude—who had certainly passed this way—thought of me when he saw the drinks and hoped there would be one remaining by the time I got here. I like to think he did.

After a silent toast to the Trail Angels and several blissful swigs, I fastened my pack. Shortly thereafter, with blood cells rehydrated and my faith in the human race restored, I stepped into the state of New York.

* * *

After three days and thirty-five miles on the Trail, I walked into the town of Unionville, a small village whose original industries have apparently found homes elsewhere. A post office, a city hall, and a couple of churches mark the town center. Small, out-of-business storefronts still advertise bygone products and services: "Vacuums

Fixed!" "Shear Delights Beauty Shop and Supplies." "Video Rentals." There was not, however—contrary to what my guidebooks had advised—a bed-and-breakfast.

It was late afternoon, and dark rain clouds were gathering. I sought information at a deli / gas station / convenience store.

"Oh, yes," the gray-haired, friendly woman behind the counter told me. "There used to be a little hotel up on the corner there, but it closed a couple of years ago."

"Oh, geez. I was hoping to stay there. Do you know of anywhere else I can get a room?"

She shook her head. "No, darling, there's nowhere here in town. You hiking the AT?"

"Yes, ma'am."

"The town lets hikers put up their tents over there." She pointed across the street to a park, complete with gazebo, playground, and a small brick restroom building.

"Just fill out this form here, you know, in case of emergency or something."

She thrust a clipboard at me, and I glanced at the list of who had recently availed themselves of Unionville hospitality. Some were familiar to me: Easygo, Yard Sale, Just Will, Antwerp, Nonesuch, Old Man. Disappointed that I would once again be sleeping on the hard ground, I provided the requisite information and expressed my gratitude.

The store was closing. I grabbed a fresh homemade sandwich from the deli case, a bag of chips, and a cold soft drink. I crossed the street as the rain clouds continued to gather and hurriedly set up my tent in a corner of the little park. Huge raindrops sporadically plopped down and soon gave way to a steady downpour. Night came on.

The initial irritation I had felt at the lack of a room eased and then disappeared altogether. I was utterly content. *There is nothing else in the whole world I need right now. I am warm and dry. I have good food and drink. My loved ones are safe in their homes, as am I in my tent.*

I thought of William Faulkner's words, "How often have I lain beneath rain on a strange roof, thinking of home." As haunting and nostalgic as this passage is, it never strikes me as sad. When I think of it—and I think of it often when I'm hiking—I am comforted with a feeling that I am exactly where I need to be.

After an hour or so, the rain tapered off, and only the occasional slow remnants plopped on the tent and bounced off. I unzipped the tent and leaned out to find the air cooler and cleaner. Small puddles glistened in Main Street potholes. It was barely eight o'clock, so I decided to take a little stroll.

I had only walked a block or so down Main Street when I heard the sound of music and laughter. A cookout was in progress at a house set near to the road. A tarp canopy had been erected in the side yard to cover picnic tables, kegs, and lawn chairs. Strings of electric lights twinkled with childlike eagerness. A couple of folks called out to me as I passed.

"Hey, are you a hiker? What's your name?" Locals always seem to get a kick out of the often bizarre appellations of the AT thru-hikers.

"Hey, I'm Sticks," I called back with a smile.

"Come have a beer! You hungry? We got plenty of food!"

"Just ate. But thanks so much all the same."

They wished me a safe journey, and I walked on.

A garish neon sign hanging out over the street caught my eye. Well, this could only mean a bar. Saturday night in Unionville was beginning to look interesting. I got close enough to read the lettering—"Wit's End"—and burst out laughing. *That is hilarious. "Hey, honey, I'll be a little late. Rough day, and I'm at Wit's End."*

I entered to find the dinner crowd, mostly families and a few elderly couples, finishing up their pizzas and burgers. The bartender had a baby. Behind the bar. I'm not saying she "had" the baby behind the bar, although who knows? At any rate, a six- or seven-month-old straddled one hip but did not appear to impede the bartender's efficiency as she pulled beers and poured drinks one-handedly.

I settled onto a stool, cold beer in hand and a happy grin pasted on my face. A very wet hiker came through the door, and all eyes turned to him as he and his pack filled the doorway. He stopped suddenly and, as if remembering the rules of civility, retreated to dump his pack on the porch. He was a big guy with a full beard and long, dark hair, both shot through with raindrops.

After a trip to the restroom, the thru-hiker, recognizing me as a fellow traveler, sat down and introduced himself as River. He had started his day very early and done twenty-plus miles, the last couple in the dark and rain. I told him of the sleeping arrangements in the park. And then, in slightly open-mouthed awe at the wonder of humans, we both silently watched the bartender and her baby.

* * *

The next day I crossed the flat, black, open prairie of the Wallkill Valley for a mile and a half before finally reentering woods. For three miles, I followed switchbacks and a stony trail up, over, and down Pochuck Mountain. Then swampland again, for several miles this time. Butterflies and twittering songbirds flitted about in the tall purple and yellow wildflowers of midsummer. I stopped to apply sunscreen to my face and legs. It is a rare thing on the AT to be exposed to the sun's glare for this length of time and distance.

It is said that from the Bearfort Mountain ridge, one can see the skyline of New York City. All I could see to the east were hazy heat waves emanating from mountain ridges. This was to be a sixteen-mile day, and I was exhausted. Dirty and dehydrated, I hiked up and down, up and down. The Trail weaves across exposed rock slabs here and then through dense, humid forest there. My goal was Greenwood Lake and the indulgences of a motel bed, a nice shower, and a cooked meal.

Guidebooks describe Greenwood Lake as a resort town. Well, I must have ended up on the wrong side of the lake because all I could see after hitching a ride from the Trail was a brownish, stagnant body of water. Worn-out-looking fishing boats tied to rotting piers sank into slimy mud flats. Drooping, weather-beaten houses and tacky 1950s-era motels lined the side streets between the highway and lake.

I paid sixty bucks—"Cash only"—for a room with peeling laminate furniture and the standard scratchy comforter. On the walkway just outside my door, a pretty glass vase filled with dead, drooping flowers; an unlabeled coffee can full of sand and lipstick-stained cigarette butts; and a framed painting of smiling clouds playing checkers were oddly, but somehow pleasingly, arranged on a small, wooden table.

I strolled down the nearly deserted streets—an old man warily watched me pass as he worked on a car in his driveway, and two women seated in frayed lawn chairs on a front porch nodded unsmilingly in return to my wave—and bought takeaway pizza from a little stand near a park. As the sun went down, I sat at a bench to eat and reflect. As pleasant as it was to have a shower and eat a hot meal, I was coming to prefer the familiarity of my tent and the routines of camp. Civilization can be overrated.

Early next morning, having no desire to linger in this strange place, I hitched a ride to the AT and stepped back into the relatively sane world of nature.

* * *

Sterling Forest is a twenty-thousand-acre oasis in the most densely populated state in our country. Hikers, environmental activists, and grassroots coalitions, to their credit, have worked diligently to keep it so. The landscape of this day's hike was diverse, wild, and charming.

I strolled along a level trail lined with dense forest, and I climbed the Eastern Pinnacles and Cat Rocks. Small brooks and pretty waterfalls abound here. Butterfly Meadow easily lives up to its name, as Queen Anne's lace sways in the breeze to entice the monarchs. Meadows give way to laurel thickets, which give way to tall oak and hickory trees, which give way to musky hemlock copses. Mushrooms and moss grow on rotting fallen logs, and delicate ferns make a fine carpet through the woods on either side of the Trail.

I climbed the rocky face of Buchanan Mountain and crossed the bridge over Mombasha Kill—*kill* being a Dutch word for creek. At Little Dam Lake, blue herons gracefully wade, and turtles lay still as statues on partially submerged stones. Descending Agony Grind to reach busy NY 17 jarred me—literally—back to consciousness. I once again became aware of the sights and sounds of humanity's loud and sometimes difficult world.

After crossing the highway, I climbed steeply up Green Pond Mountain, and then the Trail becomes a little easier as it follows old logging roads. This section encompasses the original first miles of the official Appalachian Trail and includes what is known as the Lemon Squeezer. This is a huge rock formation split in two as if by a shifting of tectonic plates, and the Trail goes up through this narrow split for several hundred feet. I am a rather small person, but even I had to take off my pack and alternately push it in front of me or tug it behind in order to squeeze between the rock walls.

I hiked into the night of this sixteen-mile day, aided by my headlamp. Near Fingerboard Mountain, the dark woods opened up onto an eerie sight in a small meadow. Several humps, like table-size spaceships, were scattered here and there. Hovering over and around them throughout the field were points of light, like fireflies, but larger and unmoving. Had I wandered into an alien encampment?

It slowly dawned on me that the rocklike humps were actually tents, inside of which were no doubt hikers, not extraterrestrials. The mysterious, hovering lights were the eyes, reflected in my headlamp, of a deer herd that had stopped to stare at my approach.

A long and interesting day indeed. Sleep did not come easily.

✳ ✳ ✳

I now had only about thirty-five miles and a few days left of this journey. The weather continued hot and stifling. I walked through heavy woods, sometimes crossing small, open fields and swamps. Pretty views of the Hudson River Valley spread out below the Hudson Highlands. The descent beyond Harriman State Park, also known as Bear Mountain State Park, brought me to the river and two iconic spots on the Appalachian Trail: Bear Mountain Inn and the Bear Mountain suspension bridge crossing the Hudson.

I reached the inn on Hessian Lake at midafternoon. On this warm July day, the picnic area was crowded with day-tripping families, many of whom had likely traveled from nearby New York City. A diverse population in all manner of ethnic dress rested on blankets and prayer rugs. Smoke rose in the air from the charcoal grills to spread the smell of spicy meat. Small, dark-skinned children laughed and played in the shallows, chattering away in languages unknown to me. For a long time, I sat at a picnic table with my pack and its meager contents and felt very alone as I watched the cheerful scene around me.

Inside the inn itself, I felt underdressed and unwelcome, which is ironic because this establishment was the original meeting place of Benton MacKaye, the "Father of the Appalachian Trail," and his cronies as they ironed out the details of the nascent AT in 1923. Deciding not to even try to bring myself up to this establishment's standards, I hitched a ride to a cheap motel out on the highway.

I returned to my hike the next morning near the inn, and the first thing I encountered was, of all things, a zoo. The Appalachian Trail goes right through it. A small sign at the front gate cheerfully proclaims "Free admission for hikers!" How bizarre to have walked 1,500 miles in the company of unfettered woodland creatures only to come across cages and bars. To be fair, this is a very small and sweet zoo, immaculately clean and—I would imagine—aimed at a young audience. There are no artificial savannahs here with giraffes and zebras and elephants, no imported polar bears trying to cool themselves in refrigerated pools. I nodded to the foxes and porcupines in their little pens and told them, "I have met some of your cousins in the wild. They are well and send their regards."

※ ※ ※

I crossed the beautifully engineered suspension bridge in the pedestrian lane and continued north on a fairly level trail for most of the day. Stepping out onto ledges, I looked to the east for the Manhattan skyline, but it remained obscured by summer haze. The only people I saw were thru-hikers, silent and determined in the oppressive heat as they made their way through the heavy woods. Planks and puncheons, sometimes slippery and rotting, make up the Trail in places where the forest floor is swampy and stagnant. Stone walls, built generations ago by Dutch settlers to mark boundaries, now trail off into impenetrable thickets.

The Trail leaves the woodland and crosses the grounds of Graymoor Monastery, home to the Franciscan Friars and Sisters of the Atonement. Even the names, not to mention the serene green acres, evoke feelings of peace and reverence. At a quiet country-road crossing just beyond the grounds, I rested in the yard of a tiny stone chapel abandoned and almost completely covered with vines. The late afternoon sun rays danced on the small, round, stained glass window, and I thought of Monet's blues and greens and yellows. The scene was one of complete serenity and a rare example of human improvement on nature. This elfin churchyard was perhaps the most beautiful place, out of a thousand beautiful places, I had yet encountered on the Appalachian Trail.

I walked a few more miles, partially along an old railroad bed, until I reached Fahnestock State Park, where Al and I had left my car all those days ago. This adventure, diverse in its beauty and challenges, emotionally taxing in its solitude, and humorously endearing in its sometimes strange brushes with humanity, was over. I headed back to home and husband—the center without which I doubted my nomadic life would hold. It seemed to me then there is not much point to going away if you don't have a place to come back to.

❊ ❊ ❊

In early August, we welcomed a new addition to our family. Kim, a 160-pound bundle of joy, arrived at Nashville International Airport as a foreign exchange student from Germany.

Earlier in the summer, a representative from the exchange program had contacted me. "Would you and your husband host a student again? For the school year?"

"Oh, no," I answered. "We're empty nesters. Our daughter's away at university. I don't think a student would want to stay with us."

"Oh, we have a lot of older host families. That's no problem at all."

I was pretty sure Tim wouldn't even consider it, and I didn't really care. But when I broached the subject a few days later, he barely looked up from the computer screen.

"Sure," he said, "but get a boy this time."

I was mildly shocked. I had fully expected him to tell me I had lost my mind.

"Older," he added. Another beat. "One who likes sports."

After I did the legwork—read the online profiles, filled out the paperwork, submitted to the home inspection—I presented a couple of possibilities to Tim.

"Here's one," I said. "Sixteen years old, plays the piano, loves soccer, basketball, and football, Swiss, speaks three languages—Oh, never mind. He's allergic to dust."

Tim snorted. "Well, he wouldn't last a day in our house."

"Okay. Well, what about this one? Sixteen-year-old from Hamburg. Crazy about soccer and American football. Name of Kim Do. Unusual name for a German."

So Kim came to live with us, and Melanie now had a new little brother. Or, as she put it, her dad got the son he never had.

✳ ✳ ✳

In mid-September, pretty darn sure they could survive without me by this time, I left Tim and Kim to their work and school and sports. Melanie had finished grad school at Appalachian State but was staying in Boone for a while to work and figure out her next move. So she and I happily took off for a six-day hike of sixty miles from New York's Fahnestock State Park, where I had finished in July, to Cornwall Bridge in Connecticut.

We flew to Newark on the fourteenth, and dear old Al was waiting for us in baggage claim, holding up a piece of cardboard on which he'd written "Sticks 1 and Sticks 2." Humor is a good way to start any adventure, and Al was never in short supply. After a grocery stop to shore up our food supply, we drove the Taconic State Parkway to Fahnestock State Park and said our farewells.

"Thank you so much. I don't know what we would have done without you," Melanie said.

"Oh, stop it," Al responded. He gave us some little gifts—candy and such—and took picture after picture of us with his cell phone. "Okay, I'll see you Saturday. About noon at Highway 4 where the AT crosses."

"We'll be there. Please don't worry about us. We'll be fine." I tried to ease Al's concerns, but this ex-Army city boy could never get his mind around the fact that some people actually *like* to walk twelve miles a day in all kinds of weather and sleep on the ground. To him it seemed like something you could only be forced—or paid very, very well—to do.

We stepped onto the Trail in midafternoon to hike the six miles to Ralphs Peak Hikers Cabin, commonly known as the RPH Shelter. We made good time in the fresh early autumn air and had the Trail largely to ourselves. For the first couple of hours, we enjoyed views of Canopus Lake sparkling below as we ascended the peak until these, too, were left behind, and it was just us, the woods, and the quiet night ahead.

* * *

The next day took us up and over forested Hosner Mountain on a smooth, dirt path onto which leaves and acorns were just beginning to fall. We climbed Stormville Mountain and Mount Egbert. Old stone walls, reminders of the farms that once dotted this land, trail off into obscurity. We strode past Nuclear Lake, eerily quiet and somber. Our guidebooks tell us that the lake contains no harmful elements, but the name does not exactly tempt one to go for a dip. After a few more miles, walking on planks over swamps and bogs, we crossed into the state of Connecticut.

The days were still long and warm, but late afternoons brought the first hints of the coming fall. Rain showers were chilly rather than refreshing, and the evening air called for jackets and even gloves. We adapted to the weather and the terrain and came to feel as if our boots were part of the Trail. Our bodies molded to our packs as naturally as the moss and lichen cleaved to softening logs strewn alongside the path.

"Mom, I'm really seriously thinking about doing a thru-hike next year," Melanie said as we rhythmically and reflectively walked through the woods.

This was not the first time she had mentioned this idea over the previous year. The several trips she had taken with me on the AT, and the hikes she had done with friends on other trails had given her a deep appreciation for the majesty of nature, the benefits of physical challenge, and the joy of minimalism. I believe Melanie saw the opportunity of thru-hiking as a chance to leave behind—for a while, at least—the clutter of life and the cobwebs it tends to collect.

"Well, it sure would be fun," I responded after a minute, "but a huge challenge."

"I know *that*, Mom. Gosh."

"Who do you think would go with you?"

"I can't depend on anybody else. I want to get a dog."

"Hmm."

"I just really love it out here," Melanie went on. "I'm so happy; there's no stress like there was in grad school or in town."

"True," I said carefully, not wanting to minimize the hardships. "Yet there's a lot of other kind of stress on the Trail, you know, like the weather, the blisters, the emotional and mental crap."

"Yeah, but it would be like the perfect time to go. Before real life begins."

She had a point. At the time, Melanie had a patchwork of jobs in Boone—nanny, barista, and teaching assistant—but nothing that seemed likely to lead to a career. She lived in a rented apartment, had little furniture or possessions, and no romantic entanglements. It would, indeed, be the opportune time for a six-month adventure.

"How would you pay for it?"

"I've got a little money in savings and what Aunt Patty left me. I'll keep working till March, and I can sell my car. That would bring in a few thousand."

Obviously, she had given the matter some thought. Mentally planning your next hike as you walk along in a pleasant reverie is not a bad way to pass the time.

* * *

Our days on the Trail were, for the most part, serene, even idyllic. We admired the quaint Bulls Bridge that crosses the Housatonic River and climbed a thousand feet through dense woods to the summit of Schaghticoke Mountain to gaze out at the river valley below. We ascended and descended peaks, some identified in our guidebooks, some anonymous. We squeezed through stiles and over fences to cross pastures and mown fields. Cattle lowed at us, and farmers on their tractors waved their hands in greeting. We slept snug in the little tent, Melanie uncharacteristically waking earlier than me each day.

"Mom, c'mon. Get up. I made coffee."

* * *

On Friday, our last full day on the Trail, we reached St. John's Ledges by lunchtime. A couple of young day-hikers were loafing near the edge of the rock outcroppings. We must have startled them because there was some hurried adjustment of clothing as we came out of the woods into their view. We talked with them for a few minutes until the young man started showing off for his pretty young companion by doing yoga poses, including an attempted headstand dangerously near the lip of the ledge.

Melanie and I moved on to another section of this remarkable stone network to give these folks—and ourselves—some privacy. We spread out our belongings on the large, flat rock and snapped some pictures of each other and the spectacular views. A bold and cheerful chipmunk climbed over our packs as we nibbled on trail mix and Fig Newtons. Our water, drawn from a pristine spring a few hours earlier, tasted like clean earth and ancient metals.

We laid back on the rocks and basked in the drowsy heat like two old cats sleeping in a sliver of sunlight in a hallway.

Melanie murmured, "Mom, I don't want to leave here."

"Mmm, I know." I couldn't keep my eyes open, and it was an effort to speak. "But we only have four miles, four *easy* miles, to camp."

A sigh. "Okay, let's go."

Five minutes passed, then ten.

Hawks circled overhead. A breeze stirred the tops of the hemlocks below the cliffs. Our shadows on the rocks lengthened until we could no longer ignore the inevitable passage of time, and we managed to pull ourselves away.

As expected, the four-mile hike to Stony Brook Campsite was

sweet and gentle. We arrived before sundown to find a fairly large clearing dotted with several tent sites and, curiously, several deep and wide indentations in the spongy ground. I wondered if these holes were old homestead cellars. We pitched our tent to stake out our own claim, and I reminded Melanie to take care if she woke in the night and stepped outside.

We broke camp early the next morning and hiked out of the woods to Cornwall Bridge, where faithful Al waited patiently. Before heading to the airport and our flight home, we stopped for lunch in the yuppie town of Kent. Seated at a small outdoor café, surrounded by happy (and clean) shoppers sipping Bloody Marys and mimosas, I felt immensely grateful for the company of Melanie and the assistance from Al. These beautiful, almost dreamlike days and nights on the Trail were only enhanced by the ease with which we'd traveled to and from it. This was truly the ultimate gift to a section hiker.

＊ ＊ ＊

That autumn, our lives were busy and full with the schedule of an active and athletic high schooler. For Kim's fall break from school, Tim's cousin Jeff and his wife, Liz, invited us to visit them in Cambridge, Massachusetts. On a crisp mid-October day, we flew into Boston, and if Tim and I found the crowded city loud and stressful, Kim found it comforting and reminiscent of Hamburg.

After a couple days of dutiful sightseeing, we drove north through small towns and countryside to Wallingford, Vermont, where Liz has an old family vacation home. Maple trees blazed proudly alongside the roads, high atop hills, and in the village squares. The red and orange of the leaves competed for attention against the blue and white of the skies. The human bustle of the compact little villages belied the solitude and grandeur of the surrounding green mountains. It is a perfect combination.

Liz's house is a weathered haven set on a low hill surrounded by emerald-colored grass even this late in the year. We found little need or excuse to leave it, but one day midweek, I rounded up Tim, Kim, Jeff, Liz, their son Augie—on break from Syracuse—and their dog Lucy for an easy six-mile day hike on the nearby Appalachian Trail. We piled into two vehicles. After leaving one at hike's end, VT 103 at Clarendon Gorge, we scrunched even closer together in one car and drove back to VT 140 (Wallingford Gulf Road) for our stroll through the woods.

The weather was New England sharp and sunny. The maple syrup tap lines stretched endlessly alongside the country roads and paths. We sauntered through meadows and on switchbacks that gently weave up and down the mountains. There was no cause for complaint or whine from anybody, for which I was grateful. (The memory of his last AT adventure was seared in Tim's mind, and he had been more than a little hesitant to trust my assurances that this was an easy stretch.) In late afternoon, Lucy anxiously herded us all across the Clarendon Gorge on a long suspension footbridge to bring us safely to hike's end. This short hike offered me a brief and tantalizing preview of the New England AT. It was a pretty little picture, but by this time, I had finally learned that first impressions can be deceptive.

* * *

For some time, my neighbor Jamie, a petite brunette about my age whom you will remember from our cemetery adventure, had been intrigued by my AT adventures. She wanted to join me on a trip but had some reservations. Number one, she didn't think she could do more than about ten miles a day. Number two, she didn't want to hike more than a couple consecutive days. Number three, she didn't want to camp.

All this was fine with me. I am not averse to the middle-aged way of doing things. I presented a manageable plan of a fifty-mile hike from the Cornwall Bridge, where Melanie and I had finished in September, to Great Barrington, Massachusetts. Jamie signed on.

On November 1, we flew into Hartford, Connecticut, rented a car, and drove to the nice little town of Salisbury. I had reserved a two-bedroom Airbnb close to restaurants and shops and within easy driving distance to the AT. We stocked up on Band-Aids, groceries, and wine. I pored over maps and read the guidebooks aloud. We were totally prepared to do the best we could do.

Early November weather in Connecticut can be indecisive but is generally cool and misty, even dreary. It is not unpleasant, however, when you are accompanied by a good friend. The New England towns are quiet, as the leaf-peepers have returned home and the ski bums have not yet arrived. The woods are still, the animals almost literally waiting to see which way the wind will blow. Jamie and I met the morning chill with proper gear and dress and the knowledge the evening would bring warm shelter.

The first day on the Trail, Monday, we dropped our car at US 7 and hitched a ride to Cornwall Bridge. I'm sure our neighbors back in Franklin would have been shocked to see Jamie—who might be fondly described as reserved—standing on the side of the road with her thumb stuck out. Nevertheless, that's what she did, and pretty enthusiastically I might add.

We crossed numerous streams and rivulets, thankful for our trekking poles in this wet time of year. I frequently looked back over my shoulder at the sound of Jamie's laughter or mild exclamation to see her sprawled on the ground, often on relatively flat, easy terrain, and once even on a simple plank bridge.

"What happened?" I would say, giving her a helping hand up.

"I don't know. I just tripped." Or slid. Or stumbled.

By the end of this first day, I had christened Jamie "She Who Falls A Lot." She was never very happy with this admittedly uncomplimentary trail name, but it has stuck surprisingly well.

The next day took us through the Housatonic River Valley and across meadows and cornfields. We squeezed through Rogers Ramp, a narrow passage through a huge split boulder, and climbed Mount Easter, with its lovely views of the Catskills to the east. At Hang Glider View, scuffed places on the grass-topped cliffs serve as launch pads for the kite-riders to get their running starts.

I have no desire to hang glide. The fear of crashing, the discomfort of the harness, the uncertainty of the kite would leave me trembling and nauseous. But to sit on a sun-warmed knoll and imagine soaring out over the valley on wind currents in the company of raptors is a very pleasant—and safe—way to pass a little time. Imagination is sometimes better than actualization.

* * *

On our third day, She Who Falls A Lot took a break from the Trail to explore the quaint towns strewn throughout this valley. She dropped me off at CT 41 where we had finished the day before, and I hiked a solitary and challenging fourteen miles to Guilder Pond.

Numerous stone walls wind through this section, reminders of how relatively populated these woods were in the not-too-distant past and how quickly man's attempts at civilization can fade back into the earth. Gorgeous views of northwestern Connecticut make it easy to see why farmers would have settled this land. Blue lakes and rivers feed the brown fields, and cattle graze on the lush green grass.

I crossed a country road where a three-sided shed had been erected as a "tiny store." The inventory consisted of a shelf of used paperbacks, a bowl of hard-boiled eggs, cartons of fresh eggs, some rather wilted autumn produce, homemade cookies and brownies wrapped in cellophane, and a small refrigerator stocked with water and soft drinks. A cigar box with an opening cut-in top had a sign taped to it exhorting patrons to "Be Honest." Several cleverly constructed beech-bark vases of different diameters and heights held brightly colored zinnias. I wanted to buy a posy for She Who Falls A Lot because I was sorry she had missed this charming tableau, but I knew it would get crushed in my pack. I settled for snapping a photo and eating a brownie in tribute to her.

I climbed Bear Mountain, at 2,100 feet, the highest point in Connecticut. A few miles later, I crossed into Massachusetts and climbed 2,600-foot Mount Everett, the highest point in *that* state. These are the Berkshires, where precipices overlook dense forests shady and dark. One is reminded of the Brothers Grimm: Red Riding Hood lost with her basket or Rapunzel locked in a tower.

My pace was slow, and by the time I reached Guilder Pond, my headlamp was casting pale and slender rays through these enchanted woods. But I felt no fear or worry; there was no doubt my friend She Who Falls a Lot would be patiently waiting for me at the end of this long day.

Our weather remained cool and pleasant, and the Trail wet and boggy as we continued our journey the next day. In contrast, sometimes we passed alongside and through cornfields of dry brown stalks, the November sky white-blue and big. The end of this day brought nostalgia already for this lovely week and this beautiful part of the country, knowing that I must push on, leaving too much unexplored and unappreciated.

She Who Falls A Lot and I finished our adventure the next day with an eight-mile hike that included a steep climb to East Mountain and some rock climbing at Ice Gulch. I felt we had left the land of plenty and were now pilgrims being tested for our determination and commitment. The day's difficulty was mitigated by the fact this was the final test of our skills, such as they were, and we finished with the knowledge we had indeed done the best we could.

✼ ✼ ✼

The end of the year came on with its dreary Tennessee winter much as it had begun. Our old dog Sadie died, and even as we mourned her death, we recognized her advanced age and found gratitude that she was now at peace. I thought of all we had lost this year but also all we had gained. Grief and joy do not cancel each other out, but one can make the other bearable.

The magic of Sterling Forest does not void the difficulty of Stairway to Heaven, and the surliness of strangers does not take away from the kindness of Trail Angels. The haunting loveliness of a sleeping camp does not make the mountains less forbidding or the rocks less treacherous. The AT is like any other path we take in life: strewn with stones and roots but also cushioned with leaves and moss. We just have to keep walking.

CHAPTER 12

2016 (260 MILES)

PART 1

GREAT BARRINGTON, MASSACHUSETTS, TO CLARENDON GORGE, VERMONT

t had taken me eleven years to hike two-thirds of the Appalachian Trail—roughly 1,400 miles out of 2,200—and the four northernmost states remained to be conquered: Massachusetts, Vermont, New Hampshire, and Maine. The complications of continuing my hike would be many: the winters in these states are extreme, and the hiking window is short; the geographical distance from my home to this area is great and would require air travel; the AT through this section is remote, and the logistics of shuttles and resupply would be daunting. It made no sense whatsoever to bop up to New England for a weekend or a few days. By necessity, any hike I attempted this year would have to be of relatively long distance and duration.

Moreover, at least through the first half of this year, we would still have Kim, our student, living with us, and Melanie would be at home until she left in the spring for her thru-hike. There was no question of trying to juggle the complications of a long hike and balancing my time between home and mountains. The latter would simply have to wait. I have no doubt the mountains did not miss me one iota, while I'm just as sure the kids and Tim needed me during this time of activity and growth. There is a saying on the AT: "Hike your own hike." There is no judgment, even—maybe especially—of yourself.

Melanie had carefully and responsibly planned her hike. She had studied maps, read blogs, and been in contact with the ATC. She had researched gear, bought what was appropriate (and what she could afford), and meticulously weighed and adjusted her pack. She had done her homework regarding dogs on the AT and, after an extensive search, found a young female Catahoula with one blue and one brown eye who answered (sometimes) to the name of Radley.

Dogs are allowed on most sections of the Appalachian Trail with a few exceptions, most notably the Great Smoky Mountains National Park and Baxter State Park. The pros in taking a dog on a thru-hike are that they provide company, they might keep wild animals at bay, and they provide at least a semblance of protection. But the cons are many. Before you enter parks where they are not allowed, you will have to make arrangements to kennel and shuttle them or enlist a friend to help you out. Dogs require food and water, just like humans, and these are heavy items. (Most thru-hiking dogs will carry at least some of their own food in custom-made packs.) Sections of the AT require difficult hand-over-hand rock climbing or dangerous river crossings, where you might have to actually carry your dog. Hostels and motels often won't allow pets or will require a deposit. It may be more difficult to hitch a ride or hire a shuttle with a dog. Paws and toenails need frequent attention, and special care must be taken regarding ticks or disease-carrying mammals, such as raccoons. Above all, his or her temperament must be suited to Trail life, such as getting along with other animals and with humans.

Pack animals (horses, mules, llamas) are not allowed anywhere on the AT. There is no policy of which I am aware that prohibits domestic cats. In fact, the ATC has recorded instances of thru-hikers completing their treks accompanied by their feline pets. I often considered taking my cat Emmie on a hike or two, and I think he would have loved it: pouncing on scurrying rodents and slinking through the underbrush by day, curled up at night by my side like a sleeping sled dog after an exhausting Iditarod race. Perhaps he and I (respectively, I should point out) would have become known as Puss n Boots; we would be the coolest kids on the Trail.

After much calculation regarding weather, stage of the moon, and for all I know, horoscope predictions, Melanie chose Wednesday, March 23, as Day One on the AT. Coincidentally, this would be during the week of Kim's spring break, which we planned to spend in Washington, DC. This meshed perfectly with the plan of taking Melanie to the trailhead. On March 22, the three of us, along with Radley, piled into the Blazer and headed southeast.

Melanie was nervous, anxious, and sometimes tearful. Tim and I were mostly quiet. Our twenty-five-year-old daughter was about to walk for six months through all kinds of weather, across all kinds of terrain, and she would face all sorts of obstacles. Kim and Radley were their usual smiling, happy-go-lucky selves, glad to be along for the ride.

After a hotel night in Ellijay, Georgia, we drove to Amicalola Falls, where Melanie registered as an official Appalachian Trail thru-hiker for the year 2016. March is a popular time for northbound hikers to start their journeys, and the visitor center was a busy place. Hikers—mostly young—weighed packs, adjusted straps, tightened laces. I heard some false bravado—"We got this, dude!"—but I sensed an undercurrent of anxiety. There is no way to minimize the seriousness of this undertaking. It is a very, very big deal.

We drove several miles on a Forest Service road to the AT crossing point that is nearest to Springer Mountain. Kim, Tim, and I tried not to hover over Melanie as she made last-minute adjustments to Radley's pack and leash. I reminded myself to not ask stupid questions or give unnecessary advice: "Do you have enough water? Did you remember to bring Advil? Don't stray off the Trail."

After final hugs and brave smiles, we watched Melanie walk away through the parking lot and into the green woods, her small body almost hidden under her pack, her little dog plodding cluelessly along-side her. I couldn't meet Tim's eyes for fear I would burst into tears and that he would turn away to hide his. All we could do now was to get in the car and continue the drive to bustling DC.

For three days, we took in the sights, the museums, the monuments. We rode the Metro to Chinatown, to Arlington, to Georgetown. The cherry trees were blooming, and the soft blossoms drifted down on us like pink snowflakes. I thought of the cold mountains and the lonely Trail.

At last, on Saturday night, my phone rang. Melanie's voice, sound-ing rough and unused, said, "Hey, it's me."

"Where are you? How's the weather? Are you staying warm?" My questions tumbled over one another. Melanie's responses were slow and measured, like those of a person suffering from PTSD.

"I'm fine. We're fine. It's cold, but I'm okay."

Tim and Kim got on the phone, and each had the wisdom not to pepper her with shrieking comments and queries. They spoke softly, offering encouragement and reassurance. "We're proud of you. You got this. Call if you need anything."

Easter Sunday morning, I dropped off Kim and Tim at Reagan to fly back to Nashville for school and work. I, in my retirement, would leisurely drive back to Franklin. None of us would say it aloud—that would have been bad karma—but if need be, I could pick up Melanie on my way home. I thought there was maybe a fifty-fifty chance of this happening. I believed that if she got through the first couple of nights sleeping alone, braving the cold, and taking care of Radley, she had a real chance to go all the way. My cell phone remained silent. *Okay, my dear, I'm heading home, away from the Trail and you.*

* * *

Melanie sounded cheerful and confident in our rare phone conversations over the next few weeks, and in early April, I drove to Fontana Dam, gateway to the Great Smoky Mountains National Park, to meet her. The park does not allow dogs, so Tim and I had agreed to take care of Radley for a couple of weeks.

I arrived to find Melanie leaning against a signpost in the parking lot of Fontana Lodge, pack and dog by her side. Her skin was tanned, with a smattering of freckles across her nose and cheeks, and she looked as if she'd lost a few pounds. A huge grin spread across her face when she saw me approaching.

I hugged her tightly and whispered, "Are you having the time of your life?"

"Yes," she answered, still grinning, with no hesitation at all.

The lobby of the lodge was filled with thru-hikers, healthy and exuberant. They all seemed to know each other; Trail Families were forming. By this time, Melanie had become known as Peanut (this was a nickname her grandfather had given her as a toddler, and I suppose when her fellow hikers discovered this, the name just stuck), and Radley had become—unsurprisingly—Boo.

The next morning, we went our separate ways—Peanut into the Smokies with all its challenges, Boo and I to Franklin with all its comforts. I felt reassured by my daughter's apparent self-confidence and well-being; I suspected she felt comforted by my presence and the knowledge of her parents' unending support.

* * *

We returned Boo to Peanut in late April at the Roan Mountain AT crossing, and they continued resolutely walking north. By the end of May, Kim was in end-of-school-year mode: regional soccer tournaments, final exams, and graduation itself. Tim and I recognized that now we served as mere backdrops to both their lives and that each now was on his or her own path.

Then, seemingly abruptly, in mid-June, Kim was out of our lives as suddenly as he had come in, and our house seemed echoingly empty. For several months, I did not enter Kim's vacated room. We left it exactly as he had, frozen in that instant he last walked out the door—the bed stripped, a rolled-up sock under a chair, a few coins forgotten in an otherwise empty drawer. Thumbtacks, once holding up calendars, maps, and sports schedules, remained on the walls. The smell of teenage boy remained until, finally, I surrendered my Miss Havisham ways and had the whole damn thing repainted.

* * *

Peanut had begun to struggle on the Trail. More accurately, Boo had begun to struggle. They were well into Virginia and should have been doing twenty-plus-mile days in order to summit Katahdin by late September. But Boo's short legs simply couldn't keep that pace.

"Mom," Melanie said when she called. "I don't know what to do. I'm taking too many zero days to let Boo rest, and even on the days we hike, she can only go about twelve miles."

She sounded crushed. *What was a parent to do?*

Tim drove to Southern Virginia in mid-June to pick up Boo and bring her back to Franklin. Our household once again became three (if we didn't count the cat, which I do, but Tim doesn't).

* * *

With 2016 half over and Kim back in Germany, I left Tim with Boo Radley in Tennessee for a two-week, 150-mile hike. I drove from Franklin on June 28 to meet Peanut at Harpers Ferry. She looked healthy and happy, her hair dyed the color of grape bubble gum in honor of the Virginia Blues. Her cheerful outward appearance, however, belied the pain she felt in her hip.

"I can't make it stop. I'm taking too much Advil, too many zero days. No matter what I do, I can't make it stop."

"You think it's your pack? Can you get it readjusted? Or make it lighter?"

"No, I've tried everything." She was almost in tears.

Someone on the Trail had given Peanut the name of a masseuse in the area who helped hikers, and she managed to get an appointment for the next day. *This was getting complicated.* But what could I do? I could hardly just dump my injured child on the side of the road and drive away, calling out "Happy Trails!"

Peanut felt like the massage did indeed help, and we drove to Duncannon (would I never be shed of this town?), arriving by late afternoon. She was skipping the section from Harpers Ferry to there because she had hiked it with me in 2015—perfectly legit. I offered to treat her to another hotel night, but she was anxious to catch up to her Trail Family. She would reach the Yardley, Pennsylvania, area in a few days, where her Uncle Tommy would pick her up, and she could spend a night or two in comfort with his family.

"All right, my love. Go slowly. Call me when you can."

She hugged me tightly, and I watched her hesitantly walk up the pathway north of busy PA 322. She crossed the railroad tracks, and then, just before the Trail entered the woods, she stopped for an instant and straightened her shoulders. Peanut lifted her eyes to the climb ahead and, without even a backward glance, walked on.

I traveled on solo to Great Barrington, Massachusetts, and left my car at the trailhead where She Who Falls A Lot and I had finished our 2015 hike. The weather was hot, my pack was heavy, and I was worried about Peanut. Also, the logistics of retrieving my car would be troublesome, and I hadn't quite figured them out yet.

But as is so often the case with the Appalachian Trail, just when you think, *Maybe all this shit isn't worth it*, she shows you her gentle side. I walked through Beartown State Forest along a soft trail bordered by Christmas-green mosses and tiny, brightly colored summer flowers. The dense forest here occasionally opens up to views of both the Catskills and the Berkshires. Beaver ponds were still and silent as the dam builders hid behind their work and shyly waited for me to pass. The burdens of life's complications started to slip from my shoulders to be replaced by a feeling of lightness as the day went on.

I climbed to the Mount Wilcox Lean-to, which is what the AT shelters are called in Massachusetts. By nightfall I was snug and happy in my sleeping bag, the soft breezes through the high branches of the trees lulling me into a deep sleep, while the night creatures accepted my presence and left me to my lonely dreams.

＊ ＊ ＊

The next day was, in a word, wet. A light rain fell, and the Trail here crosses numerous streams and frequently borders small ponds. Fortunately, the path between Mount Wilcox and Upper Goose Pond is wide and relatively flat. A dark and quiet gulch strewn with tumbled boulders and fallen hemlocks provides some variation. It is a lovely and somber Tolkien Hobbit world. A climb out of the Tyringham Valley up Baldy Mountain leads yet again to the marshy plateaus. I felt as if I were a time traveler and had visited four or five temperate zones in one day.

The cabin at Upper Goose Pond is a half mile off the Trail, which is a long detour, but the virtues—proximity to the pond, the free pancake breakfast, the roomy and well-maintained accommodations—are much touted in guidebooks and along the Trail. It is one of the very few sites along the AT where a caretaker is present for maintenance and supervision. As I approached the pond, I heard the call of waterfowl. *The loons! The loons!* I smiled. Then, alas, once again, my serenity was threatened by the complications of a world inhabited by other humans.

I reached the establishment—which is indeed an enclosed cabin, not a three-sided shelter—in early evening under a light rainfall. Several thru-hikers lounged about on the spacious front porch. Clothing and gear were draped over bushes and railings waiting for the sun.

I climbed the few stairs to the front door, where the caretaker, I assume, stood.

She looked me up and down. "Can I help you?"

"Yeah. Hey, I'm Sticks. Just want to let you know I'd like to stay here tonight if that's okay."

"Well, the lower bunks are all full," she said. "But I'm sure we could get somebody to switch and take a top one."

I did not get her meaning at first. I stared for a second and then… wait…*Was she saying she didn't think I was capable of climbing three or four steps to get to an upper bunk or pulling myself up to it some way?*

Now, I admit I was probably not a very prepossessing sight with my bedraggled appearance and slight, middle-aged frame. However, this woman acted like I should be in a nursing home with a walker and a bib. How did she think I managed the 1,500 miles to get to this overrated, pretentious shack? Did she think I had been airdropped on the Trail from a fucking helicopter?

I was furious and embarrassed. "No," I said as coldly as possible. "I don't need a bunk. I had planned to pitch my tent in the back there." With shoulders back and chin up, I turned and walked off the porch, the eyes of the thru-hikers following me pityingly.

The next day, after a disappointing breakfast of rationed pancakes (only two each, please) and a weak cup of coffee, I followed the half-mile side trail to rejoin the AT. The sight of the beloved white blazes reminded me of my true place and purpose, and once again, I could slip back into my belonging, leaving behind the judgmental and parsimonious nature of humankind.

❋ ❋ ❋

This was to be an eighteen-mile day with almost no change in an elevation of 1,800 feet. The rain had stopped, and the air was again hot, but not stifling. I went through October Mountain State Forest and over Becket Mountain, Walling Mountain, Bald Top Mountain, and October Mountain itself. These are really just benign bumps rising above a base of buggy, quicksand-like ooze. My poles, on either side of the planks and puncheons, at times threatened to disappear into the black marsh. When no walkway or conveniently situated stones were available, my boots sank into the quagmire. I lifted my feet carefully, the boots separating from the mud with a sucking pressure that threatened to strip them clean off. I felt brave and daring and adventurous, perhaps like Percy Fawcett as he strode on the banks of the Amazon.

I walked on through the early July days with a feeling of progress and accomplishment. Massachusetts has only ninety-one miles of the Appalachian Trail, and I found most of them to be pleasant and not particularly difficult. Several communities along the way make for nice breaks and easy resupplies. I strolled through the hospitable town of Dalton and then, after another seven easy northbound miles, into the equally charming town of Cheshire.

The Trail goes through town, and I followed the blazes to a conveniently located ice cream shop. It would be an extremely rare and strong-willed hiker who could pass this up. I know I couldn't. I signed the hiker log next to the cash register, mindful that Peanut would be coming along behind me within a few weeks. *Hey, I had a Diet Coke float; can you guess who this is?*

Continuing on through town, I came to the Catholic Church known to accommodate, on its basement floor, long-distance hikers. I had no desire to be a part of this group, but I hung about there for a bit, asking occasional passersby if they knew how I could get a ride back to Great Barrington to retrieve my car. "No, sorry. No taxis. Don't know of any shuttles." Lyft and Uber had yet to make an appearance in this corner of Massachusetts. Troublesome logistics again reared their ugly heads.

I had been on the Trail for four days. I was hot and tired, and I wanted my car and the freedom that comes with it to find a motel and a grocery store. I hung around in front of a liquor store, asking patrons if they were going south. "Money is no object!" I wanted to scream out loud. "Just take me! I'll give you fifty, no, a hundred bucks!" Finally, one young woman apparently decided I didn't seem too disreputable or dangerous and took pity on me. I was near delirious with relief as she drove me to Great Barrington.

A good night's sleep restored my energy and attitude. I left the car at a public parking area in Cheshire and stepped back on the AT after a resupply to see me through the next few days. This was the Fourth of July—a warm and beautiful day—and I would spend it on what is widely accepted as one of the most scenic sections of the Trail.

From the town of Cheshire at one thousand feet, the AT climbs for seven miles through dense forest to Mount Greylock at almost 3,500 feet. The first couple of hours were an aerobic challenge, but the ascent becomes gentler after about mile four. I strolled along happily in the peaceful forest until I stepped out of the woods onto the parking lot of Bascom Lodge at the summit.

Leaving the deep woods just at midday, I squinted my eyes in the bright sunlight of the summit's bald and dug my rarely used sunglasses out of my pack. While rummaging in there, I retrieved a light jacket because a cool breeze that had not penetrated the closeness of the forest swept across this treeless expanse. The biggest change, however, came not from the sun or the wind, but from other humans.

Transitioning from a wilderness area to a popular tourist destination is always somewhat jarring, but the contrasts of this day's adventure were almost surreal. Mount Greylock can be reached by car, and on this Independence Day, a lot of folks had chosen that option— so many that a crossing guard was directing traffic in the parking lot. I stood at the edge of the pavement, disoriented and overwhelmed by the sights and sounds, until he blew his whistle, held up his hand to stop an oncoming car, and graciously waved me through.

The large and beautifully proportioned Bascom Lodge is perched proudly on the eastern flank of the summit. To the north is a wide, grassy expanse free of rocks and trees. Here, young lovers relaxed on blankets, adoring parents chased after their toddlers, and photographers tried, futilely, to capture the glory of the views from this paradise. It is a poignant reminder to northbound AT hikers that it is almost time to put the beautiful Berkshire range behind us.

Picnicking families, day-trippers, and a few thru-hikers filled the patio and picnic area of the lodge. I divested myself of pack and poles and took a seat at a wooden table out front. At the table next to me, a large multigenerational family laughed and chatted as they set out the contents of their baskets. It was time to eat, and I went searching for sustenance.

It is no secret that long-distance hikers tend to be a bit hyperbolic when it comes to their descriptions of food. But I will tell you without exaggeration the best goddam grilled cheese sandwich I ever ate was on July 4, 2016, and it was purchased from Bascom Lodge atop Mount Greylock. A thick slab of nutty Gruyère oozed between slices of chewy, buttery bread browned to perfection. I slowly drank ice-cold lemonade with this masterpiece and finished with a slab of orange pound cake so moist I almost had to eat it with a spoon. *Criminy.*

Reluctantly, after a nice little catnap in the sun-warmed grass, I roused myself and left the summit. I stepped back into the solitary woods and hiked several miles down to Wilbur Clearing Lean-to. As I stretched out in my sleeping bag on the wooden floor—a few thru-hikers settling into their own dreams beside me—I thought of the pleasant hike, the stunning scenery, the delicious lunch. From very, very far away, I thought I heard the sound of Independence Day fireworks. But perhaps I only imagined it.

* * *

The weather remained warm for my ten-mile hike the next day. The Trail descends seriously for three miles to the town of North Adams, where I did not linger. Two more miles brought me to the state line, and I bade farewell to Massachusetts and greeted Vermont. Here, the AT merges with the Long Trail and the two journey together for a hundred miles or so. At this point, the AT-LT ascends again for six or seven miles to the Seth Warner Shelter. Looking back at the views of Greylock, I felt the pride of accomplishment tempered by a sense of unease. Each step I took, each mountain I climbed—while undeniably bringing me closer to the end goal—was also a reminder of the challenges yet to come.

After a comfortable and solitary night at Seth Warner Shelter, I navigated a steep descent and a tricky boulder field. Streams and marshes continued to be ubiquitous and the terrain rugged, but the views remained stunning and the weather pleasant. I felt strong and self-satisfied on this eleven-mile day, and I confidently reached the road crossing near Bennington, a "real" town with all the amenities that implies.

I easily got a hitch into town and found a cheap motel with laundry facilities. It was time to take stock and make a plan for the next phase of the adventure. I consulted my AWOL guide and decided to retrieve my car from Cheshire, drive it to Bennington (which boasts a bus station), and leave it until the end of my hike at Wallingford. When I got to Wallingford in about six days, I could get the bus back to Bennington.

"AWOL" is the commonly used nickname for *The A.T. Guide: A Handbook for Hiking the Appalachian Trail*, by David "AWOL" Miller. One of the very helpful things about AWOL's guide, which is revised yearly and has editions for both northbounders and southbounders, is that it is meticulously up to date with information about motels, hostels, etc., in the towns on or near the Trail. AWOL provides contact information for schedules and stops of busses, trains, and shuttle services. This guide is widely used among thru-hikers and had been highly recommended to me by Peanut. (This was also the time when certain phone apps like Guthook Guides were becoming popular, but I can shamefully say I was clueless about things like that.)

Plans firmly, if not easy to implement or cheap to accomplish, in place, I finally located a cab driver to take me to Cheshire, at least sixty miles south by road. For quite a hefty price, he picked me up at the motel just before dusk. We traveled on rural roads and through small mountain towns to my car, parked safely where I had left it.

The next day was warm and got warmer, but with car now parked safely at the Bennington bus station, laundry done, pack resupplied, body clean and rested, I felt energetic enough to face whatever Vermont chose to throw at me.

The Trail was boggy as I hiked through the Glastenbury Wilderness. I believe Vermont is the wettest state in our union. Water soaked through my gaiters, boots, and socks in spite of the planks, puncheons, and footbridges. When I removed my footwear at each day's end through this section, layers of white, prunish skin simply sloughed off.

In the early evening of July 7, after an eleven-mile (mostly upwards) day, I reached the Goddard Shelter, an elevated, roomy space with a picnic table and a nearby creek bed. As I munched on my cheese and crackers, looking forward to a dessert of a Snickers bar, a northbound solo hiker appeared through the tree line twenty or thirty yards from the shelter.

"Hey," she called. "Anybody here?"

"Hey," I called back. "I'm here. Sticks."

She approached the picnic table with quick, almost running, steps. "I'm Scout," she said, flinging off her pack and tossing it up onto the floor of the shelter.

In her late forties or maybe early fifties, Scout was beautiful in a completely natural and unadorned way. Her hair was a nest of long, snaky dreadlocks, as if she just couldn't be bothered to brush it or tend to it in any way, and this was the result. The blondish-brown locks were pulled back from her forehead, with a wide buff above her thick eyebrows and clear, hazel eyes. Her face was wide, her lips chapped. High cheekbones stretched her skin, rendering the laugh lines and crow's feet insignificant or even transforming them into welcome additions.

Aside from conventional hiking boots, Scout's wardrobe seemed to have been chosen from a Goodwill bargain bin or a hiker box. She wore a faded, lilac-colored cotton tank top over tanned shoulders and lean biceps. Her multicolored skirt's ruffled hem hung almost to the top of her boots, and only a few inches of dirty, muscular calf was visible. She carried no trekking poles; I am sure they would have only been in her way.

As Scout cooked her dinner over her little stove at the picnic table, she told me her story, jumping from subject to subject.

"Yeah, I'm sort of a thru-hiker, I guess. Been hiking the AT for years. I just hike a few hundred miles here and there, sort of hop around." She turned off the flame and stirred her rice. "Done most of it though, I think, over the years."

She took a small bottle of Tabasco sauce from her food bag and sprinkled some into the pot.

We were quiet for a few minutes while Scout thoughtfully chewed her dinner, her eyes fixed somewhere in the middle distance. Dusk settled in, and we turned on headlamps to clean up the remnants of our meals.

With sleeping bags and pads laid out, Scout rolled a cigarette and leaned back against the shelter's outside wall.

"Yeah, I just like to walk, to move. I like the people out here too. People in towns and cities—I don't know, I feel like they judge me sometimes."

Yes, I could definitely see that happening. The women would be jealous of her beauty and free spirit; the men would want to own the former and conquer the latter.

* * *

The next day dawned hot, and the woods seemed close and foreboding as I went on alone. Storm clouds were building in the northeast, and I moved easily on a boggy downhill trail. Quiet, determined thru-hikers passed me with only smiles and a few words of acknowledgment. Sixteen hundred miles into their hike, their mud-splattered legs were lean and corded with muscle. Having already come this far by early July, they would easily reach Katahdin before the snows did.

After thirteen miles, I arrived, sweaty and itchy, at Arlington-West Wardsboro Road just before sunset. A dirty, beat-up RV adorned with bumper stickers was parked in the small lot. Just as I crossed the clearing, the side door opened, and Scout, looking light and carefree without pack or shoes, leaned out.

"Sticks!" she called happily. "I been waiting for you! Get in here."

I eased off my heavy pack and placed it, with my poles, on the ground in the shade of the camper. Scout held open the door for me and waved me inside, chatting all the while.

A handsome, tanned, smiling man sat behind the steering wheel with his feet on the passenger seat, his body turned to face us. Scout flounced down on the rumpled bed, and I perched on a scarred plastic cooler.

"This is Onesimus, the greatest Trail Angel on the AT," she declared.

Trying not to mispronounce this unfamiliar name, I said, "Onesimus, it's great to meet you. I'm Sticks."

"Sticks, glad you're here. Get whatever you want from the fridge. There's some cold drinks—no beer, sorry; I'm recovering—and some popsicles in the freezer."

I asked Onesimus how he came to be a traveling man. He told me he had been in the Army for a long time and served a few tours in the Middle East.

"That kind of sucked, you know. So I retired, and now I get a little pension, enough to live on. I don't have many bills or need much stuff."

I looked around at the off-brand canned food on a shelf, the duct tape securing the fridge door, the split Naugahyde bench cover. Yes, it was apparent that our friend Onesimus did not require much in the way of material items.

I pitched my tent at the campsite just north of the road crossing. Heat and humidity persisted, and mosquitos hung thick in the air. Six or eight thru-hikers sat around a campfire, but I was too tired to join in their discussions of the merits of one type of gear over another. *Who cares?* I thought churlishly as I drifted off to sleep, exhausted from the pace of my day in the dank humidity. The tides of the AT again turned, and the confidence with which I began this section ebbed, and stomach-churning trepidation rose.

The wind picked up during the night, and I woke to the sound of treetops roaring. Onesimus came into the campsite carrying an old, dented percolator. His headlamp was on even though it was after dawn—the sun had not penetrated the black clouds.

"Anybody want coffee?" He moved from tent to tent as we held out our cups through the flaps. "It's about to rain really hard. They're predicting storms all day."

I hurriedly began to break camp. I wanted to be in my raincoat with my gear safely stowed and my pack securely covered before the downpour.

Onesimus made an offer to the assembly at large. "I will be at the next road crossing, Highway 11, at the end of the day. About seven-teen miles north. Anybody want to slackpack, throw your shit in the camper. I'll meet you there tonight."

> *Slackpack* is a term used to describe a hike in which one carries only the basic necessities in a pack, leaving heavy items such as tents, sleeping bags, etc., either with someone or in a safe place to retrieve later. It's not often done by thru-hikers because they are hiking a linear path as opposed to a loop hike or in-and-out, although some hostels or outfitters will offer this service. In any case, a slackpack opportunity is always met with jubilation by a long-distance hiker who will be able to walk more quickly and joyously without the burden of a heavy pack.

"Hell, yes!" the thru-hikers cheered and proceeded to take up the offer by immediately taking down tents and packing up gear.

I quickly debated. Seventeen miles was a long day for me. I had not planned to get all the way to VT 11 on this day; my schedule called for me to camp on the Trail for another night. On the other hand, the thought of traveling with a light pack and getting to a dry motel was pretty enticing. Scout walked hurriedly through our midst, heading for the northbound Trail. She threw me a quick smile and wave.

A blinding bolt of lightning and an almost simultaneous clap of thunder hastened my decision. I hurriedly pulled everything out of my pack except food, water, and basic emergency items. Just as the first fat raindrops fell, I dumped my tent, sleeping bag, pad, and extra clothes into a corner of the camper. With the hood of my raincoat tightly cinched and the cover on my now comparatively light pack securely in place, I stepped onto the northbound AT.

"See you tonight, Onesimus!" I called back. "Thanks so much."

* * *

All day the rain fell. Thankfully, the predicted storm—after its initial flirtation—passed us by and left us with only occasional gusts of wind and distant claps of thunder. I slogged on through the day, walking quickly, ever mindful of the challenge of seventeen miles. I climbed

Stratton Mountain and at midday passed a ski area complete with gondola, closed at this time of the year. I hurried by Stratton Pond, and the mournful loons called just as the sun, which had been shy all day, began not so much to set as to fade. The rain tapered off and finally stopped altogether as I stepped out of the woods onto VT 11.

I had walked seventeen miles through sloppy conditions in what I thought was a fairly reasonable amount of time. I had barely rested all day. I was tired but now giddy with relief and pride to have reached my destination relatively unscathed. Feeling pretty damn good about myself, I hurried to the camper parked along the north side of the road. Onesimus opened the door and leaned out with a big smile and a welcoming wave.

"Hey, Sticks," he called. "We thought you'd never get here!"

The other hikers who had slackpacked this day had long since retrieved their gear and continued on their way. Humility again came to claim me as its victim.

"So what's your plan, Sticks?" Onesimus asked. "You want us to take you somewhere?"

"Heck, yeah," I answered. "I need to dry out. Can you just drive me into town? I think there's a cheap little motel on the highway. The Red Sled."

"Sure thing." After a few false starts, the engine on the RV roared to life, and we happily motored into the metropolis of Manchester Center, Vermont.

Onesimus pulled into the parking lot of the Red Sled Motel, a one-story brick building on VT 11 a few miles west of the Trail. He left the motor idling as I went into the office and forked over my credit card for a one-night stay. After a trip to the local Price Chopper, he and Scout accepted my offer to use my shower, and then they clambered back into the RV and continued on to whatever destiny awaited them. Our paths never crossed again, but I often heard hikers mention the kindness of Onesimus. Of Scout, I never had any further word.

* * *

I spread out my wet clothes to dry on the bed in my room and planned to leave early the next day. Now resupplied, I had no reason to linger here. I had hiked for eight days and only had about thirty-five more miles to Wallingford, which could easily be done in two or three days' time. I fell asleep to the sound of yet another rain shower passing over.

Leaden clouds hung low over the Red Sled Motel and obscured the mountaintops to the northeast as I looked out the window the next morning. Several hikers in raingear stood at the roadside in the chilly gloom, trying to hitch a ride to the trailhead. It utterly exhausted me to even think about the long, wet hike ahead of me, which would include the difficult ascent of Bromley Mountain. I slowly got dressed and made my way to the little diner across the street. Eggs, toast, and coffee only added to my stupor.

Walking back to the motel, I stopped to stare down the slick, blacktopped road, empty now of hitchhikers and passing traffic. Mist swirled about me. To take up my pack—once again heavy with camping gear—and poles, to try to catch a ride on this bleak morning, to step back into the wilderness of the dark-green mountains seemed a task too monumental to even contemplate.

Then I had a revelation.

I don't have to do it! I have walked for over a hundred miles in eight days over rough terrain in alternating heat and rain. The car shuttles have been complicated and arduous. My body is tired; my spirit is tired. I am fifty-six years old, and I can do whatever I want to do.

I marched into the office of the Red Sled.

"I will need my room for another night, and I will need fresh towels. Thank you."

The gray drizzle continued falling outside my window onto the black and now-deserted parking lot. My room was adequate: two double beds—one now strewn with my damp clothing—covered with floral print spreads, the flat pillows, the cheaply framed landscape print hanging too high on the wall, the nightstand with its somewhat sticky and suspect surface, the gifted Bible atop an extremely thin telephone book on the lower shelf.

The TV, which I had not turned on the night before, hung suspended from the ceiling at a rather odd angle. I perched at the end of the bed with my head tilted far back and tried to figure out the remote. Two fuzzy channels were all that appeared. I considered contacting the motel management for explanation or instruction but decided I really didn't give a shit.

All day, lying between worn sheets that smelled of bleach, I dozed, waking every so often to the sounds of distant doors opening and closing or the passing wheels of a cleaning cart. I flipped between the two channels and occasionally drifted off to either the peaceful noises of nature from a National Geographic special or the somber narration of a Ken Burns documentary. The whistling call of the osprey alternated with Prohibition-era jazz in my semidreams until, finally, the day turned into night without any discernible difference in light or noise or even in time and space, and I slept deeply till dawn.

When I woke early the next morning, I thought briskly, *Well, I must press on.* With gear neatly stowed in my pack and the sun finally making intermittent appearances over the mountains, I enjoyed another breakfast at the roadside diner.

A young dad and his little boy sat in the booth across from me. The towheaded, adorable child was fidgety, and his father exhorted him gently to "Sit down, son" and "Finish your milk" and "Eat your pancakes."

Two thru-hikers waited at the edge of the diner's parking lot for a lift to the trailhead. I joined them, now anxious to get moving. The father from the restaurant, a wide-faced, stocky man, buckled his son into a car seat in the back of a pickup truck's cab and then turned to call to us.

"You guys going to the AT? Sorry, I only got room for one."

I motioned to the other hikers. "One of you want to go? You were here first."

Oh, no, they assured me. They wanted to stay together and would wait for another ride.

I climbed into the truck and positioned my pack in my lap, noticing that there were two car seats in the extended cab. The little boy, unafraid and curious, watched me.

"Where we going, Daddy?"

"Let's take this lady to her hike, and then we'll run our errands, okay?"

The child nodded serenely. I turned to face him more fully.

"Hi. I'm Sticks."

He considered this information. Then, with the thumb and finger of his right hand, he configured the fingers of his left, raised it to show me, and proudly said, "I'm three."

I smiled. Long-distance hikers rarely see children, and though this seems strange, you forget how small they are, how sweet their voices, how soft their hair. This little reminder of humanity stayed with me for days.

* * *

It was July 11, and I was in the Green Mountain National Forest. This fifteen-mile day on the AT-LT took me up and down Bromley Mountain, Styles Peak, and Peru Peak. I passed Griffith Lake and crossed numerous streams now full and rushing from the previous days' rain. I marched on, my body feeling stronger after the day of rest. This night was spent in the company of thru-hikers at Lost Pond Shelter, and again the rains came.

On July 12, the sun shone brightly through the evergreens, but it would take many days of dry weather to diminish the puddles of water or harden the boggy trail. I cruised about ten miles, at one point skirting Little Rock Pond, on this pretty hike down to Greenwall Shelter. The sun, when it penetrated the tall branches and cast its rays onto the narrow path, warmed me, and I felt that summer had returned after a sabbatical. The air smelled of clean pine, and I was reminded that Vermont is known as the Green Mountain State. *This is why.*

I had but a few AT miles to do on the next and final morning of this trek. When I reached the road that would take me to Wallingford, I didn't even try to get a ride. This was a sign of just how muddy my boots were; I didn't want to mess up anyone's car. I trudged on, facing the minimal traffic, for the couple of miles that it took me to get to the Gulf station where I could meet the bus. There, I changed into camp shoes, bought some doughnuts and coffee, and hunkered down against the side of the building. A few locals looked at me strangely. One elderly lady approached and asked, "Are you okay, dear? Do you need anything?"

I'm sure she had mistaken me, in my dirty clothes and bulging pack, for a homeless person. Who could blame her? She seemed relieved when I told her I was a hiker waiting for the bus to Bennington. At the appointed hour, the big Greyhound pulled alongside the gas station, pausing just long enough for me to hop on and hand over my nine bucks. In just over an hour traveling south along VT 7, I was delivered safely back to my car and back into the world of responsibility for those other than myself.

❋ ❋ ❋

When I reached my car at Bennington, I headed south. Peanut was back on the Trail in the Lehigh Valley area after several days of resting her hip at her Uncle Tom's house in Yardley. A mother-daughter reunion was imminent.

We met up in a sports bar in the hiker-friendly town of Wind Gap, Pennsylvania. Her spirits were high, and she was realistic about her hip.

"I'll keep walking, and if it gets too bad, I'll quit. But I really think I'll make it. I just have a good feeling about the whole thing." Peanut was anxious to catch up with her Trail Family, and after a motel night, I took her to the Trail crossing very early in the morning.

"I love you; hang in there," I called after her as she headed into the woods. She, still with a slight limp and a hesitant gait, smiled back over her shoulder and lifted a pole in farewell.

There were no plans to see Peanut again until she completed her thru-hike in October. I turned away from the Trail and offered up a silent heartfelt plea to the Angels and Mother Nature to be kind to my only child.

PART 2

CLARENDON GORGE, VERMONT, TO KINSMAN NOTCH, NEW HAMPSHIRE

At home, we turned the calendar tacked to our kitchen wall from July to August, and then that month too was behind us. The summer, with its family vacations and obligations, was waning but not yet over. There was time for a hike.

She Who Falls A Lot and I flew from Nashville to Manchester, New Hampshire, on September 7. We rented a car and drove to Wallingford, Vermont, where I had finished my hike in July. Tim's cousin Jeff and his wife, Liz, had graciously consented to my request of using their vacation farm as a home base for our day hikes. The plan was to hike ten to twelve miles a day for five days.

She Who Falls A Lot would then drive the car back to Manchester and fly home. I would continue hiking north solo for several more days before making my way back by bus or shuttle for my flight home on the twentieth. Although the devil may be in the details, I took some pleasure in arranging these logistics. It took my mind off the true devil in this picture: the AT's entry into the White Mountains.

Jeff happened to be at the farm for a one-day overlap with our visit. On his way back to Cambridge, he shuttled us to VT 103, and we were grateful that at least for this day, we wouldn't have the stress of hitchhiking. The weather was perfect, warm but with almost no humidity, and our planned hike for this first day was only about eight miles. Life was simple and good.

We quickly realized that while the plan was simple, the hike was not. Difficulty began immediately with strenuous boulder-climbing through a ravine. Our pace was very slow, but once we cleared the ravine, we were able to step it up a bit as we crossed farm fields and animal pastures, where our biggest concerns were crossing stiles and avoiding cow shit. In late afternoon, we reached our car at Upper Cold River Road, happy that the night would bring relative luxury at the farm.

Day Two looked to be another difficult hike, including the ascent and descent of Killington Peak, where temperatures can drop dramatically and winds can be brutal. We parked our car at US 4 and hitched a ride back to Upper Cold River Road to begin our twelve-mile day. Luckily, the weather remained decent—warm and dry. We kept a slow but steady pace as we climbed up, up, up over rugged terrain, gaining 1,700 feet elevation in just under four miles.

Just before we arrived at the side trail to Killington Peak (the AT does not directly cross the summit), She Who Falls A Lot—living up to her name—stumbled on a pile of rocks and fell. I hurried to help.

"I'm okay," she said, grimacing a bit. "Let me just sit here a minute."

After a second, she rolled to a seated position on a footstool-size rock. "It's my ankle. I think I sprained it."

Yes, I could see already some swelling above her low-topped hiking socks. She started to unlace the boot.

"No, wait," I said. "I'm afraid if you take it off, you won't be able to get it back on."

We sat a few minutes in silence.

"Do you think you can walk on it?" I finally asked.

"I don't think it's too bad. Let me try."

She stood up gingerly and, leaning heavily on her poles, took a few tentative steps.

"Okay, let's give it a go."

We walked on slowly and arrived at the clearly marked spur trail leading up to the peak. This junction is a tumble of rocks where hikers on the AT-LT, north and southbound, take a break or move on down to the nearby shelter.

"How's the foot?" I asked as we eased off our packs.

"Not too bad, but I need to stop for a minute." She Who Falls a Lot lowered herself to take a seat on a fallen log. The swelling of her left foot was even more clearly visible.

We had intended to take the spur trail up to the summit, have some lunch and admire the view, then return to the AT to finish up the several miles remaining to reach US 4.

"What do you think, my friend? We still have about six miles to the car. But it's downhill, so maybe it won't be too hard." I tried to sound encouraging.

"I'm going so slow, though. It'll take forever."

"Or," I continued, "we can take the path here to the lodge and the gondola. You can ride it down if you want, and I'll hike quickly to the car."

"Okay. Well, let's at least go up there and check it out, and then I guess we can decide."

The climb to Killington Peak from the AT is a half mile series of rock scrambles, some dangerously precipitous. It is a difficult climb for all but the most experienced rock climbers. We often resorted to crawling on our hands and knees, stopping to throw our sticks ahead of us and giving one another a hand up and over boulders.

We continued the laborious ascent, finally reaching Killington Peak. On the bald summit, we met once again with civilization. The clanging gondola, packed with a group of boisterous merrymakers, was just making its U-turn to head back down the mountain. People attired in linen suits and chiffon dresses posed for pictures outside the glass-fronted restaurant, the blue sky and green mountains serving as a majestic background.

"The restaurant is closed," the friendly fellow operating the gondola told us. "Private party." We had come upon a wedding rehearsal luncheon, seemingly on top of the world.

Well, darn. So much for the idea of a nice lunch. We dug some snacks from our packs and sat at a picnic table to admire the vista.

"What do you think?" I asked. "Can you keep going?"

"I am *not* going back down that rocky trail. I'd never make it, not even if my foot was okay."

"No problem. Take the gondola down, and I'll hike to the car. Pick you up in a few hours."

She paid the twenty bucks or whatever and climbed aboard the next outgoing gondola with some slightly rowdy members of the wedding party. I waved goodbye and turned to make my way back to the AT. *Crisis averted.* Worry over my friend's injury was mitigated by the relief I felt that we had not been miles from an exit and that common sense had prevailed.

* * *

Rain came the next day. We had taped up She Who Falls A Lot's foot the night before, and she declared it was on the mend but still not one hundred percent. With the promise of a chilly, wet day and a slippery trail, she opted out of the day's hike.

"No worries," I told her. "You can take me to the trailhead and pick me up."

For some reason—perhaps because the northbound ascent of Quimby Mountain looked pretty daunting—I decided to do the eleven-mile section southbound. She Who Falls A Lot dropped me off at Stony Brook Road and would pick me up at US 4 (Sherburne Pass) at day's end.

This is a lovely hike even on a damp, cool day. I began by climbing an eight- or ten-foot ladder that had been placed by thoughtful human hands against a sheer rock face just south of where the AT crosses remote Stony Brook Road. There are some ups and downs, including Quimby Mountain, but meandering switchbacks and occasional meadows make for fairly easy terrain. This is also the section in which the Appalachian Trail and the Long Trail part company—the former heading northeast to Maine, the latter heading northwest to Canada.

A few miles into this hike, as the day warmed, I stretched out for a break on the banks of Kent Pond near Mountain Meadows Inn. As I sipped a bottle of grape juice and munched on a PBJ sandwich (there is such joy to be had in packing fresh food daily) a stocky, dark-haired hiker approached me.

"Hey, mind if I join you?" she asked cheerfully. She sat down beside me and started rummaging through a dirty, patched pack. "I'm Sherlock Holmes."

This woman looked to be about my age, and she wore a long-sleeve turtleneck knit shirt and tight polyester pants in spite of the heat. Her clothing was all black, and she had very white skin, giving one the impression of a vampire. The chest strap on her pack was broken, one side of it dangling uselessly, the other side missing altogether. Duct tape bound the waist strap to the main frame.

"I'm Sticks." I offered some Pringles, which were graciously accepted. "Are you a southbound thru-hiker?"

"Yeah, started in Katahdin. Did all of Maine, but skipped the Whites and got a ride to Vermont." Sherlock here was apparently using the phrase thru-hiker pretty loosely. "I'm just gonna walk as far south as I can until bad weather. Or I run out of money."

"How did you get your trail name?" I asked. "It's really cool."

She answered with no sign of shame or embarrassment. "Well, my real name is Shirley. And I don't have a fucking clue what I'm doing out here, so hikers just started calling me Sherlock Holmes. Like I started out with this kid's school backpack from Walmart, and it fell apart, so I got this one from a hiker's box at a hostel near Woodstock."

"Well, good for you. You've made it this far." I tried to sound encouraging.

Sherlock Holmes and I walked south together for several miles through the damp afternoon. She was surprisingly quick and agile, and my pace increased to keep up with her.

"My friend She Who Falls A Lot is picking me up at the road crossing. You need a ride anywhere? We're going into Rutland."

"Sure!"

We met She Who Falls A Lot at the appointed hour and place, and drove the short distance to Rutland, a quaint and friendly town. We dropped Sherlock off and continued on to our quarters at the farm. The next day, as we were car shuttling, we saw her with a group of hikers walking north on US 4. Should we stop and tell her she was going the wrong way? *No.* Clueless is sometimes the only way to go.

* * *

She Who Falls A Lot was back on the Trail with me for the next couple of days. We managed to hike twelve to thirteen miles each day, doing the hitchhiker shuffle. This was fairly easy hiking fortunately, because our pace was pretty slow in light of the injured ankle. We traveled north through rolling hills and quiet forests. The weather had cleared and was sunny, even a bit autumnal.

These days were simply beautiful; we were near the town of Woodstock, and the area is as idyllic as the name. We walked through hushed and fragrant woods and crossed farmland golden in this late summer month. For a bit, we followed a section known as the King's Highway, now just part of the AT bordered by a low stone wall. I was reminded of England's narrow lanes hemmed in by tall hedgerows. I imagined horses and carriages traveling this road 250 years ago, the riders and occupants wearing cravats and shirtwaists and speaking with British accents. The flat, spongy trail made me feel as if I could walk forever, and I practiced living in the moment, knowing that the ease of this section would, too, pass.

We crossed over the White River on an old iron bridge and went through the little town of West Hartford. From there, we walked to Norwich—yet another charming village—just a couple of miles south of the Vermont–New Hampshire state line. On this section of the AT, you feel like you are always within shouting distance of civilization. The views from the low mountains almost always include towns and fairly busy streets. Nevertheless, there is also the sense of anticipation that very, very soon, you will be leaving the populated world and entering the final two states, New Hampshire and Maine, the most remote section of the Trail.

✽ ✽ ✽

On the morning of September 13, She Who Falls A Lot dropped me off at Norwich on her way to the airport. With seven days of solo hiking ahead of me and once again burdened by a full pack, I walked across the bridge into the state of New Hampshire. There would be no more day-tripping for me.

Blazes are painted on the sidewalks and signposts of the streets of Hanover. The town, on this lovely early autumn day, bustled with the lunchtime crowd of Dartmouth College students and local shoppers. I lingered for a while on the green, repacking my pack and studying maps, reluctant to return to the solitary Trail. A cloud blocked the sun for a moment and threw the grassy lawn into shadow, reminding me of the lateness of the afternoon and the beginning of a chill in the air. I strapped on my pack and headed, alone once again, out of town and into the woods.

I reached Velvet Rocks Shelter near dusk. A small, comfortable shelter in a nice little glade a quarter mile off the Trail, it is maintained by the venerable Dartmouth Outing Club (DOC). Located so near town, it is a well-used site. Several trail runners, out for their evening exercise, jogged through the clearing as I set about making camp.

I made a note in the shelter register. "If I was rich and/or smart, Dartmouth is the college I would have chosen. Sticks."

She Who Falls A Lot and I had regularly checked the Trail registers, hoping to see an entry from Peanut, who by now was a couple hundred miles north of here. We had not seen any, but here at Velvet Rocks Shelter was her unmistakable scribble.

The entry, dated some two weeks previous, was not signed, but I would recognize that handwriting, which has not changed or improved since about fourth grade, anywhere:

I am very dissapointed in this shelter. It is more than .2 off the trail and is not very clean!!!

Oh, Peanut. I flipped forward to the page where I had just posted my words and added a postscript.

*I am very **disappointed** in Peanut's entry for August 16th. Obviously, she did **not** go to Dartmouth. Sticks.*

The next morning, I discovered why New Hampshire is called the Granite State. I scrambled and crawled over black-banded slabs bordered by tall evergreens. There was little change in elevation for several miles, but my pace was hesitant as a light drizzle made the rocks dangerously slick. A steep climb—one thousand feet in a few miles—to the summit of Moose Mountain took me to its namesake shelter. This had been a lonely and difficult ten-mile day. I was happy to share this space with a hale and hearty group of DOC members out for a midweek ramble.

✳ ✳ ✳

The next day did not so much break as slowly fracture. Snuggled in my sleeping bag, I heard the sound of rain dripping from the shelter eaves and the hushed conversation of my fellow hikers. The acrid smell of a campfire stung my nose, not unpleasantly. I opened my eyes to see only a whitish-gray mist where the three-sided shelter opened to what would have been, on a clear day, a view of the distant mountains. I closed my eyes again.

When next I opened them, the skies had somewhat cleared. The tents had been taken down, and the group of hikers were packing up, their voices louder now as they tamped out the campfire. The odor of fresh pine and stale boots mingled in the shelter. I dozed off again.

Complete silence and stillness woke me. Not a squirrel scampered or a bird tweeted. I sat up, confused. *What time is it?* The sky, dark gray, was no help. I groped about for my watch and glasses. *10:30! What the…?* The mountain creatures surely were watching me, sitting up on their haunches or peering down from their perches, wondering when this lazy human was going to be on her way and thinking, *We must get about our business here, and she is really throwing us off our game.*

I hurriedly got my ass moving, disgusted with myself for sleeping half the morning away. Quickly climbing the second peak of Moose Mountain, I forced myself to calm down. *What does it matter?*

I was soon to find out it mattered a great deal.

The second summit of Moose Mountain gives way to a very steep descent. I plummeted 1,500 feet in a mile and a half. I had no more reached bottom than the steep ascent of Holts Ledge began. This is not easy hiking, my friends; no walk in the woods, no stroll in the park. This is serious, rugged, wild mountaineering.

The descent of Holts Ledge took me to Lyme-Dorchester Road and the Dartmouth Skiway. Stunned by the realities of the northern Appalachian Mountains, I figured my pace for the day had been, at best, one mile an hour. I sat by the side of the road, almost too weary to remove my pack, and assessed the situation.

My plan had been to hike another five miles and sleep at the Fire Warden's Cabin, a small, enclosed building located on the AT and available for use by hikers. *That ain't gonna happen.* I was wet and cold—in fact, had been wet and cold for more than twenty-four hours. The trail to the cabin is a two-thousand-foot climb up Smarts Mountain, and due to my late start and my slow pace, I would be doing it mostly in the dark.

Well, shit. I thumbed through AWOL's guide and found a number for Dowds' Country Inn in Lyme.

"I'm a hiker," I told the voice on the other end of the line. "Do you have a room for the night? Can you come pick me up on the highway?"

Yes and yes.

* * *

Although this unexpected stop had thrown me off my schedule, I would just have to make up the miles. The good news was that I dried out, slept in a beautiful room, had a hot shower, ate a delicious meal, and was driven back to the trailhead. I tried not to let it bother me that this little detour had cost me upward of 150 bucks.

The weather remained damp and cold as I stepped back on the Trail. I was determined to stay in the Fire Warden's Cabin this evening, even though it was only about five miles in. A rarity on the AT, the cabin is an actual four-sided building closed to the elements. I envisioned a snug little cottage where I could snuggle in a corner with my book and listen to the rain on the roof, safe and warm. I'm sorry to report that the cabin fell well short of these expectations.

I walked along ridges and climbed over ledges, where lovely mountain views no doubt could have been admired had the day been clear. My pace was slow, and the damp seemed to seep through all my layers of clothes and chill my very bones. Occasionally, thru-hikers passed me.

"Hey, y'all," I would call out. "Staying at the Fire Warden's Cabin tonight?"

"No, pushing on, I think. Try to make it to Glencliff."

Thru-hikers have a communication system to rival AT&T, and the fact that none seemed excited about this cabin paradise should have been a clue.

I arrived at the clearing well before dark to find, as advertised, a small four-sided building complete with windows and a door. Charmless and forlorn-looking, the cabin nevertheless did promise shelter from what was now a downright cold evening. With relief and gratitude, I opened the creaky wooden door and entered.

Mouse droppings and bits of hiker trash—Band-Aid backings, empty fuel containers, a forgotten sock or two—littered the splintered floor. A slow drip from a leaky ceiling added its mark to the mildewed walls. It felt as if decades of chill were contained in this room. My heart sank. *Why, it might be warmer to sleep outside in my tent!*

I just had to make the best of it. I swept out a corner and spread out my sleeping pad and bag. I popped a couple of Advil and, leaving my pack and contents propped against the wall, stepped back outside.

A campfire ring offered some hope of comfort. I gathered kindling and firewood, most of it damp and soft. With some effort, I eventually had a nice fire ablaze, just as true and utter darkness fell over the clearing.

Two tall, heavily burdened, thickly bearded hikers crashed into the circle of firelight.

"Hey, whassup? Room in the cabin for us?" A forty-something-year-old man made the introductions. "I'm Camel; this is Loco. Northbound."

We made the usual chitchat about the weather, about food, about upcoming Mount Moosilauke. Camel was talkative, brash, authoritative. Loco, also about forty, tall and stooped, was near mute. They fired up their stoves to boil water.

"We been soaking lentils all day," Camel said. "Making some soup." He emptied a ziplock bag of what appeared to be mushy, brownish peas into the pot. "Want to try some?"

"No, I'm good," I answered, savoring the sandwich I'd brought from Dowds'.

With dinner finished and the fire dying down, I went back into the cabin. *Sonofabitch.* Mice had gotten into my first aid kit, which I had carelessly left open, and had chewed through the small ziplock bag containing Advil. They had nibbled on the candy-like orange coating until all that remained were the white tablets, now scattered about and soggy.

I dejectedly packed up the trash and arranged my bag and pad. Shivering almost uncontrollably, disillusioned by this difficult day and apprehensive about the next, I slept fitfully. When dawn finally reached the cabin's dirty window, I quickly packed up my gear and stole away quietly, leaving Loco and Camel snoring softly.

Still cold, still anxious, I continued up Smarts Mountain and then began the long, difficult hike to my next destination, Ore Hill campsite. A three-mile descent took me to Eastman Ledges. Then, mockingly, the Trail climbs right back up again for three miles to Mount Cube. Next—you guessed it—three miles down to the lonely campsite. The day's views had been of the north: the White Mountains, patiently waiting for their prey.

Only two more days of this, I promised myself as I climbed out of my tent on the chilly morning of September 18. The day warmed up as I walked the eight miles through the woods to Glencliff. The Trail here was relatively flat, and I felt a bit of confidence returning. *Don't get cocky, Sticks.* Tomorrow—my last day on this hike—would be only the beginning of the notorious Whites.

> The White Mountains consist of several ranges, including the Presidential and Mahoosuc Ranges, in New Hampshire and Southern Maine. There are upwards of forty-five peaks that summit at more than four thousand feet, and the tallest, Mount Washington, is over six thousand feet. The trails, including the Appalachian Trail, that are hacked out of this wilderness are often above tree line and follow crevices of rock formations, like the Trail in the southern Appalachians follows gaps and ridgetops. Very few centers of human population are anywhere near trail accesses; blazes and markings are few and far between. But it is the weather that gives these Whites their fearsome reputation: snow can fall in any month of the year, the temperature can plummet within minutes, and winds are often brutally dangerous.

This section of the AT in Southwest New Hampshire is very remote—although one can argue that New Hampshire itself is remote. The population of the largest city, Manchester, is only 110,000. The remaining million or so people are scattered about the state in unincorporated little communities like Glencliff.

Glencliff is within the White Mountain National Forest, and to my knowledge, there is no Main Street, no business district, no Motel 6. What there is, is a road—NH 25, also known as Moosilauke Highway. And on this road, just where the AT crosses, is a hostel known as Hikers Welcome.

I felt shy and out of place as hikers came and went on the grounds of Hikers Welcome. Everyone seemed younger, more experienced, healthier than I. This trip had diminished me in many ways. I had lost several pounds from an already small frame, and my slow pace and ineptitude had struck a blow to my ego from which I feared I'd never recover.

A tall, very fit-looking young man approached me as I sat at the corner of a picnic table out front. He removed his pack and smiled shyly. "Do you know what we do here?" he asked with a strong French accent. "Can I stay here?"

"Well, I'm not sure. I think there's a sign-up sheet over by the door." We walked the few steps to the table where a clipboard with registration forms awaited our particulars.

"Okay, here we go." I read the instructions. "You just put your name here and how many nights you intend to stay. Shower? Laundry? Ride to store? Everything is sort of à la carte, price-wise."

"Name?" he asked. "Do they want my real name or trail name?"

"I don't know. Let's just put both names. What is your trail name?"

"Yao Ming."

I looked up quickly and studied his fair-skinned face and long blond hair. "Like the really tall Chinese basketball player?" I asked, taken aback.

He nodded.

"Are you Chinese?"

He shook his head.

"Do you play basketball?"

Again, no.

"So why is this your trail name? Because you're tall?"

Yao Ming shrugged. "I guess. This is what they call me."

I considered this for a minute. "Well, you're not really that tall," I finally said.

"I know! This is what I think too!"

Snorts of laughter overtook us as we tried to complete the registration forms.

Oh, lordy, I thought, wiping my eyes with a dirty sleeve. As difficult as this journey is, at least I'm not having to do it in a foreign language or with a ridiculous trail name.

The Hikers Welcome proprietors were very friendly and accommodating, providing rides to a store for resupply and to Kinsman Notch at NH 112, the other end of what is known as the Moosilauke hike. The hostel itself is a neatly maintained, two-story clapboard affair perched at the roadside.

A two-story bunkhouse to which I was assigned, some thirty or forty yards from the main facility, still had that lovely smell of new construction. Eight or ten bunk beds on each floor were laid with clean, soft mattresses. Electric lights burned brightly.

My circle of friends grew by two when I met Darth Vader, a middle-age, soft-spoken fellow, and his polite, twenty-something son, Skywalker. They turned out to be from—of all places—Franklin, Tennessee. Darth Vader and Skywalker had claimed their stakes along with several other guys on the downstairs level. Yao Ming and I made our way upstairs.

I stretched out luxuriously in my bunk, cheered by my new friends who had hiked Moosilauke this day and told me (gallantly lying with straight faces) that I could handle it just fine. Yao, who had chivalrously taken a bed on the other side of the room, turned out his light.

"Hey, Yao Ming," I called.

"Yes?" he answered softly.

"Your big ole feet aren't hanging off the end of that bed, are they?"

He snickered. "Oh, Steeks, you are so funny."

❋ ❋ ❋

Mount Moosilauke is considered the southern gateway to the White Mountains of New Hampshire. It peaks at just under five thousand feet, rising almost four thousand feet in less than six miles from the gap at Glencliff. For nine to ten months of the year, it is snow- and ice-covered, making it impassable for most of us mere mortals. These are the cold, hard facts about Moosilauke that any map or guidebook could tell you.

What I can tell you is that it kicked my ass, and anybody who says it's not that tough is either a big, fat liar or Alex Honnold.

Advice from other hikers led me to the decision to tackle the nine-mile Moosilauke hike from north to south. I was told it is a bit easier to climb up the gorge and get it out of the way early on. The clincher for me was that I could have the hostel folks drop me off early at Kinsman Notch, and then my southbound hike would take me back to the hostel at the road crossing. I could slackpack and would not have to worry about meeting a driver at a certain time. There was absolutely no doubt in my mind that my pace would be very slow.

The weather was cool and gray, but no rain fell. The nice woman from the hostel dropped me off at Kinsman Notch, where the AT crosses NH 112 at exactly 7:00 a.m. Just as I stepped on the Trail to begin my journey, I saw a small sign nailed to a beech tree. On this sign are the familiar AT symbol and these crudely etched words in all capital letters:

THIS TRAIL IS EXTREMELY TOUGH. IF YOU LACK EXPE-RIENCE PLEASE USE ANOTHER TRAIL.

There's another trail?

TAKE SPECIAL CARE AT THE CASCADES TO AVOID TRAGIC RESULTS.

The Trail climbs two thousand feet in just over a mile. Imagine a StairMaster, except on one side is a tall, dense forest and on the other is a gorge filled with churning cascades. This is the inaptly named Beaver Brook—it should be called something like Death Watch. Your steps are slick slabs and your handrail is the next rock up. Occasionally, there are iron rungs the DOC has hammered into place. However, often one end of a rung has pulled away from the granite, which doesn't inspire much confidence that the other end will hold. I inched along, at each step thinking carefully about the placement of my hands and feet. Two agonizing hours passed before I completed this one intimidating mile.

Any relief or feeling of accomplishment about putting the gorge behind me was short-lived; I still had a long trying hike ahead of me. Two more miles of tough climbing over boulders and fallen trees that nature had twisted and piled on top of each other tested every muscle in my body: arms to pull me up, quads and glutes to hoist myself up, back and core to balance myself on slivers of ledges. I was grateful for the light pack and thought several times that any additional weight would have simply toppled me.

Finally, the forest was left behind as I neared the summit of Mount Moosilauke at 4,800 feet. The evergreen trees here are stunted and twisted, reminding one of gorse bushes on Scottish moors. The path is marked by three- to four-foot tall rock cairns that appear through the mist like ghostly beacons. Several northbound hikers, including Yao Ming, were taking photos of the summit marker and contemplating the White Mountains to the north, which they would reach in only another day or two. I wished them all well, high-fiving Yao Ming, and continued picking my solitary way south at my laborious pace.

The Moosilauke descent took me another several hours as I inched my way back down through the tortuous and twisted mountainside. It was almost dusk when I reached Sanitarium Road, where a small cemetery tucked back in the woods added a note of eeriness to the solitary remoteness of this area. I rested a bit with my back against a crumbling old fence and felt the beginnings of a return to civilization and humanity even in this place of transition.

But this day and hike were not done with me yet. A wide river crossing tested my last reserve. For some time, I walked up and down the bank, looking for the safest route across. A rope, tied to two trees on either side of the river, could serve as an overhead handhold. I considered this option, but it had been overused, and now the path that it served was deep, and the rope would be largely out of my reach.

Just do it, I finally decided. Relying heavily on my poles and luck, I waded across the rushing stream without even trying to hop from stone to stone. The frigid water was often over my knees, and I dared not hesitate lest the current knock me down. Moving as quickly as possible, I reached the safety of the side bank and, not stopping to look back, moved on. The dusk was quickly becoming night, and I dug out my headlamp and switched it on to hike along a now-flat trail bordering a marshy pond. It occurred to me I might see a moose, and I stopped to gaze out over the still water.

Moose are common in the northern Appalachian Mountains, particularly in New York and the New England states. They wander through the deciduous forests, huge and mostly silent. Complete herbivores, they feed off the water plants that grow in the marshes and ponds throughout the mountains; they are not at all interested in hikers or their food. An adult male can weigh over 1,200 pounds and a female up to 800. They are not an endangered species, and they are hunted for sport and food in the fall and winter. Although moose aren't usually aggressive toward humans, like any animal, they can be dangerous if provoked or if a calf is threatened. If you see one, it's best to ignore him and let him continue on with his business. They often cross the AT or even follow its path, as evidenced by the enormous piles of droppings a hiker will encounter on certain sections. Oddly, moose poop—which consists of large marble-size droppings—has little or no odor. Some gift shops in Maine carry kitschy souvenirs made by local craftspeople from these droppings. (Before you judge, remember winters are long in New England.) I once met a man who kept two moose pellets dangling from his truck's rearview mirror like a pair of dice.

No moose appeared, but the stillness provided me with an opportunity for reflection. The events of this year—the complicated intersections of life on and off the Trail—reminded me I was not getting younger, not getting healthier, not getting richer. I would not be able to hike these trails—which would only get harder—forever. I needed to finish this journey while I was still able to handle the arduous arrangements, not to mention the difficulty of the Trail itself. If I did not finish the AT next year, it might never happen. So I came to a decision, as I had before the river crossing. *Just do it.* I would finish my hike next year, the thirteenth year, 2017.

✳ ✳ ✳

An employee of the hostel took me to Manchester to meet my flight the next day, and I went home to Tim and Boo. In October, Peanut, having successfully and joyfully completed her thru-hike at Katahdin, arrived. Her journey had lasted exactly six months. Now, back in the world of warm dry clothes, of soft clean beds, of hot nourishing food, she seemed to feel unanchored and restless. The demands of everyday life—getting a job, interacting socially, dressing professionally—were overwhelming.

A phrase, widely attributed to the hiker Flash, neatly sums up the posthike hangover: "Life on the Trail is hard, but living is easy; life at home is easy, but the living is hard." Peanut told me it was difficult to come to terms with the fact that the most challenging and the most remarkable—*the best*—thing she'd ever done or would ever do was already behind her at the tender age of twenty-five.

I consoled her with murmurs of encouragement. "There'll be other hikes, other adventures."

But I understood. As harrowing as my hikes had been this year—with the tall rugged mountains, the complicated logistics, the brutal weather, the lonely campsites, the sheer audacity of the Trail—they had also held many moments of exquisite beauty and countless examples of the indomitable human spirit. To contemplate a future in which all this would only be a past seemed an impossible task.

CHAPTER 13

2017 (400 MILES)

PART 1

KINSMAN NOTCH, NEW HAMPSHIRE, TO ANDOVER, MAINE

A note on my calendar for Sunday, January 1, 2017, says the year began with a hike. There it is, in my blue-ink scrawl: 11:00 a.m. hike. I have no recollection of where I hiked—undoubtedly one of our trails here in Middle Tennessee—with whom, how long, how far, or what the weather was, but it makes me happy now to see this is how I started what was to be my final year on the Appalachian Trail.

Through the dreary months of late winter and then through the green months of early spring, I thought of the Trail ahead. There was not much to do really in terms of preparation; I had the gear, the maps, the time. All I lacked was confidence and guts. *Just do it*, I thought, *or don't*.

Four hundred rugged, dangerous miles awaited me in New England, and the weather window was small for New Hampshire and Maine. Finally, I made a definite plan: I would spend most of June on the Trail, come home for the month of July, and then return to make the final push in August. It was not inevitable that I would finish the Trail. But it was inevitable that I would try.

* * *

On June 1, I flew into Portland, Maine, and took a bus to North Woodstock, New Hampshire. I intended to hike solo two hundred miles from Kinsman Notch to Stratton, Maine, in twenty-five days. An average of just eight miles a day, this seemed a simple, straight-forward strategy. In reality, these miles would reduce me to a ragged winter bone from which all the marrow had been sucked until even the hungriest dog would disdain it.

Per arrangement, Anne, a friendly woman in her early fifties who was proprietress of the Autumn Breeze Motor Lodge, picked me up at the gas station that serves as North Woodstock's bus station. She showed me to a clean, comfortable room, where I obsessively pored over AWOL and refined my itinerary.

Early the next morning, Anne drove me thirty miles in her little four-wheel-drive car to the trailhead at Kinsman Notch.

"I've lived in a lot of places," she said in answer to my questions.

"Different states, Texas, Louisiana. But I just moved here from Florida. Always wanted to own a bed-and-breakfast—a little inn—in Vermont or New Hampshire. I found this little hotel for sale and decided to give it a go while I still have a few years left in me. The deal clincher was that I could live in it, have a little apartment on-site."

"It's just charming," I said and meant it.

"Yeah, it really is going well. In the summer, I get hikers. In the winter, skiers. I think offering the shuttle drives and free laundry helps."

I nodded again. "I can't speak for the skiers, but it will certainly attract the hikers. We're a stingy lot."

As we pulled into the trailhead parking area at Kinsman Notch, I said, "Okay, Anne. My plan is to hike north for a couple of days. Can you pick me up late afternoon or early evening on Saturday? Franconia Notch, where the AT crosses Highway 3?"

"Oh, sure. Just call when you get there. You should have cell service."

"Awesome." I thanked her and strapped on my pack.

"Oh, but try to call before six," Anne added from the open car window as she pulled out of the parking lot. "That's when my cocktail hour starts!"

Not a bad gig for our Anne, I thought as I stepped onto the AT this cool and pleasant day. You gotta applaud a gal who has a dream and follows up on it.

✳ ✳ ✳

A quick, steep ascent from the Notch began my eight-mile hike to Eliza Brook Shelter. The weather remained temperate as I walked down to Gordon Pond and then back up through woods of beech and evergreen to the peak of Mount Wolf. My pace was slow on the rocky trail, but I had planned these low-mileage days in a nod to my senior status.

The relative ease of Day One with its mild weather and moderate challenge became a distant memory on Day Two. I needed to reach Franconia Notch some nine miles north before Anne's cocktail hour pulled her away from her driving duties.

I started out in a chilly rain with a couple of friendly, middle-aged thru-hikers who had also slept at the shelter. At first, the Trail isn't too difficult, as it follows Eliza Brook and crosses Harrington Pond, but then it gains altitude, and as luck would have it, the rain turned to sleet. The other hikers pulled away from me as my steps grew slow and unsteady. An extremely strenuous climb over pitch after pitch of slippery granite boulders took me to the summit of South Kinsman Mountain at 4,500 feet. The mist obscured any distant views, and my world was limited to the rock cairns positioned among the gnarled alpine bushes on the tundra.

I could have been a lonely, wounded reindeer searching for her herd.

A rocky, steep descent of a couple hundred feet offered no respite. The AT, in her perversity, climbs again to the summit of North Kinsman Mountain. *Jesus Christ, one Kinsman wasn't enough?*

I picked my way down from the mountains, heading to Franconia Notch. Lonesome Lake Hut is about three miles shy of the Notch, and I stopped, shaken and bruised, for a short rest.

The hut system of New Hampshire, maintained by the Appalachian Mountain Club (AMC) and not to be confused with the Appalachian Trail Conservancy (ATC), consists of eight separate facilities scattered throughout the White Mountains. Lonesome Lake Hut—really a system of wooden buildings complete with bunkrooms, dining room, and bathrooms—is the first of the AMC hut system that a northbound AT hiker will encounter. It is a marvel of engineering ingenuity and a tribute to the hardy souls who built it in 1876 and to those who now maintain it.

None of the huts have electricity, central heat, or running water, but they do boast compost toilets. Extremely remote, none are anywhere near a road but can be accessed by a variety of trails, including the AT. Each hut is unique in size and style. The sleeping accommodations consist of bunk rooms either inside the main building or in small outbuildings.

Staffers—known as the "Croo"—cook and serve two meals a day, family style. Every item necessary for daily operations is brought in on the backs of Croo members. Laden with wooden crates fastened to archaic wooden packs, these (usually young) men and women almost unbelievably walk miles up and down the mountains to reach a supply station and then return. They are like human-sized, indefatigable ants.

The huts are beautiful and the food delicious, but they are pricey. Reservations are required and usually must be made well in advance. The clientele seems to consist primarily of hiking clubs and Scout groups. (But don't misunderstand: these folks are no wimps. To hike the trails into any of these hut sites requires stamina and skill.) It is easy to differentiate these folks from the few scruffy AT thru-hikers who come through and who sometimes, depending on the Croo boss and floor-space availability, are allowed to stay for the night in exchange for a few hours of work. The former are hale and hearty, well and expensively dressed, cheerful and talkative. The latter are wan and haggard, clothing worn and tattered, vacant-eyed and taciturn. As a section hiker, I suppose I was somewhere in between.

I continued making my way toward the Notch, rock-hopping across streams and sloshing through muddy quagmires, interrupted by slick, tricky boulder scrambles. The difficulty of this day was mitigated only by the knowledge I would be out of the elements by nightfall. My note scratched in the margins of my AWOL guide simply reads, "hard." I reached the road crossing with only minutes to spare before Anne's cocktail hour began.

❋ ❋ ❋

An overnight retreat at the Autumn Breeze provided some relief from the difficulty of this long hike and the miseries of the wet weather. Anne washed my dirty clothes, and I dried out my wet gear. A trip to the convenience store was my last opportunity to replenish my food bag and first aid kit. I would not again see a hotel or a town for some time, and it would be eight days before I next combed my hair.

Anne dropped me off at Franconia Notch in the early afternoon, and we said our final farewells. The temperature had risen dramatically from the previous day, and I was simply hot as I climbed the three miles to Liberty Springs Campsite, an ascent of over two thousand feet. This is a stunningly beautiful hike, where gorges and cascades border the slick, steep trail, and the surrounding hemlocks reach dizzying heights. On this warm, sunny day, many lightly burdened hikers had walked in from various side trails that radiate through Franconia State Park. They scampered and chattered through the woods like Patagonia-clothed squirrels.

I pitched my tent among several others at the campsite. The night brought falling temperatures to the mountains and anxiety to my soul. Tomorrow would bring Franconia Ridge and the start of the forbidding Presidential Range of the White Mountains.

It also brought hail. I woke up to icy marbles dancing on my little tent. *Dear lord, what next? A hurricane?* Well, yeah, maybe.

The hail turned to sleet as I climbed Little Haystack Mountain. The steep, rocky trail emerges from the woods near the summit and turns into what is essentially a knife edge above tree line for the next two miles. I picked my way along the alpine path from cairn to cairn in the sleety, swirling mist. A few other northbound hikers passed me quickly, their bodies bent into the fierce wind. Less than a mile north of Haystack, I reached the summit of Mount Lincoln at 5,100 feet, scared and miserable. I knew what was coming next.

* * *

Mount Lafayette peaks at over 5,200 feet and, like its brothers, Mount Washington and Mount Madison, is famous for wind speeds of well over a hundred miles an hour. All AT hikers are aware of the extreme danger here, but I had a more personal reason why the words *Mount Lafayette* churned the pit of my stomach to sicken me with dread.

On the evening of August 22, 2016, Peanut had tried to reach me several times, but the call kept dropping. I knew she was in the New Hampshire section of her thru-hike, but at that time, I had no reference point for the sheer brutality of the Whites. Finally, we made a connection.

"Mom, can you hear me?"

Peanut's voice was shaky. Even though she was speaking loudly, her words were almost drowned by howls and roars.

"Are you okay? Yes, I can hear you, but hardly. What's going on?"

"We're stuck on Lafayette. We can't get back to tree line; the wind's too strong. Afraid we're gonna get blown off the mountain." I could hear, in the background, a man's voice telling someone to "Stay down, stay down."

I tried to stay calm and speak deliberately. "Okay, who are you with? You must stay together."

"We set up my tent, me and Wolverine and Flash and Rumblejunk. We just set it up right here on the Trail, and all four of us are in it. But we're all really scared."

"Sounds like you did the right thing. The weight of all four of you should keep you safe. Don't go outside the tent, not even to pee. You have to stay connected."

"I love you. I need to get off the phone. Will call when we get off the mountain."

"I love you too. You'll be okay. Stay together. Stay there as long as you need to. Call me as soon as you can."

Tim and I spent the wee hours before dawn tossing and turning fitfully. Each of us occasionally reached out to check our phones to see if we had missed a call or text. Finally, just as the very beginning of daylight seeped through the bedroom window, my phone rang.

"Mom?"

Just from the sound of her voice—calmer, happier—I knew the danger had passed. I turned to Tim, smiled, and nodded.

He slumped back onto the pillow, pulled the covers up to his chin, and turned over on his side to face the wall away from the window, muttering, "That girl is going to give me a heart attack yet."

The wind had calmed. Peanut and her friends were moving on. They later learned the winds on Mount Lafayette on that date had been clocked at 110 miles per hour—one mile per hour below those of a Category 3 hurricane.

❊ ❊ ❊

This terrifying episode hung in my mind as I made my own ascent of Mount Lafayette and the winds picked up. *I must keep going, I must keep going*, was my refrain each time I staggered. The Trail here consists of pointed, craggy rocks studded with twisted, prickly bushes. On either side of the path, the mountain slides away under more of these rocks until even the bushes are eradicated. There is nothing in the surrounding landscape to indicate that you are anywhere but in a lonely forbidden slice of earth never intended to support human (or, for that matter, any) life form. I simply could not see any possible place to pitch a tent. How Peanut and her friends had managed it was beyond my comprehension.

My stomach lurched as a gust of wind snatched my pack cover and lifted it into the air, keeping it aloft like a dancing kite several feet above my head until it disappeared into the clouds. The thought of littering upset me, but I dared not take my eyes off the trail ahead to see if a rock or scraggly bush might have caught the pack cover.

An hour of agony passed until finally I dropped below tree line again. This brought almost no relief from the wind but did offer some reassurance that at least I would not be blown off the knife-edge ridge. My fear now, as I began the four-mile descent to Garfield Ridge Shelter, was that a falling tree would kill me. Beech and birch and pine, some ten to twelve inches in diameter, were in danger of being sucked up by their roots like boots being pulled from quicksand. The trunks rose and fell with the gusts, and I walked as quickly as possible, low branches whipping my face and tearing at my clothes.

I reached the shelter just before dark, chilled to the bone. More alarmingly, my gear was also wet because of the loss of the pack cover. I simply could not stop shivering as I huddled in my sleeping bag with a toboggan pulled low over my ears. My teeth chattered loudly. I kept apologizing to my shelter mate, Bobby, a young man who was in the Whites for a few days testing his gear for an upcoming European hike.

This was the closest I have ever come to hypothermia. Fortunately, I had borrowed Peanut's sleeping bag liner, which offered another layer of protection, but I still shivered violently until finally, deep in the night, I managed to fall asleep.

Bobby woke me apologetically at dawn.

"Hey, Sticks," he softly called. I opened my eyes to see him, pack strapped on and poles in hand, framed in the shelter opening, another gray day around him. "Sorry to wake you."

"No problem," I said as I slowly sat up, keeping my sleeping bag wrapped around my shoulders.

"I'm pushing on south; just wanted to make sure you're okay."

"Okay, thanks. Good luck on Lafayette. I'm fine."

I'm not sure he was convinced; I know I wasn't.

* * *

The clouds had not dissipated nor the temperatures risen during the night. Rain continued intermittently. The wind was unrelenting, whipping through the treetops as if it were riding a wild bull. I stumbled down the three miles to the Galehead Hut, which held the promise of, if not warmth, at least a dry interlude.

I had had the foresight to become a member of the AMC, which entitled me to discounts at the huts. Luckily, the Galehead Hut has a small inventory of basic hiking supplies for sale, so I was able to replace my pack rain cover. My membership also provided some coupons for soups and treats. Otherwise, the hut caretakers are reluctant to provide food to thru-hikers; supplies are strictly for the paying guests.

As I sat there enjoying a warm bowl of spicy bean soup with one or two others in the small dining room, a tall young man burst in. He looked like the dude from *The Revenant*. Wild-eyed, his hair matted and beard icy, a bear might have been at his heels. He staggered against the table, then sank into a chair.

"I almost died. I seriously almost died," he said after catching his breath.

"Did you do Lafayette today?"

He nodded and shook his head as if to clear his mind of the memory.

"I did it yesterday. Probably even windier today," I commiserated.

We compared notes about our brushes with mortality and then fell silent. I finished my soup, wished all present well, and walked back out into New Hampshire, where—I was learning—the maxim that everyone talks about the weather but nobody does a thing about it is absolutely true.

* * *

The evening brought relative comfort at Guyot Shelter, and then Day Five ended up being a short one. I only hiked four miles, but this included the strenuous climb up Mount Guyot. I had intended to hike nine miles to the Ethan Pond campsite, but I quickly set aside that notion when I arrived at the Zealand Falls Hut. The day had warmed up, and now Croo members and guests lazed about on the rocks in the falls like sea lions on the piers in San Francisco. I was quite happy to take off my pack and rest on the porch.

The caretaker offered sleeping space on the floor in exchange for clearing dishes and sweeping up after the evening meal. *Sure.* Whatever pride I once had was now long gone, swept away by the gales of Mount Lafayette.

The next day was a fourteen-miler. It started out easy enough, several miles along ridgeline below three thousand feet before dropping even farther to Ethan Pond at 1,200 feet. But along with the elevation, the pleasant temperatures from the previous day fell precipitously, and the winds again picked up.

I climbed the Webster Cliffs on steep switchbacks that travel through hardwood forest before giving way to twists and turns through tall evergreens. I scrambled over rocky ledges and followed cairns to the summit at four thousand feet, where clouds once again closed over to obscure the views. The afternoon brought a scary little descent on slippery rocks, followed by a steep climb up Mount Jackson. The Trail then dips a bit and goes through a muddy marsh until it finally spit me out, like a chewed-up tasteless wad of tobacco, at my destination for the evening, the Nauman Tent Site at Mizpah Spring Hut. My body, stooped and small under the heavy pack, had been battered all this day by the howling winds. I felt as achy and tender as if I had been pelted by stones. There was no inch of skin or spirit which was not bruised.

It was nearly dark as I set up my tent after paying my discount rate of five bucks to the caretaker. I was the sole camper on this lonely, wooded piece of land a few hundred feet from the hut itself. I made a cup of tea in my camp stove and looked out at the dripping trees from my little platform, dreaming of Gorham, New Hampshire, my next town stop. Prior to this adventure, I had never heard of Gorham, but now, to my mind, it had taken on the qualities of Mecca.

Only twenty Trail miles lay between me and Gorham. Unfortunately, a line of sentinels named after long-dead statesmen stretched along the path. Pierce, Franklin, Monroe, Washington, Jefferson, and Madison waited stern and unsmiling, their pates snow-patched like bad comb-overs at this time of year. I feared they would not be kind.

All night the wind roared in the trees surrounding my desolate campsite. When I peered out the tent flap into the dismal gray morning, I thought, *Abandon hope, all ye who enter here.* With its cold, miserable rain, this day was simply not fit for human consumption.

Nevertheless, one does have to pee. I forced myself to rise, donned rain gear, and stepped into the bleak landscape.

I found the day's forecast for Mount Washington and surrounding peaks handwritten on a sheet of paper that had been slipped into a plastic sleeve and tacked to a tall hemlock. As I was peering at it, letting the phrase "100 mph winds" register in my befuddled mind, the very young camp caretaker passed by.

"Excuse me," I said. "I don't have my glasses. Does this say one hundred miles per hour?"

She glanced at the sign. "Yeah, not good," she said with a rueful headshake.

"Does this mean I shouldn't try?"

The woman—really just a girl—answered, "We're not supposed to give advice, you know. We just post the signs." She paused for a second. "But I wouldn't do it."

Well, that was enough advice for me. I thanked her and turned to walk the couple hundred yards to the hut.

"On the other hand," the girl called after me, "it could be worse tomorrow."

The Mizpah Spring Hut is a typical, eco-friendly AMC structure, its unique feature being a well-stocked library. Don't envision a baronial, wainscoted den with a railed ladder. A few shelves along the kitchen wall hold well-used volumes of local history, adventure stories, and geographical treatises.

The book I chose to keep me company as I huddled in my tent like a woodchuck had a no-frills title, something like *A Documentation of All Deaths Ever Recorded on Mount Washington*. In hindsight, probably not a wise choice.

This charming tome provides an account of all the deaths that have occurred on Mount Washington since recreational hiking in the White Mountains began in the mid-1800s. We can probably assume the indigenous people here may have lost a brother or two to the extreme weather also, but I think, by and large, they had the good sense to stay in the valleys and leave the mountaintops to the gods.

Anyway, I learned that since the early nineteenth century, 150 people have died on Mount Washington. Sprinkle in another couple of dozen who have succumbed on neighboring peaks, and we're closing in on two hundred lost souls. To provide some context, approximately three hundred people have died on Everest in the same time frame. To be fair, far fewer people attempt to climb Everest, so the fatality *rate* there is much higher. This knowledge gave me no comfort at all.

* * *

Finally, finally, I woke to a day of relatively decent weather. Not sparkling sunshine and a gentle breeze—it was still cold and gray. But the wind had died down, and the temperature had risen to the high forties. Our weather forecast, again delivered in the form of a handwritten note on the hemlock tree, called for only sixty- to seventy-mile-per-hour winds at the Mount Washington summit. This news cheered me, and the day of rest had partially restored me. Gorham awaited.

The first ascent was of Mount Pierce, which I tackled with a fairly steady pace and some semblance of adequacy; at least I wasn't keening like a banshee to warn of impending death. From the Pierce summit, I warily eyed Mount Washington to the north, the clouds parting occasionally to reveal the snow patches and distant weather station.

The Trail skirts Mount Eisenhower and then summits Mount Franklin, rising above tree line at times. This is a pleasant hike if you're lucky enough to have calm winds and no precipitation. I trod carefully, avoiding the pretty, delicate alpine flowers, as instructed by the AMC. It takes everything this flora has to survive the cold temperatures, the harsh winds, the arid soil. They don't need some big old boot or pointy trekking pole coming down on their fragile leaves and blooms.

I reached the Lake of the Clouds Hut, situated just below the Mount Washington peak, before lunchtime. This is the most popular of the AMC Huts, and at the time of my visit, it was a bustling and cheerful place.

"Hey, Sticks," someone called out to me from a corner of the large dining room. I settled in next to a group of hikers I'd crossed paths with over the last several days to exchange tales of our adventures.

"You staying here tonight?" one asked. "It's early, but this is such a nice place, and they let you sleep for free in the dungeon." (I knew from my guidebooks that this simply referred to the basement and did not infer any torture would be dispensed. One could simply walk north a hundred yards to find that.)

"No, I want to summit Washington by this afternoon and then hike down to Madison Spring Hut."

After a few more minutes of chitchat, a couple of the hikers accompanied me outside. As I walked away, I turned around several times to wave goodbye. My bright-yellow, puffy jacket would be easy to spot as I climbed slowly but steadily up the whitish-gray granite rocks that give these mountains their name.

I picked my way, one step and one stone at a time, to the summit. The climb was not quite as difficult as I had expected, due to the (relatively) calm winds and my extreme caution. But also because by now, my expectations of what the Whites could hold was somewhere just short of Armageddon. My gingerly careful pace brought me safely to the doors of the visitor center at Mount Washington summit. I paused to enviously watch passengers disembarking from the cheerful little passenger train. A pleasant park ranger stopped to chat with me and, learning of my plan, kindly advised me to get moving.

"Temperatures are dropping," he said. "And winds are rising."

In New Hampshire, there are forty-eight summits of over four thousand feet, and a hiker who attempts to claim the honor of reaching all of those is called a peak bagger. It is a daunting challenge and, like the challenge of the AT, can be done all in one season or spread out over the years.

The tallest peak is Mount Washington at just under 6,300 feet. The weather station perched on the summit once documented the strongest winds ever recorded on Earth—over 230 miles per hour. The visitor center / café / gift shop / ranger station can be reached (aside from the hiking trails) via cog railroad or a winding, paved road motorway. The day tourists spill out of the visitor center to walk twenty or thirty yards to the designated high point marked by a pole emblazoned with the AT symbol. Dressed in T-shirts and shorts appropriate to the weather in the valley below, they shiver and shriek in the cold and wind.

Those who do not venture into the chilly outdoors browse in the crowded lobby of the center. They gaze at the oversize maps on the wall to read the alarming statistics of Mount Washington, no doubt wondering about the sanity of any person choosing to be out in these elements (or as I overheard more than once: "Man, they're fucking crazy.")

The five miles from the 6,300-foot summit of Mount Washington to the Madison Springs Hut at 5,100 feet are sheer, rocky hell that include a traverse of Mount Jefferson. For the entire last mile, as I hesitantly sidestepped down the uneven and unsteady granite stairway still above tree line, I could see the tiny hut far below. My focus zeroed in on my carefully placed footsteps, and I forced myself to ignore the ragged and rugged surrounding landscape that seemed to encompass the universe itself. *All I have to do is take this step and then this one and now this one. The hut will eventually rise to meet me.*

Several hours of this descent, and just before dark, I made it to the front porch, rocks leading right up to the heavy wooden door where a Croo member quickly appeared.

She greeted me with, "We've been watching you come down the mountain. We didn't know if you were hurt or just slow."

Ouch. "I guess I'm just slow." I paused for effect and then said, "But I made it."

I did not want to sleep on the floor. I did not want to sweep up and clean up and be pitied as a second-class citizen. But the Croo told me there was no tent camping (in spite of what guidebooks advised), and the bunkhouse rooms were reserved. I felt as insignificant as a mote of dust and that my absence in this world of haughty grandeur and severe austerity would not be missed and in fact would probably be welcomed. Like a whipped dog licking her wounds, I retreated (literally) under a table and spent an uncomfortable, sleepless night in my stinking sleeping bag surrounded by exhausted, snoring thru-hikers. The next morning, per the instructions of the Croo, my fellow outcasts and I rose early and got out of the way for the paying guests to have their morning meal.

The hut was surrounded by a cold, swirling mist, and winds on the summits were expected to be as high as ninety-plus miles per hour. To me, this seemed like a fairly ominous forecast, but no one else seemed to be particularly bothered. Hikers began heading out to seek various trails. One energetic group was training for an upcoming trip to Kilimanjaro. Others were heading south to Mount Washington. Some, like me, were planning to summit Mount Madison and continue north on the AT. I layered on clothes, strapped on my pack, and walked out into a landscape of sleety forlornness, the other hikers melting away almost immediately into the fog.

Eight miles of extremely rugged terrain—much of it above tree line and in no way sheltered from the weather—lay ahead before the Trail would reach a road crossing. By the time I had gone no more than a half mile or so from the hut, I was on my hands and knees. The summit, which I could not even see due to the icy sleet the ferocious wind pelted into my eyes, was less than a mile away. I crawled from cairn to cairn, aware that to stray off the Trail would mean disaster. When I dared to glance down at the plummeting slopes on either side, the nausea of vertigo threatened to overtake whatever shred was left of courage. It was impossible for me to stand on my feet. The few times I attempted, the horizontal gale staggered me and knocked me back to the rocky ground. Other hikers—amazingly upright but always unsteady—occasionally materialized out of the mist.

"Are you okay?" Their lips formed the words that were lost to the winds.

I nodded time after time, crawling another inch, up and then up, another foot over pile after pile of rocks, and thought of T.S. Eliot: *I should have been a pair of ragged claws scuttling across the floors of silent seas.*

A group of three or four young men, peak baggers whom I'd met the day before on Mount Washington, staggered toward me. I had christened them Team Gary—peak baggers apparently don't have Trail names.

"Sticks, can we help?" Gary screamed against the gale.

I shook my head as I lay on the ground holding onto a football-size piece of granite, and Team Gary moved on. For an instant, I regretted letting them go.

What am I doing here? I am no Sacagawea, no Ernest Shackleford, no Conrad fucking Anker. I am a hiker, not a mountain climber. I am retired. I don't even have to be here. I had a very clear vision of myself curled up on my living room couch, reading a good book, cup of hot chocolate at hand. This desire was so visceral, so intense, that I wondered if I was hallucinating.

I really, *really* wanted to be off that mountain. There were only two ways to achieve that. I could get my ass moving on my own steam, or they could carry my dead body down. While I was considering the latter, prone and terrified, the wind seeming to blow even more fiercely by the second, something caught my watery, half-blinded eye.

A small black item, wedged between two coffee-table-size rocks about six feet off the Trail, winked at me. My mind required a few minutes to register what my eyes, through the cobweb of frozen droplets on my lashes, were seeing. Unbelievably, it was my watch! I had not even noticed it wasn't on my wrist. The gale had simply stripped it from my arm and flung it against the mountain like a jilted bridegroom flinging his beloved's ring at the altar.

I considered just leaving it. Retrieving it would require crawling an extra twelve feet, round trip. *No,* I decided. *It is a sign.* Tim had given me this watch during my early years of hiking, and it had been with me almost every step of the AT. I never wore it except while hiking, and I kept it set on Eastern Time.

Yes. I would retrieve it, put it safely in my pack, and move on. I would surely die someday, but it would not be this day. And it would not be on this fucking mountain.

* * *

Two miserable hours later, I made it to tree line. From that point and for the following six hours, I plunged through lonely forestland, not stopping to eat or rest. The black ribbon of NH 16—the road to Gorham—finally appeared just as the mountains began to blot out what little sun the day had held. It had taken me thirteen hours to travel eight miles.

Gorham is ten miles west of where the AT crosses the highway. I put on my headlamp and started walking on the blacktop. Car after car passed without stopping, and my feet began to ache from the hard surface under my worn-out boots. I was close to tears when a dirty Subaru pulled over, driven by a young man who introduced himself as Mash. He was soft-spoken as he told me he was a former thru-hiker, class of 2015. He knew these mountains, and there was no need for questions, for exclamation, for drama.

"Mash, just take me to any hotel in Gorham," I said. "I'm done. I'm just…done."

"Yeah," he said softly. "These Whites will take it out of you. But there's a good hiker hostel, cheap, right in town."

I shook my head. It was well after dark, probably nine o'clock or so, and I didn't want to disturb the hikers or the landlords. Also—and you will rarely hear these words from me—I really needed a phone and a TV.

We approached the lights of Gorham. The golden arches of McDonald's shone brightly next to a strip motel with a VA_AN_Y sign intermittently blinking red. Mash pulled into the parking lot and insisted on carrying my dirty pack into the dim lobby before bidding me farewell.

A large, loud woman dressed in tight black stretch pants, knock-off Ugg boots, and—incongruously—a bright-red tube top was near hysteria as she talked to the clerk at the registration counter. I stood patiently in a corner.

"Lord have mercy!" she shrieked. "I liked to have just hit a moose! Damn road was icy—in June!—and I like to slid plumb off the road."

The brown-skinned, black-haired man behind the counter did

not seem impressed. The woman turned to me and did an almost comically classic double take.

"Girl, what happened to you? You okay?"

I nodded. Not having seen a mirror in eight days, I had no idea of the picture I presented.

"Well, I don't know where you from," she continued, "but I'm from Florida. Now sometimes a dog or cat or maybe an armadillo might run across the road—but a *moose*!" The woman shook her head. "Mm, mm, mm. I like to died."

The clerk pushed a room key across the counter. Snatching it up, the woman went on, "I just drove twenty hours up here to see my fiancé over at the penitentiary."

She paused for a breath and looked at me again. "What are you doing here?" she asked, as if no one would ever visit this town or state unless there was an extremely pressing reason, such as visiting an incarcerated loved one.

I managed one word. "Hiking."

"Mm, mm, mm," she muttered again. "Everybody done gone crazy."

* * *

My room at this hotel was, in a word, yucky—and I think by this time, we can all agree my standards are hardly exacting. After more than a week in the bracing air of the mountains, the smell of stale cigarettes and old sex made me feel slightly nauseous.

Still, I needed to eat. I was seriously calorie-deprived and probably dehydrated. Even more important, I needed to call my family.

While my phone was charging, I walked over to McDonald's (the only game in town at this hour) and bought a to-go hamburger and fries. I got rid of the meat, which left me with a surprisingly tasty sandwich of ketchup, mustard, and pickles. Careful to not let the food touch any surface of the hotel room, I flipped through the TV channels until I found the Nashville Predators–Pittsburgh Penguins National Hockey League playoff game.

Text after text had come from Tim and Peanut: *Are you okay? Call when you can. Where are you?*

I texted back with greasy, salty fingers. *I'm fine. In Gorham. I know you're at game. Enjoy. Will call later.*

The puck slapped back and forth as I watched in silence. The fans roared; the whistle blew. When the camera panned the arena, I searched the crowd for the faces of my loved ones. The final moments ticked down. The Predators' chance for a Stanley Cup slipped away.

You have fought the good fight, I thought. *Now rest.*

* * *

Next morning the unfamiliar sight and feel of sunshine through a crack in the heavy, dust-laden drapes woke me. A careful inventory of my body revealed no major damage or unsurmountable incapacities. Week-old scabs from scrapes on shins and forearms now had an overlay of fresh red cuts. Old, greenish bruises were fading under new purple ones across my hips and shoulders. Ugly, broken toenails capped swollen feet crisscrossed with peeling strips of dirty moleskin. The water pooled at my feet in the shower ran rusty brown from mud and blood.

The first order of business was to check out of the Ritz Gorham and find more pleasant accommodations. I had no intention of hiking this day and every intention of savoring this respite in a comfortable space.

I wandered into the street that is Gorham. Helmetless motorcyclists on huge Harleys rumbled past on their way to the road that leads to Mount Washington. The manic-depressive weather of New Hampshire now produced a hot and humid day, and exhaust from the bikes and cars hung above the asphalt. I found the city smell of gasoline and oil strangely comforting.

Just across the street from the motel stood a few tired businesses—an auto parts store, a junk shop, a laundromat. *Aha!* That would be my first errand of the day.

I lugged my heavy, battered pack into a small room with a linoleum-covered floor and drop-tiled ceiling. It smelled cleanly of laundry detergent and dryer sheets. An extremely thin young man with multiple facial piercings was loading a washing machine. He barely glanced at me. Curiously, he wore a bag—like a small purse or fanny pack—in the shape of a monkey strapped around his waist so that it hung at crotch area.

Could things get any weirder, I thought and then shrugged. Who was I to judge the fashion choices of the residents of Coos County? An alien could have walked in, and I would have simply nodded, so emptied was I of curiosity and energy.

I set about unloading my pack, throwing away the trash from my food bag, and removing the dirty clothes—a few pairs of thick socks and thin liners, two pairs of base leggings, some panties, a bandana or two, one long-sleeved shirt, two short-sleeved shirts, two pairs of nylon shorts, and one pair of outer pants. There was also a down vest, a rain jacket, and my puffy coat.

All of this could easily go into one load, but I also wanted to wash the shorts, athletic bra, and cotton T-shirt I had on. However, it would hardly do to stand around naked in the Gorham laundromat, even though it was entirely possible I wouldn't be the first person to do that.

This establishment had no restroom or broom closet or other such private place where I might strip down. I chose the puffy coat and the cleanest pair of dirty shorts for my ensemble and then addressed Mr. Monkey Crotch.

"Uh, excuse me?"

The young man, slouching against a sloshing washing machine, looked up from his cell phone.

"Yeah, hey. I've been hiking, and I need to wash these clothes I'm wearing."

He looked at me, waiting for further explanation.

"So…I need to change real quick, but there's really no place to do that here. I was wondering if you could maybe turn your back for a second." I snickered a bit just to let him know I recognized the absurdity of the situation. His eyes widened, and then he quickly turned away to face a back wall.

I hurriedly took off shirt and bra and donned the jacket. Then off with the shorts and on with the slightly cleaner pair. This costume change took a matter of seconds.

"Okay," I called out. "All set here. Thank you."

* * *

With my pack orderly and filled with fresh, clean clothes, I ventured back onto the street and into the hot day. I headed east toward another clump of buildings and found a post office, an outfitter, and a convenience store—all three necessary for the day's agenda.

At the post office, I mailed Peanut's stove home. I had only used it a couple of times and didn't want to haul around fuel and mess with cooking. I mailed some postcards. To Tim and Peanut: *I'm fine, having a blast, miss you, see you soon.* To Jen and She Who Falls a Lot: *These Whites are terrifying, I'm scared to death, don't tell Tim and Peanut.*

At the outfitter, I bought a pair of replacement hiking boots. One of mine had blown out on the Presidential rocks. My old boots had served me well for hundreds of miles and several years, and I threw them in the trash with no regrets. The new boots were comfortable, lightweight, and on sale. I left the outfitters with a smug feeling of accomplishment.

Next stop: convenience store. The next leg of this journey would last about three days, and that requires a lot of junk food. Chips, crackers, candy bars, Pop-Tarts, dry cereal. My food bag looked as if a seven-year-old packed it.

At the margin of this business district but still on the main road was the Libby Bed and Breakfast, a New England saltbox dressed up as one of San Francisco's Painted Ladies. Pastel hues of purple, lilac, and lavender colored the latticework and porch railings. Attached to the aspiring Victorian structure was a one-story addition that serves as a more humble hostel for the redheaded stepchildren, the hikers.

The Libby B&B, I learned, was operated by two burly and surprisingly urbane men—cousins, I believe. The younger of the two detached himself from a small group of ragged thru-hikers as I entered the kitchen/lobby/sitting room of the hostel.

"Welcome, welcome," he said, introducing himself as Johnny. "You needing a place to stay? We got cots out here or rooms in the house."

"Yes, definitely a room if you got one to spare. Single. And a bathroom?"

Outside and around the porch to the main entrance, we stepped into a Victorian parlor and back in time a hundred years. Soft, faded Oriental rugs blanketed worn oak-plank floors. Snow-white doilies peeked from beneath fluted lamps perched on cherrywood tables. A horsehair sofa covered with needlepoint pillows sagged invitingly in a corner. Black-and-white portraits of stern, unsmiling ancestors peered at us from the rose print–papered walls.

I followed Johnny up a flight of stairs, where carefully framed newspaper articles depicted a younger Johnny in various starring roles of a local theater company.

"I can give you this room here for forty dollars," he said, using an old-fashioned skeleton key to open a heavy, solid wood door. "The bathroom is down the hall, but I think you'll have it to yourself tonight."

The room's decor echoed that of downstairs, except it included a four-poster, lace-canopied bed piled with gleaming white pillows. I thought of my evening accommodations for the past eight days.

"I'll take it."

* * *

This was already my second zero day of the trip, and I had only hiked a total of seventy miles in ten days. Moreover, the miles ahead would not be easy. Clearly, my goal of Stratton, Maine, was unattainable, and I adjusted my sights for Andover, seventy-five miles over the mountains and through the woods.

Johnny and company provided rides to the trailhead, so on the morning of June 13, I scrunched into his vintage Buick with several other hikers. My plan was to hike three days, spending two nights on the Trail, and then return to Gorham for another night of luxury at chez Libby.

At town level, the day was warm—even hot—and I started my hike in shorts, to the delight of the mosquito hordes. I ambled along for a mile on flat, marshy trail bordering Lost Pond. The mosquitoes gave way to cooling winds as I climbed two thousand feet to scramble across the peaks of Wildcat Mountain. These peaks are unimaginatively named, from south to north, Peak E, Peak D, Peak C, Peak B, and Peak A.

Hikers, myself included, have been known to quite literally shudder when speaking of the Presidential Range of the White Mountains. However, it is my humble opinion that Wildcat is just as treacherous, just as heart-stopping, as the more southern sentinels. But because of its lower altitude—four thousand feet to Washington's six thousand–plus—the wind is not as ferocious. Hiking the Whites is all about the weather. Had I climbed Wildcat on an inclement day, I would have felt every bit as defeated as I had on Madison. As it was, my stomach lurched each time the wind picked up or I felt a sudden gust.

Steep jumbles of stone protect dark caves and lairs where the ice of October still lives even in June. The Trail cuts through the mountain as if hacked out by a dull chainsaw. "Hike" is a misnomer. I crawled and scrambled and scooched.

Finally, after six miles and with the day already almost gone, I reached the spur trail to Carter Notch Hut. I had intended to go a few more miles and camp on the Trail, but there you have it: I was old and slow.

The one-hundred-year-old Carter Notch Hut, only a tenth of a mile off the Trail, is a small stone building nestled in the woods.

"We have no room on the floor," the smiley Croo member told me. "My boss only lets a couple of thru-hikers stay each night because our hut is so small."

"Can I camp?"

Again, no.

"Is there a bunk? I can pay. I have an AMC card."

"Oh, yeah, sure. Plenty of bunks left."

Eighty bucks later, I was standing in a tiny, four-bed wooden box in a bunkhouse separate from the main hut. It was immaculately clean and unoccupied. I undressed and crawled under the heavy blanket, the soft pillow beneath my head. I had borrowed a British cozy mystery from Libby's meager library, and now, headlamp on, I happily anticipated the comforting images of hearth fires, tea services, and gentlemanly white-haired inspectors.

Oh, dear. I soon discovered the book was missing the first thirty pages. No matter. I caught onto the plot soon enough and read myself to sleep.

* * *

From Carter Notch Hut to my next destination, Imp campsite, was only seven miles, and it was gorgeous. This was rugged, wild country where one can easily expect to come across an enchanted cottage nestled in a copse and a lonely misunderstood ogre peering out from within it. Cliffs and boulders push up out of the forest floor, releasing the luscious smell of musk. Towering hardwoods link limbs high above the hiker's head to create a greenish-black sky. On this breeze-less day, the woods were still and the animals—large or small—silently let me pass without making their presence known.

The weather remained fine as I climbed out of the Notch to the 4,700-foot summit of Carter Dome, then down one hundred feet to the summit of Mount Hight. These peaks, as well as those of South Carter Mountain, Middle Carter Mountain, and North Carter Mountain, offer the hiker incredible panoramic views of the Presidentials to the west and the Mahoosuc Range of Maine to the north.

To reach each summit requires navigating cliffs and climbing steeply. These mountains are jealous of their peaks. They will hold you back and thwart your moves to keep you locked in their viny arms. But by very late afternoon, I had slowly sidestepped down the rocky staircase that is the AT descent of North Carter Mountain.

I slept in my tent, happy with the day's beauty and challenge. In the morning, I woke to rain once again. This would be, after the four-thousand-foot summit of Mount Moriah, a mostly downhill day. Seven miles would take me to US 2 and then a three-mile hitch to the beloved Libby House.

Cold rain followed me all day as I slipped and slid on the Trail alongside and through cascades, falls, bogs, and marshes. At five miles in, I waded across the Rattle River and splashed across stream after stream of its tributaries. Water was present in every conceivable incar-nation. My new boots were supposedly semiwaterproof, but they were no match for this Trail, and now, with each squelching step, I could feel the wetness seeping through my thick socks. The setting was more appropriate to an otter than a human being.

＊ ＊ ＊

Night Two at Libby's in Gorham was just as pleasant as Night One had been. I had certainly not planned on a Night Three—I already had two zero days out of fourteen total, a not-very-impressive statistic. But I woke late on the morning of the sixteenth to the rumble of thunder, and only the slightest hint of what could be called "day" filtering in through the lace curtains. Rain spit at the windows.

I. Can. Not. Do. It.

A light tapping on the door was followed by soft words. "Sticks, I've brought your breakfast tray. I'll just leave it right here."

Would it be unethical to just linger here for the next week and a half and simply tell my friends and family that I had hiked the AT? No one would ever know…

I ate the pastries and the fruit, drank the orange juice and hot coffee, and called Johnny from my cell phone. "Hey, it's Sticks. If you don't have this room booked, I want it for another night."

The long, rainy day passed in a posthike fog of *Gunsmoke* reruns, my British detective story, and delicious catnaps. By late afternoon, the skies cleared, and the urge to stretch my legs, to clear my head, to wipe the cobwebs from my mind—in short, to get out of my funk—moved me. I sat at a table in the side yard with my maps and a bottle of white wine. An occasional car passed by on the main street. Intermittent bursts of laughter from the hiker hostel cheered me. I could procrastinate no longer.

Mahoosuc Notch awaited my arrival. Only twenty-three miles stood between me and what is widely considered the most difficult mile on the entire Appalachian Trail.

But I had to get there first.

＊ ＊ ＊

Johnny took me to the trailhead at US 2 the next morning. I had a rather ambitious day of twelve miles to Gentian Pond Shelter planned. The Trail here is at relatively low altitude—one- to three-thousand feet—compared to the four- to six-thousand feet I'd faced for the previous two weeks and hundred miles. There are a couple of gradual climbs at Mount Hayes (one of our more benign presidents, at least in terms of their mountainous namesakes) and Cascade Mountain.

I hiked across several long, flat sections through the warm day, greatly bothered by mosquitoes but surprisingly unmolested by the biting black flies that are infamous in northern New Hampshire and Maine. One hiker told me that they are at their most fierce in the period between Mother's Day and Father's Day. As I was still a bit south of their primary habitat, my timing was (uncharacteristically) good.

Never going above tree line, I walked through pleasant spruce forest and hopped across several brooks. Beech trees, with their peeling white bark, line the Trail. I reached Page Pond by late afternoon and stopped for a while, hoping to see moose. I saw none, but here I began to see their droppings, which I would continue to see in almost unbelievable quantities for the next two hundred miles.

The remaining four miles to Gentian Pond Shelter took me across boggy and soggy trail to Dream Lake, which I reached just at dusk. This is a typical New England pond where dragonflies dart about like air-to-sea missiles and ducks placidly swim with their tiny, downy offspring following like well-behaved puppies. Another bit of hiker lore: dragonflies eat the black flies, so when you see these insects with their diaphanous blue wings, you know the flies are on their way out. Note to dragonflies—can you please eat the mosquitoes too?

* * *

Piper, with whom I shared the shelter on this muggy summer night, was a small, wiry man well into his sixties.

"I'm finishing up my thru-hike," he cheerfully told me as he stirred the contents of his cook pot. "Started five years ago but lost a toe and had to quit. Back before the Whites."

Lost a toe? This would be a good story.

"Yeah, I woke up one morning in a shelter, and when I stumbled out, I stubbed my big toe really bad. Broke it."

"Wow, that sucks."

"I tried to hike for a few days, but it hurt too bad. Had to go off Trail." Piper turned off his little stove. "So by that time, it was infected. Nasty. Doctors tried to save it, but it just got worse and worse."

He sat back against a rock and dipped a fork into the noodles. "They cut if off. And had to cut off a good part of the side of my foot too. Lot of rehab. You wouldn't think just one toe is so important for walking. But it is."

I reflected on his story. "You know, Piper, that's how Jack Daniels died."

He stopped, fork halfway to mouth. "The whiskey guy?"

"Yep. True story. He got frustrated when he couldn't open a safe in his office. So he kicked it. His toe got infected, and he died a few weeks later. Gangrene."

Piper shook his head. "Mercy. Well, at least I didn't die."

Yes, I'm sure we were both thinking, *things could always be worse*.

All the livelong night, I scratched. The bug repellent that I religiously apply—mostly due to fear of disease-carrying ticks—had failed me. My legs and arms were covered with irritating red welts. When I scratched the mosquito bites, blood ran freely from dislodged scabs. I felt like a mangy old flea-bitten dog. The sound of the scratching must have been very irritating to Piper as he tried to sleep. I kept apologizing.

"No worries," he said. "It could be worse."

❋ ❋ ❋

The next day was much cooler as I started my planned ten-mile hike over the Mahoosuc range to Full Goose Shelter, the last stop before the Mahoosuc Notch itself. I had done twelve miles the day before with a little time to spare, so I didn't think ten miles was an unreasonable goal.

The Trail did not agree.

My pace was ridiculously slow as I climbed the boulders, the cliffs, the slabs that make up the ascent of Mount Success. It took me five hours to hike the two-mile, 1,500-foot elevation change. Boggy intervals offer some diversity, but they are no easier to navigate. This is rugged terrain, lonely and forbidding. I saw no clean, fresh day-trippers out for a merry stroll, only a few dirty, weary thru-hikers masochistically pushing north.

At the 3,500-foot-plus summit, I had no cause for celebration. It was already after noon, and several peaks stood between me and Full Goose Shelter. *I will go as far as I can today*, I decided, *and then reassess.*

"As far as I could" turned out to be three more miles. *Pathetic.* However, there was some good news. A half mile shy of the Carlo Col Shelter, I said farewell to New Hampshire, that most befuddling of the AT states, and stepped into Maine, the fourteenth and final state of my adventure.

* * *

Rain came during the night as I tossed and turned in my little tent at Carlo Col campsite. There were only four and a half miles from here to the Full Goose Shelter, and I had all day to hike them. I tried to sleep late, to wait for the rain to clear, and to muster my inner resources for the challenge of Mahoosuc Notch.

None of these things happened. I couldn't sleep for anxiety. The rain continued to fall. Whatever resources I once could claim had been left far behind in New Hampshire.

Miserably, I broke camp and simply conceded that this would be a long, cold, wet, difficult day. Strangely, that acknowledgment motivated me. *That which doesn't kill you will make you stronger! If it was easy, everybody would do it! When the going gets tough, the tough get going!* I could say these clichéd gems to myself; if someone else had uttered them, I probably would have smacked him in the mouth.

Agonizingly slowly, I climbed the steep, rocky ledges of Mount Carlo and the peaks of Goose Eye Mountain. The steady rain made rocks slick, and the Trail itself sometimes turned into a gully. The huge slabs of lichen-covered granite that mark these hills offered no purchase for boots and poles. Afraid of my feet flying out from under me on the wet, mossy surface, I often just sat down and scooched.

I wasn't above tree line here, but in many sections, the slabs of rocks prevent the growth of tall woods. The plant life is sedge-like brush. I often came across small brown grouse nesting near the scruffy bushes that grow from the cracks in the rocks. The birds just looked at this awkward interloper with their glassy black eyes, ruffled their feathers a bit, and turned their attention back to their chicks.

The rain turned to cool mist in the afternoon. The cairns that mark the Trail over the moors and heaths add to the illusion that one has been transported in time and space from the AT of today to the England of Brontë. I kept my eyes peeled for werewolves and listened for the sound of their howling. It would not have been shocking to come across the carcass of a sheep with its throat torn and bloody. Fortunately, only a few harmless rabbits hopped across my path, their eyes bright and noses twitching, chasing prey much smaller than I.

It was nearly dark when I dipped back down into the woods and arrived at the ladder that leads to Full Goose Shelter. Yes, that's right. The shelter is perched atop a ledge, and reaching it from the Trail requires climbing a crudely built five-foot ladder. Embarrassingly, I had some trouble navigating this, burdened as I was by pack and poles. A couple of fellows behind me patiently waited their turns, but I'm sure they were thinking, *How the heck is this woman going to hike the Notch if she can't even make it up a ladder?* It was a valid question.

Several hikers had already staked their claims inside the shelter, where there was floor space for eight or ten. Wind Chimes had hung his hammock from corner to corner. I had intended to pitch my tent but was discouraged by the light drizzle and falling temperatures. I laid out my pad and bag next to a side wall of the shelter, taking as little space as possible. The night settled around me and the shivering, snoring thru-hikers. Dread of the day to come colored my dreams, and morning found me reluctant to stir.

* * *

The mile-and-a-half path from the shelter to Mahoosuc Notch is a steep descent through thick hardwood forest, and I walked every step with trepidation. Mahoosuc Notch is widely known as the most difficult mile of the Appalachian Trail. Some hikers claim it is also the most fun. This was the position my daughter took during her 2016 thru-hike.

I might have thought the same thing had I been thirty years younger, accompanied by friends, well rested and well fed, carrying a light pack, with long arms and legs, and good weather. Since none of those things were true, it was decidedly not fun.

This mile of the AT is basically a gap at 2,200-feet elevation between two 3,600-foot peaks. It is a gorge, really, where the surrounding mountains have seen fit over the millennia to dump all their unwanted boulders. Think of making your way through a twenty-foot-wide obstacle course of huge, jagged rocks. You must either climb over them, between them, or under them. You cannot go around them. Believe me, I tried.

It takes even the most capable of hikers a solid two hours to traverse this gift from nature. For a long time I was too embarrassed to tell anyone how long it took me. But I will whisper it to you now if you promise not to tell anyone: *eight hours*. One mile. Eight hours. Nature was rolling in the aisles with laughter at my antics.

Each boulder must be tackled separately. Like snowflakes, no two are the same. I climbed. I fell. I tried again. I gave up carrying my pack on my back, as I was constantly taking it off to squeeze through the narrow gaps. I tied a rope to the shoulder strap and drug it behind me, heaving it to the top of the rock ahead of me. Sometimes it was necessary to position it upright at the rock's base to use as a stepstool and pull it up by the rope when I got to the top.

A sleety rain fell from the low, gray clouds most of the day. There were patches of snow and ice in the crevasses where the sun's rays never quite reach. Other hikers scrambled past me, some graciously offering a hand or a boost, but I always declined. I had gotten myself into this mess, and I would get myself out of it.

The end—when it finally did come—was abrupt. Peanut had told me that at the north end of the Notch was a campsite big enough for maybe two tents. Sure enough, the boulders eventually thinned out, I turned a corner through a copse, and there it was. Perched in the clearing was a small, blue tent, and I heard the sound of women's laughter.

Peanut had advised me to camp here for the evening if I was late getting out of the gorge.

"Mom, nobody talks about how tough the climb up the Arm (the ascent out of the gorge) is. Everybody freaks out about the Notch, but the Arm is really, really hard too."

I recalled these words of daughterly advice as I rested on my poles. Did I heed them?

No. Speck Pond Shelter was only a mile-and-a-half north, and I figured I could get there in the two hours of daylight remaining. But immediately the Trail steepened. My quads burned with each step, reminding me my muscles had been pushed to their maximum capacity for eight hours. I was shaky, lightheaded, and nauseous. I had neither eaten nor drank much of anything all day. The woods were quiet as dusk deepened, and I began to regret my decision to continue on.

After a miserable and totally wasted half hour, I turned back. Peanut was right, and her advice was good. It would have taken me hours, well into the dangerous night, to reach the next shelter. Assuming I ever did.

Back at the clearing, I wearily set up my tent and exchanged a few words with my campmates. They were a very fit couple in their late thirties who had cheerfully scampered past me halfway through the gorge. I had noticed them at that time because they seemed remarkably happy, as they still seemed now. They were apparently of the "Mahoosuc Notch is fun!" school.

Next morning I rose knowing I faced seven more miles before reaching the ME 26 highway crossing at Grafton Notch. I was filthy, exhausted, battered, and bruised. My food supply was down to a few crackers and a bite or two of chocolate. Because I had planned to hike this section in three days, and it had actually taken me five, I was woefully undersupplied. I broke camp as wearily as I had made it the night before.

✳ ✳ ✳

The rain had ceased, and the day was warm as I climbed the Arm, which rises from the gorge almost two thousand feet in a mile and a half. I felt justified in my decision to turn back the night before; this was extremely serious hiking. The Trail then plummets just as steeply to the banks of Speck Pond, with its shelter and campsites, before climbing the cliffs and ledges of Old Speck to 4,100 feet, the highest peak of the Mahoosuc Range. *When will this Trail have mercy?*

The AT skirts the summit of Old Speck by a third of a mile. Should hikers be thankful we are spared the grueling extra climb up or dismayed that, after the brutal, unending switchbacks, we are robbed of the views from the peak? Of course, one can choose to take the round-trip, .6 mile spur trail. I think it will come as no surprise I declined that option and continued on my way.

I didn't so much arrive at Grafton Notch State Park as fall into it. There were a few cars in the parking lot awaiting the day-hikers who were out on the park's various trails. I sat immobile on a berm until a group of three or four high-spirited young people emerged from the woods and approached a dirty Toyota. I was prepared to beg.

"Hey, guys. Which way you going? Can you take me a few miles to the Rostay Inn?"

"Sure. Hop in."

Grafton Notch is not really a town, or if it is, I missed it. What I saw of it was a convenience store / gas station, a restaurant, and the Rostay Inn clustered around an intersection. This was enough for me.

* * *

The Trail north from Grafton Notch State Park crosses the west and east summits of Baldpate Mountain with an overall rise in elevation from 2,000 feet to 3,500 feet. The day was warm and the ascent through the woods sometimes steep, but the night at the very comfortable and hospitable inn had somewhat restored me. I was once again clean and resupplied. Hikers are gullible creatures; a little encouraging pat on the head, and we are right back to thinking we are worthy.

The hike up the East Peak from the gap between the two summits is rocky and challenging. But I felt strong on this pleasant day as I alternately hopped, jumped, and skipped up to the exposed bald. The view of Maine from here is amazing, and I began to feel that perhaps the worst was behind me or at least that I would live to tell the tale.

From the East Peak I cruised down to Frye Notch Lean-to. A small stream provided a soft lullaby as I slept soundly in the snug shelter. A few northbound thru-hikers, all of us strangers in a strange land, kept me company. They had over 250 miles ahead of them to complete their odyssey, while I had but twenty-five miles to walk before my June sally ended, and I could return to hearth and home.

The first three and a half miles of the AT from Frye Notch Shelter to East B Hill Road is a pleasant walk in the woods, fairly level, and without the brutal rocks of the previous days. But then the Trail gets slippery as it borders a gorge filled with a series of sparkling cascades. Not much stands between you and the churning water.

I picked my way tentatively through this section, and by midafternoon, I could see the road. Unfortunately, it was on the other side of the twenty-foot-wide Ellis River. *Sigh.* Well, it couldn't be helped. After some useless standing around as if waiting for a bridge to miraculously appear, I stepped into the high, fast-moving current.

I reached the far side without incident, took off my heavy, wet boots, replaced them with camp shoes, and sat down on the grassy shoulder of East B Hill Road. I was a woman with a plan.

The date was June 23. I had a plane ticket for June 26 to fly to Nashville. During my stay in Grafton Notch, I had contacted the Pine Ellis Lodging in Andover, Maine, requesting a single room, shuttle service, and a ride to the airport in Portland. Between the initial pickup at the trailhead and the ride to the airport, I intended to hike for two days.

Now, when I say "lodge" and "shuttle" here, please do not envision balconied chalets, bustling bellboys, and a smart, white van with the name of the establishment emblazoned on the side. Dave, a member of the extended multigenerational family who owned and operated the Pine Ellis, picked me up at East B Hill Road in an old Suburban, from which the back seats had been removed to make room for hikers' gear.

"Are you Sticks?" Dave was a handsome, middle-aged man whom

I initially took to be of Native American descent, but he told me later his heritage was Guatemalan. "You been waiting long?"

"No, not too long. No problem." (There was no cell coverage in this area, and when I had made the arrangements from Grafton Notch, I had said I'd be at the road by midafternoon. The voice on the other end of the phone had replied, "Someone will be there sometime.")

Dave motioned to a gallon jug on the back floorboard next to a stack of plastic cups. "Help yourself to lemonade." I gladly accepted the offer and gratefully, but probably not very politely, drank cup after cup.

We rattled along the scenic road for eight miles to the town of Andover, as stereotypical a Maine community as you can imagine with its extreme remoteness and taciturn characters. There is a nice little community park, a school that instructs a dozen or so young students (the older kids are bused elsewhere), a couple of deli-style restaurants, and a gas station / convenience store. Pine Ellis Lodging is one of two hostels.

Dave pulled up in front of a sagging frame house, the wood so dark-colored as to be almost black, with a wide front porch complete with swing and several comfortable-looking chairs, now occupied by hikers in various stages of relaxation. A reserved, plain-faced woman who appeared to be perhaps of the middle generation of the extended-family proprietors met us at the door. She smiled slightly and recited a canned speech.

"No boots inside. You can leave them here on the porch. Washer and dryer in the garage. Bunks upstairs behind the kitchen. You can use refrigerator that has a sign on it for hikers. Bathroom at bottom of stairs. Put dirty towels in the basket. Coffee and pastries for breakfast at seven. Shuttle leaves at eight for trailhead. Supplies here."

The woman opened a freestanding cabinet on a corner of the porch. In it were some candy bars and other snacks, a few cans of stove fuel, and miscellaneous items such as bug spray and moleskin.

"Take what you need on honor system. We settle bills first thing every morning."

I love this place. "I'm Sticks. I called about a private room."

"Oh, sure, Sticks. Just come on in after you take off your boots."

After divesting myself of boots, pack, and poles, I opened the screen door to a small foyer, which in turn opened into a large kitchen. Scarred yellow linoleum covered the floor, and ancient appliances lined the walls. I followed our hostess through a small living room. Dave, beer in hand, sat on a floral-print couch, eyes turned toward a large console TV airing the evening news.

We continued our journey up an enclosed back stairway that ended in a small hallway with two or three closed doors. The woman opened one of them. "This do?" she asked.

The room was almost entirely taken up by a sagging double bed neatly made up with crisp, white cases on the two flat pillows. I smiled and nodded at the landlady, who seemed genuinely anxious for my approval. She smiled back at me and went on her way.

* * *

Pine Ellis provides rides to the trailheads at East B Hill Road and South Arm Road. The distance on the AT between these two points is ten miles. Most people hike this section in one day, but it is not an easy trail. Because I had two days before my departure, I decided to not push myself. I was even going to attempt to enjoy the final chapter of this trip.

With warm weather forecast and no rain expected, I packed as lightly as I could for Saturday and Sunday on the Trail. A couple of days' food, no extra clothes, and—taking a chance there would be room at the Hall Mountain Lean-to—no tent. Leaving the superfluous items at the lodge, I rode with Dave to East B Hill Road.

The Trail here winds its way gradually for a couple of miles through deep woods, ascending ridges and crossing streams before it finally reaches Surplus Pond and begins its climb up Wyman Mountain. The hours whittled away the miles, and by early afternoon, I had descended Wyman. This was a day of solitude. I wondered where all the other hikers were. Was there a party somewhere, and I hadn't been invited?

I began the climb to Hall Mountain and realized I would reach the lean-to hours before dark. The woods were very, very quiet, and

I was acutely aware of the sound of my solitary footsteps and ragged breathing.

Company would be nice when I reach the shelter. Or better yet, a book. I will make a campfire and shake off this unsettling feeling of loneliness.

The heat of the afternoon lessened as the day waned. A foggy mist had settled in the gap where the small wooden shelter perched. It looked sadly deserted, like a playhouse when the children who once joyfully visited have all grown up and moved away. Bits of leaves had blown in, and the floor was unswept. On the back wall, cobwebs hung between the pegs meant to hold hikers' packs. A couple of half-full fuel canisters had been left behind on a shelf. I saw a book, a thick paperback with the front cover torn off, in a dark corner. *Wonderful! Now I will have a way to fill the hours before dark.*

Spirits lifted, I quickly unpacked and set about sweeping out the shelter and arranging my sleeping bag and pad. I neatly lined up the items I would need for the night: headlamp, Advil, water bottle. The day continued its long goodbye, and I put on my puffy jacket and clean, thick socks to greet the dusk.

The campfire sent tall, thin smoke signals into the air, where they flattened out above the shelter eaves. I blew at the kindling until bright flames fluttered and the clean smell of burning wood filled the glen. With dinner—a deli sandwich saved all day just for this moment and a small plastic bottle of red wine—laid out on a nearby rock, I retrieved the abandoned book from the shelter.

Now, I ask you, if you had spent the entire day walking through a remote, dense forest to reach a lonely, forsaken cabin; if you had felt a certain unexplained spookiness for the last miles and hours; if the mist and the smoke now surrounded you like a ghostly caul in this silent-as-a-graveyard place, what book would you most want to read?

I'm guessing probably not *Pet Sematary*. But that was what some hiker with a twisted sense of humor had, no doubt gleefully, left behind for some unsuspecting traveler.

This is Stephen King's chilling account of a long-deserted and mostly forgotten burial place for cats and dogs hidden away in the deep woods of Maine. But now, here by myself in these same Maine woods, alone and defenseless on a fallen log, I felt spooked as I read the familiar words about a cemetery that is not only a resting place for pets, but also for a person or two—and burial in it is not really final.

I ate my sandwich and drank my wine, sitting on that log in front of the fire and turning the pages. Darkness fell. I turned on my headlamp. Now whenever I looked up, a ray of light disrupted the mist and made the night seem even darker in contrast.

Footsteps approached. Stopped. Approached again. I held my breath. *Please, oh please, please, please, let it be a hiker. A live one. Not some large, fierce animal come back from the dead.*

"Hello?" A man's voice. Sweet relief washed over me.

"Yes? Hello! Come on in."

A heavily burdened, stubble-faced man clomped out of the woods into the clearing.

"Make yourself at home," I said, gesturing to the shelter. "Plenty of room."

"Thanks. Good to come home to a nice fire," the man said, grinning as he shrugged off his pack.

"I'm Sticks."

"I'm Chris."

"Just Chris?" I asked, noting the lack of a Trail name.

"Yep, just Chris."

"Well, Just Chris"—it was my turn to smile—"I'm really glad you're here." And I was.

He said he was recently retired and was traveling southbound, planning to hike the AT until the weather forced him to stop.

"Some chance I might make it all the way to Georgia."

"Sure. It's early yet."

I told him of the joys and challenges ahead, and he asked many questions. Somewhat envious that he still had this amazing adventure ahead of him, I reminded myself of the Whites, and the envy disappeared.

✳ ✳ ✳

My last day on the Trail dawned cool with a weak sun filtering through trees still lightly shrouded in mist left over from the previous evening.

After a breakfast of strawberry Pop-Tarts, I pressed what was left of my food—a Snickers bar and a bag of salted peanuts—on Just Chris and stepped on the Trail to tackle the four miles to South Arm Road.

I stumbled and tumbled 1,500 feet down Hall Mountain over a trail of rocks that would turn into a river in heavy rain—fortunately, the day stayed sunny—and then, as always, the Trail went right back up another mountain.

The ascent of Moody Mountain is a lung-searing, quad-burning, mother of a climb, rising more than 1,200 feet in less than a mile. To see this depicted on a relief map is to be reminded of the north face of Eiger or the flat side of Half Dome.

The summit, however, offered lovely views of the little village of Andover. I tried to locate the Pine Ellis Lodging from this aerie and imagined I saw its rambling footprint at the edge of town. Hawks floated on the current. I wished to be one of them and drift down into the valley. When this transformation did not occur, I shouldered my pack and gathered my wits to sidestep the last two miles down to the road where my chariot and the end of this part of my adventure awaited.

PART 2

ANDOVER, MAINE, TO MOUNT KATAHDIN, MAINE

July in Franklin is always hot. It is often brutally hot. Such was the case in 2017, but I seemed unable to get enough of the sun. My legs and mind were always restless. I ran for miles on shadeless streets until my clothes dripped sweat. My shoulders turned brown as I pulled garden weeds that had been left to their own unrestrained devices in my absence. I lounged poolside at the homes of friends and neighbors, near mute in the presence of civic normalcy.

When I returned home from the Trail in June, the crepe myrtles at the back of our house had fully bloomed in deep pink profusion, as had the delicate purple petals of the rose of Sharon bushes in the side yard. By early August, they were so laden with clusters of flowers the boughs bent toward the earth with the burden. Dazed bumblebees browsed among the sprays like the heat-stupefied tourists, wandering in and out of the air-conditioned shops on Franklin's Main Street. The time had come for me to return to the cooler climes of Maine, to the mountains. To the Trail.

* * *

My friend Dave from Pine Ellis Lodging, wearing his jaunty feathered hat, was waiting for me at baggage claim in Portland. We drove the couple of hours to Andover, and once again, I had a comfortable night at the lodge and stocked my food bag with goodies from the convenience store.

Another wave of thru-hikers lolled about on Pine Ellis's wide front porch, resting before the final push. Two hundred fifty miles lie between here and Katahdin, and then we could all lay our burdens down.

Northbound from South Arm Road, the AT begins an almost immediate ascent of Old Blue Mountain. Rising almost two thousand feet in less than three miles to its 3,600-foot summit, Old Blue is an irascible old fart. Hikers awkwardly blunder through the nearly impenetrable underbrush that threatens to engulf the Trail, and we heave ourselves up and over the narrow rock staircases. The mountain seems to say to us, "Ayuh, you tenderfoots, you city slickers! Thought you had it made, didn't ya, after the Whites and Wildcat? You got another think coming. Look at you! Sweating and panting and slipping and cussing. Well, get on with it. I'm sick of the sight of you."

The afternoon provided some relief as I wearily descended the north slope to walk on a boggy and relatively flat path for a couple of miles. Then, finally, the last climb of the day, Bemis Mountain, kinder and gentler than Old Blue.

For the first day back on the Trail, nine miles through the Maine ruggedness was not a small accomplishment. I reached Bemis Mountain Lean-to before dark and gratefully spread out sleeping pad and bag. Shortly, I was joined by a small group of southbounders, and we sat at the open side of the shelter, our legs dangling off the floor and into the moat, a feature found at many of the Maine lean-tos. Some of the moats are so wide and deep that when I first encountered one, I thought they were meant to deter moose. No, they are there to discourage hungry porcupines from climbing into the wooden structures. I am told porcupines like the salt from the sweat sleeping hikers leave behind. This is also why you don't want to leave your boots lying around outside; to these critters, a boot is just a bag of salty potato chips.

* * *

The distance from Bemis Mountain Lean-to to Sabbath Day Pond Lean-to is just over eight miles. The first four miles travel over the peaks of the Bemis Mountain range, and the next four along soft, flat trail with ponds to left and right. This hike is neatly intersected halfway through by a drop to Bemis Stream, followed by a climb up to ME 17. Here, on this cool, overcast day, I gave myself a little treat and hitched a ride into the quaint little town of Oquossoc for a real lunch and a cold drink.

Back on the Trail within a couple of hours and with a light rain falling, I began to frequently pass lakes, which in Maine are called "carry ponds." I think it's because they are used to "carry" your things—food, supplies, people—from one side to the other, avoiding the dense forest.

On more than one occasion, I saw floatplanes landing on the flat, still surfaces. Men dressed in waders and many-pocketed vests, their brimmed hats adorned with colorful feathered fishing lures, stepped from the pontoons into the clear and apparently shallow water. Fiberglass rowboats and wooden scows are strategically scattered lakeside, tied to sturdy trees. I wondered how on earth they came to be there; I saw no roads on which they could have been transported. There are any number of things about the people and places of Maine that puzzle me.

I passed Moxie Pond and Long Pond and crossed several streams as I hiked north through the afternoon. The soft rain had ceased, and now the woods smelled of clean, fresh spruce. Immensely pleased with the day, I arrived at Sabbath Day Pond Lean-to in good spirits.

Squatch, Stretch, and Squire were but a few of the thru-hikers enjoying the swimming hole at the nearby beach. The shelters, by this date, were becoming more and more crowded as I pushed north. This was the peak time for the northbounders to be closing in on their journey's end. I smiled to see their hiker tans—faces, arms, legs, hands as brown as Smoky Mountain acorns, but their feet and ankles, perpetually covered by socks and boots, as white as Katahdin snow.

✽ ✽ ✽

My lovely, peaceful ramble continued the next day on smooth, easy trail for eleven miles to the next shelter, Piazza Rock Lean-to. I stayed below three thousand feet all day; peaks seemed to have been replaced by ponds.

Traveling on trail markedly abundant with moose droppings, I passed Little Swift River Pond and South Pond. I crossed ME 4, the highway leading to the town of Rangeley, a well-loved resupply stop for thru-hikers, but I pushed on. Soft rain again fell in the afternoon, and when I reached Piazza Rock, I saw the shelter was full. No problem. I was completely happy in my tent, pleased with how far I had advanced, and not a bit worried about upcoming Saddleback and Saddleback Junior. I would later ruefully recall that bliss of ignorance.

The climb from Piazza Rock Lean-to to the summit of Saddleback Mountain is two thousand feet to above tree line at over four thousand feet. I again skirted ponds and stepped around moose poop. As I laboriously made my way up the slope, I nodded to the grouse that nonchalantly nest alongside the Trail. I crossed the open, barren summit, my stomach sometimes giving a sickening lurch as frequent gusts of wind reminded me of the evils of Lafayette and Madison.

The Trail from here to Saddleback Junior shows signs of ice and wind erosion, and the poor little spruce bushes grow horizontally to protect themselves from Mother Nature. I carefully picked my way down to Poplar Ridge Lean-to for the night. This had been a nine-mile day of physical challenge and harsh beauty. Complete exhaustion dulled my mind and, in blessed survival mode, I could not think of the trail ahead or the trail behind, only of what was necessary at this exact moment. And that, my friends, was sleep.

The next day, I planned to hike only eight miles to the next shelter, Spaulding Mountain Lean-to. But the Trail proved fun and interesting as I forded Orbeton Stream and climbed the gentle slope of Lone Mountain. I reached the shelter by midafternoon and thought, *Well, heck, I can keep on walking!* Maps indicated a tent site on the north side of the Carrabassett River five miles ahead.

I climbed Spaulding Mountain and Sugarloaf Mountain, enjoying the mild day and the panoramic views of Maine's peaks and valleys. All was right with the world.

The descent of Sugarloaf nixed that naive notion. Two miles of tumbled rocks fall over a thousand feet drop in elevation, and my pace slowed to that of a snail. This was lonely, hard work. *Step down. Find placement for trekking pole. Make sure it is secure. Take another step.* I wiped away tears of frustration, as I could see the river at the bottom of this misery but could not seem to get close. The sun began its descent into the western sky, and I feared it would reach its destination before I reached mine. I won, but within minutes. Two hikers on the opposite bank called to me encouragingly and pointed out the easiest place to ford. It was all I could do to set up my tent, and all I could hang on to was the thought, *Tomorrow, town.*

Eight miles and two mountains to Stratton. I climbed from the river to South Crocker Mountain at four thousand feet and then to North Crocker at 4,300 feet. Again, this is rugged, steep hiking, but also again, there is variety in views and terrain. The path goes through woods, then over rockslides, and then through woods again, and all around are the views of the mountains. After a mildly steep descent of North Crocker, the AT turns gentle again, and I coasted a few more miles to Stratton.

The houses in rural Maine seem to all be made from wooden Erector Sets. They sit close to the road, in this case ME 27, which took me the five miles from the trailhead into Stratton on a hitched ride. It seems the homes start off as a few separate buildings—here the main structure, there a garage, yonder a shed—but then the owner decides at various times that it's way too damn cold to walk from one building to another without cover, so he walls and roofs the passageways until there is a little compound consisting of joined boxes of varying heights and sizes. Cords of firewood are stacked under eaves, and moose antlers often adorn the siding. The overall effect is brave and charming.

* * *

In the no-nonsense, utilitarian town of Stratton, I bedded down at a similarly practical motel/hostel. It was here I first met Skeeter and Aussie, who, like me, made an odd contrast to the hikers hanging around out front—the young men with their heavy beards and the young women with their tangled hair, both sexes wearing bandanas, faded shorts, and hemp bracelets, and who seemed uninterested in anything but each other.

Aussie was in his early to midsixties, clean-shaven with combed-back silver hair. He seemed smaller than he probably actually was because his wiry, compact body appeared to have no excess fat whatsoever but was comprised only of bone, muscle, and tendon. Even his face seemed stretched over teeth and skull.

Although at least a decade younger, Skeeter was similar in body type. She was of average height and lean as a gazelle. Her hair was a completely natural combination of white and blonde strands that framed her face and softly touched the back of her collar. The slight burnish of her cheekbones and the pale blue of her eyes gave Skeeter the look of a beautiful mannequin. Both were dressed impeccably in long pants, button-up shirts, and safari hats, all khaki or pale green. I hiked on and off with them from Stratton to Katahdin, and neither ever seemed to get dirty. It was unbelievable. I always looked like I lived in a refugee camp with no running water.

Skeeter and Aussie were typically enigmatic long-distance hikers. Over these weeks and miles, we talked only of the Trail and the weather, never learning of each other's lives outside the hike. It is strange that you walk and eat and sleep with these people and never find out if they have kids, what their professions are, what their political leanings might be. No matter; we all had one shared single goal.

* * *

Resupplied and refreshed, I left Stratton the next morning to spend four nights on the Trail before I reached the next town, Caratunk. For the first three days, the weather was perfect, with clear skies and cool temperatures.

This is the Bigelow Mountain range, and it is breathtakingly beautiful, remote, and rugged, yet gentler than its southern neighbors. I strolled along the ridges through beech forests on a path sometimes rocky but not unforgiving. Ponds and streams and rivers abound in this section. The shelters were crowded with the northbounders anticipating a Katahdin summit for Labor Day. I climbed Avery Peak and the peaks of Bigelow Mountain and Little Bigelow. I shared the crowded shelters with Seamstress, Tunnel Rat, Turmeric, Mosey, and Eager Beaver. Aussie and Skeeter's tent could often be seen on lonely campsites along the Trail.

Day Four of this segment brought a constant steady rain that made rocks treacherous, and it obscured any views. The log bridges across the swamps turned into oil slicks. We all trudged on in our muddy boots, our bodies and packs covered tortoise-like with polyester shells.

It was late afternoon, almost evening, when I reached the small shelter at Pierce Pond. This lean-to comfortably accommodates only about six hikers, and eight were already crammed into it, their gear scattered everywhere. Aussie and Skeeter had their tent set up on a tiny site in the shadow of the shelter.

Ghosthiker, a tall thin young man, stepped into the clearing from an eastbound side trail. The other hikers had told me he was on a scouting mission to check out a nearby fishing camp.

"Hey, gang. Harrison's got three spaces left."

I perked up. My original plan had been to tent-camp, but if I could get out of the rain, I was willing to walk a little farther.

Ghosthiker continued. "About .4 east through the woods. Forty bucks, bed, dinner, and breakfast."

Those of us not hunkered down in the shelter were huddled under its eaves. Seamstress straightened up and pulled her hood over her head. "I'm in," she said cheerfully.

"Me too." I hoisted my pack while the others discussed the pros and cons of pitching tents or spending money.

"Thing is," Ghosthiker warned, "he only takes cash."

My heart sank. I again took off my pack and fished out my hiker's wallet. "I have twenty-two dollars."

Aussie didn't hesitate. "I got cash. Take it. You can pay me back in town."

Harrison's Camp is basically an old wooden house with a narrow porch running along its side. Bear rugs cover the floors and all manner of animal heads hang on the walls. Lights and appliances are powered by a humming generator. There is a small bathroom outside that houses a shower and, luxuriously, a flush toilet. Two old pickup trucks loaded with firewood were parked in an unpaved driveway that turned off a rough dirt road that led to…somewhere, I assume. The back of the house faced the pond, where raindrops speckled the surface and loons cried mournfully.

I was assigned to a tiny cabin a stone's throw from the main building. In here were a couple of iron bedsteads and a wood stove. The starkness pleased me, as did the simplicity of dinner. Steak, bread, green salad, and baked potato were served family style to about ten hikers in the spacious dining room of the main house. With no pretense of manners, I scraped the potato peel with my teeth and sopped up the salad dressing with leftover bread crust. No one judged me as they sucked the bones of the meat, and I did not judge them.

The rain stopped during the night, and stillness woke me early.

Anxious now to get moving, I returned to the Trail. Less than four miles on easy, sloping trail took me to the banks of the Kennebec River, where I joined Seamstress and a couple of other hikers waiting for the ferry, a rowboat that can carry about four hikers at a time across the four-hundred-foot-wide river. It operates during hiking season and is free. This is the only official part of the AT where your boots don't trod the earth. There is a white blaze painted on the floor of the rowboat to provide authenticity.

On the day we were there, the river seemed placid enough, but they say it's a nasty piece of water with a swift and unpredictable current. Before the Maine Appalachian Trail Club took over and paid for the operation of the ferry, hikers often tried to ford the Kennebec instead of paying a fee, and the results were sometimes disastrous. Even now there are tales of locals fishing an occasional errant hiker out of the river somewhere downstream.

* * *

Shortly after crossing the Kennebec, the AT crosses US 201 at Caratunk. I walked about a mile along the highway to the beautiful Sterling Inn, which offers reasonable prices to hikers but also caters to weekend travelers wishing to stay in a quaint New England bed-and-breakfast. A wide front porch, complete with cushioned, comfortable rocking chairs and softly humming ceiling fans, wraps around the building. Here, freshly showered and resupplied, I spent the late afternoon and evening alternately reading a paperback Thoreau from the inn's bookshelves and watching the traffic that seemed to fly by on the highway.

The roughly forty AT miles from Caratunk to Monson, Maine, is a low-elevation trail at about one thousand feet, with the exceptions of Pleasant Pond Mountain and Moxie Bald Mountain, which rise to nearly three thousand feet. For two-and-a-half days, I walked serenely and unhurriedly through beech and maple, fording small streams. Blueberry bushes yielded the very last of the season's fruits, and the very first dead leaves begin to drift from the trees. Autumn was near.

* * *

Monson, Maine, normally has a population of less than a thousand people. I assume that doesn't include hikers who swell those ranks considerably in August and September. Like most small towns in Maine, Monson is remote, although ME 15, a major road catering to the rumbling logging trucks, runs right through it. It is near dead center of the state, and it is the gateway to the last hundred miles of the northbound Appalachian Trail.

I, along with Aussie and Skeeter, hitched a ride from the trailhead for the few miles into Monson, where we found that the residents come across as self-sufficient and unusually erudite. The bulletin board at the post office displayed notices regarding meetings of the historical society and lectures from naturalists. An amateur theater group called for auditions for *The Glass Menagerie*, and the library book club was to discuss *The Taming of the Shrew* at its next gathering.

Here we also found Shaw's. Probably the most well-known hostel on the entire Appalachian Trail, it was overflowing. This hostel is a sprawling old house with a detached hiker barn, a garage where business is transacted and supplies are sold, and a yard where the thriftier hikers can pitch a tent for a minimal fee. At the time of our stay, Shaw's was operated by Poet and Hippie Chick, hikers them-selves who now had a couple of young children, one still at the breast. This is a convivial place, where hikers swap tales, cut pack weight, and enjoy the famous all-you-can-eat pancake breakfasts. Some find it so comfortable that it becomes easy to procrastinate about getting back on the Trail. I met one young woman who'd been there for two weeks.

Laundry done, belly full, email checked, I spent the rest of this day and all night awaiting the arrival of my daughter. Peanut was to accompany me on the last segment of this great adventure.

She flew into Portland on August 23 and arrived in Monson by bus in midmorning. My anxiety lessened and my excitement grew. Now two-thirds of our little family was in one place, and moreover, I had an experienced hiker to push me up the formidable Mount Katahdin.

We consolidated our gear (Peanut had come straight to Maine from a Western Canadian ten-day hike) and mailed the excess home, but she decided to carry her tent just in case she wanted some pri-vacy. We would be eight nights on the Trail, and I suppose she was a little worried this might be too much mother-daughter quality time. We bought food for nine days and divided in into two portions. One four-day portion would be delivered by Shaw's midway into the Hundred Mile Wilderness, the section between Monson and Baxter State Park—the latter home to Mount Katahdin and the northern terminus of the Appalachian Trail.

❊ ❊ ❊

Poet took several of us hikers to the trailhead at ME 15 on Thursday morning, a sunny, cool day on which to begin the end. Shortly after stepping on the Trail, we encountered a wooden sign etched with the message:

> CAUTION. There are no places to obtain supplies or help until you reach Abol Bridge 100 miles north. You should not attempt this section unless you carry a minimum of ten days' supplies. Do not underestimate the difficulty of this section. Good hiking!—MATC.

The first day was difficult, and our pace was slow. We forded several streams and climbed up and down with numbing regularity. We stayed Thursday night at the Wilson Valley Lean-to. The next day was a repeat in its difficulty, with a tough climb up Barren Mountain thrown in. On this night, Peanut and I camped, sharing my tent, between Third Mountain and Fourth Mountain at a rise interestingly called Mount Three and a Half. I looked forward to the flat and easy Red Carpet, which is what thru-hikers call the last sixty or so miles of the AT prior to Katahdin. At that point, some hikers (not I) will easily do twenty-five-plus mile days.

Our weather continued fine, cool with no precipitation. On Saturday the Trail became forgiving and smooth. This was a very pretty hike with lovely views of the rolling Maine hills and dense, late-summer forest. After a tent night at Carl A. Newhall Lean-to, we celebrated Sunday with another sweet and easy day. At the 3,500-foot summit of White Cap Mountain, Peanut pointed north. Looming in the far distance was my final destination.

Katahdin in view! Oh, the joy!

* * *

Although no public roads run through the Hundred Mile Wilderness, there is a private road owned by a logging company that allows Shaw's to make its delivery of resupply. After we gratefully retrieved our box, we literally just strolled for four more days on almost flat trail through deep woods, camping on the banks of the ponds. In the evenings, Peanut stripped down and bathed in the still waters. The loons cried loudly in the night, often waking me in my tent, reminding me this magical time was not a dream.

We shared campfires with thru-hikers, who by now had been walking for six months from Springer and were simply exhausted. The talk was of the summit. "When will you try? Labor Day? Weather moving in but supposed to clear Sunday." I was particularly worried about Irish, a young man who seemed to be suffering from starvation or at least severe malnutrition. He was a tall, wide-shouldered fellow—it would have taken many calories to fill him—and the whites of his eyes were completely red. I noticed a collapsible fishing pole sticking up from his pack.

"Have you had much luck with the fish?" I asked one evening as several hikers gathered around the fire.

"No." Irish shook his head. "Not up here anyway. No luck really since before the Whites."

I passed around a bag of gingersnaps, and each hiker politely took a couple. When the bag came back around to me, I gave it again to Irish seated to my right. "Here, take the rest. We had a resupply from Shaw's. We have plenty of food. Please."

On Thursday, we reached Abol Bridge and relative civilization—a bridge, a road, and a small generator-powered cafeteria. It was strange to smell the odor of grease, hear the clink of glasses and the calls of the waitress, read a menu under a dim bulb. We walked unsteadily on the wooden floors and touched the insides of the walls as if to test their solidity.

Ten more easy miles brought us to Abol Pines Campground,

where I spent my last night on the AT. A private three-sided shelter, with a picnic table and views of the mountains and lake, was ours for a few bucks. Peanut cooked our dinner, and I did not pause to examine my feelings. I was tired to the point of emotional depletion. One more mountain to climb. A couple more nights in a hostel. Another hitchhike and another shuttle. The long plane ride home.

The temperature fell during the night, and Peanut snuggled her sleeping bag close to mine. We woke to a cold drizzle but an easy hike to Baxter State Park, reaching it by midday. Here, we registered at the ranger station and ran into a group of thru-hikers we'd camped with in the Hundred Mile Wilderness. They had summited Katahdin this day in the cold and told us there had been snow at the top. I was delighted to see Irish among them and told him I had been thinking of him.

He grinned, his eyes still bloodshot but his expression happy. "I made it," he said. "I'm going home."

Peanut and I got a ride into Millinocket, a typically austere Maine town with most of its businesses clustered onto two or three streets. We checked into the "family suite" at a hostel. My first order of business was to visit a local secondhand store to buy a warm, cuddly sweatshirt. Pack weight and excessive belongings would no longer be concerns of mine.

The second order of business was to browse through an establishment next to our hostel called Turn the Page, a combination bookstore and wine bar, which seemed to me to be a brilliant idea. I took a seat at a window, where I frequently looked up from my book and glass. Tim was going to join us for our post-Katahdin celebration, and I was keeping watch for his rental car. When I saw a clean, new sedan hesitantly making its way along the street, I stepped outside to wave him down and welcome him to Maine.

Our words tumbled over each other as we ate an excellent dinner at a local restaurant. "How was the hike? How was the flight? How's Radley? Weather sucked today, but supposed to be good tomorrow."

The family suite at the hostel consisted of a tiny kitchen, a tiny sitting room, and two tiny bedrooms. Peanut and I stripped everything from our packs except the very basic necessities for the summit: water, food, first aid kit, and extra clothes, including gloves and hats.

Sleeping bags, dirty clothes, stove were left strewn about on the couch, on the foot of the bed, on the small kitchen table. We gave Tim instructions for the next day.

"We will take the hostel shuttle to Baxter very early in the morning. By late afternoon, we should be finished, and we will meet you in the park where the Katahdin Trail ends."

The weather forecast called for mild temperatures, no precipitation, and light winds. There was nothing else to be done except get up, leave my husband sleeping in the warm bed, and walk out the door.

* * *

From the ranger station in Baxter State Park to the summit of Mount Katahdin and the northern terminus of the Appalachian Trail is five miles. The gain in elevation is a staggering 4,200 feet. This mountain is basically a big pile of granite, unadorned and solitary, rising from the forest floor like a rogue wave might push its way up over the ocean. Later, a friend sent me a bumper sticker that said, "I climbed Katahdin." Thank you, but "I crawled Katahdin" would be a more appropriate sentiment.

This is an extremely challenging hike, but decent weather and the company of Peanut gave me at least a little better chance in this game of woman versus nature. The ascent is immediate and relentless. Tumbled boulders rise precipitously on either side of the path or in many cases directly on it. Short, scruffy bushes and stony earth border the trail, and there is no forest or woodland to block your view of the piles of jagged rocks that make up the landscape.

The imperious power of this mountain is too much to contemplate in its entirety. I focused on each obstacle, each rock, individually as if it were a lone piece of a jigsaw puzzle or a single knot in a tangled necklace. Each step required negotiation as I slowly and carefully considered the precise placement of boots and poles. Peanut, who could have easily leapt from rock to rock, patiently matched my pace, offering words of encouragement. She often stopped above and ahead of me to lean back with a supporting hand.

Finally, after a climb of several hours measured stone by stone and inch by inch, the terrain leveled off onto the mesa-like plateau that is the summit.

If you have made it this far—whether you have walked five miles from the Baxter State Park parking lot or 2,200 miles from the Springer Mountain terminus—you will see a sign. And on this spot of earth that never sees the sun or moon through the constant low clouds, that knows only the most resilient of plant life and the hardiest of animals, that for three seasons of each year is snow-blanketed and ice-rimmed, wind-whipped and hail-pelted, revered and cursed, here is what the sign says:

KATAHDIN

BAXTER PEAK Elevation – 5267 ft

NORTHERN TERMINUS OF THE APPALACHIAN TRAIL

The words are written in white paint on a weathered plank of wood perhaps three feet by three feet. Notations below these words indicate mileage to various points on the AT. The sign is secured to a wide-based ladder-like structure with a couple of crossbars on the back side to serve as steps. There are no other man-made structures (except a few discreet wooden markers indicating various exit trails) on the summit of Katahdin. Camping is not allowed here, and the park stewards expect hikers to keep celebrations muted and respectful. There is no popping of champagne corks or at least none openly displayed. Tears are shed, but it's hard to say if they are tears of triumph or of grief.

A group of thirty or so hikers—thru-hikers, section-hikers, day-hikers—stood in a wavy, uncontrolled queue leading up to this iconic sign. The day still young and the weather fine, no one seemed to be in any particular hurry. Peanut and I joined Aussie and Skeeter to wait our turns to climb onto the crossbars. We took the typical photos of one another—poles aloft, faces wind-chapped, grins wide.

What am I supposed to do with this momentous occasion? What had I expected to feel?

I had expected, at the beginning of this year, to finish the AT. Well, I had done it. I had expected tough mountains and bad weather and remote towns and shitty food and cold nights. I found these. I had expected unsurpassed beauty, the generosity of strangers, the support of my husband, the company of my daughter, and the worry from my mother and friends. These I found too. But for this moment and for this place, I had made no plans and had harbored no expectations. The reality of the end was simply a gut punch that left me breathless and numb.

Dear people, I wish I could tell you that I wandered away from the others and found a rock to sit on, to stare out into the foggy distance and meditate in a yogi-like posture. A place to calmly reflect and remember, to mark the moment, to bask in my accomplishment. Yes, here would be a time for complete self-awareness and inner peace.

I would like to say that I looked back and thought of all those friends who traveled with me over many miles—Jen, Smokin' Goat, Denise Wolfe, Cecilia, Heather, Sebastian, She Who Falls A Lot— and those who accompanied me only for a day or so—Amanda, Teresa, Kelley, Allie, Lynn, Diane, Kim Commando.

I should have at least said a prayer or two for all the Angels—Bob, Al, Tommy, Lynne, Onecimus, Bill, Randy, Anne, Jeff, Liz, and the countless others whose names I never even learned—who picked me up from airports, let me sleep in spare rooms, gave me rides, and made my nomadic life easier.

What would it have hurt for me to just take a little time to mentally remark on the miracles of Trail Magic: *Oh, that bowl of cool slippery peaches on a hot summer afternoon! Oh, Almond Joy, that tiny candy bar left hanging in a tree for the weary traveler!*

It would have been wholly appropriate to turn my face up to the sky and close my eyes and remember the sweet little towns—Hot Springs, Damascus, Harpers Ferry, Gorham, Monson—which had provided me with succor and relief, rest and resupply. I should have smiled at the notion that without this hike, I would never have visited or even known of these lovely places. (Who chooses to vacation in Troutdale, Virginia?)

To take a little while and pay homage to the Trail itself with its formidable obstacles—Clingmans Dome, Mahoosuc Notch, Lehigh Gap, Stairway to Heaven, Mount Lafayette—would have been the right thing to do. Oh, and its unquestionable beauty—Roan Mountain, Grayson Highlands, Sterling Forest, Shenandoah Valley. Why, the names of these places are carved on my heart and are as much a part of me now as my fingerprints. It shames me to say I didn't even think of them on this stony mountain.

And the hike! Hot and cold, rain and drought, sleet and sunshine, blisters and bruises, sprains and vertigo, thirst and hunger. The ups and downs over and through switchbacks, valleys, meadows, forests, cow pastures, dirt roads, bridges, overpasses, tunnels, sidewalks, cliffs, and ledges. The lonely tents, the crowded shelters, the cheerful hostels, and the miserable rooms. Happiness and joy, solitude and companionship, pride and humility, failure and accomplishment. Certainly all this deserved at least a nod.

Oh, and nature. Shouldn't I have acknowledged its awful grandeur and its intricately simple design? The resiliency of flora to survive or resurrect after catastrophic fire, hurricane, disease? The gentle forbearance of all the animals—the brassy chipmunk, the startled deer, the watchful owl, the slithering snake, the shy bear, the patient moose, the mournful coyote—who, in fear or disdain (or amusement), quietly let us pass by?

And, no, I didn't pause to think of the hikers. The eagerness of a first-time AT adventurer out for a day or two, overpacked and wide-eyed as a child. The tenacious section-hikers anxiously counting the years as they slipped away even while appreciating every single mile. And above all, the thru-hikers with their desiccated bodies and indomitable spirits: Rodeo, Just Chris, Meticulous, Peanut, Cricket, Seamstress, Aussie, Piper, Scout, Skeeter. I should have wept in admiration for all they went through and with gratitude for all they taught me.

What of the world outside the Trail? Thirteen years of changing seasons, of war and elections, of crises and negotiations, of deserts and cities and oceans, of new students and old dogs, of graduations and anniversaries, of assignments and retirements, of dying siblings and motherless children and childless mothers. Wouldn't you think all these things deserved a moment of silence?

Should I have recited a poem from Eliot? A passage from Muir, from Thoreau, from Faulkner? Undoubtedly.

Yes, I should have sat there on that breezy mountaintop, fourteen states north from where this journey began, and thought of all this and more. I should have made an accounting and a reckoning, a tally of gratitude and grievance.

But I didn't.

I was just too tired and too old, and—in hindsight—too sad. I wanted to get off the damn mountain, take a hot shower, eat a good meal, and sleep with my husband in a warm bed in a cold Maine town.

* * *

Peanut and I laid out our picnic on some flat rocks on the windswept, stone-strewn mountainside. Aussie and Skeeter wandered over to join us in some desultory conversation.

"What trail you taking down?" Aussie asked. It was a brutal fact that we still had to get down off the mountain, and there was the option of a few trails, including backtracking on the AT. Nobody wanted to do that. It would be like visiting your child at college the day after you dropped her off. The wounds were too fresh.

"I don't know," I answered tonelessly. "I guess the Hunt Trail, it's supposed to be easiest, at least relatively."

"Yeah." Aussie's gaze turned to the horizon. "We might take the Knife Edge route. Might be interesting." As the name implies, the Knife Edge is an extremely narrow and dangerous path with drop-offs of two thousand feet on either side of the Trail.

Peanut's eyebrows lifted, and a wide smile started to lift the corners of her mouth as Aussie put forth this idea. The grin quickly faded when she turned to see the stern, disbelieving look on my face. She might have been fourteen, asking me if she could get a tattoo or pierce her lip.

"Okay, we'll take the Hunt Trail down," she conceded.

Skeeter asked Peanut about her future plans, and we all perked up: much better to think of other hikes, of other trails.

"Planning a thru-hike, for next year, on the PCT," Peanut said. "Probably start in April."

Skeeter turned to me. "What about you, Sticks? PCT?"

"Oh no, way too long and far away for me. Me and my friend Jen are talking about starting the Mountains-to-Sea Trail. Come with us."

She smiled and her blue eyes crinkled. "Might do that."

We gathered up our belongings and stuffed the leftover food and stray bits of trash into our packs. The wind was picking up and the mist swirled coldly about us as the temperature dropped. Autumn does not linger in Maine, and the chill of the approaching winter was coming on quickly. Hikers were beginning to disperse into the fog, and there was no longer a queue at the sign; no one else would summit at this late hour. The air smelled of snow. I was keenly aware that we had more of the day behind us than we had ahead of us, and that the night, on a rocky mountain descent, is not our friend. Soon only the starless sky would be witness to this place.

I nodded farewell to my fellow hikers as I hoisted my pack and tightened my straps for the last time. With a final backward glance at the rustic sign, anchored on black rocks and framed by a gray world, I stepped onto the blue-marked side trail. The constant search for the two-by-four-inch white blaze was over.

EPILOGUE

Exactly one month after the Katahdin summit, Tim turned sixty. We celebrated his birthday at our home in Franklin, friends and family traveling in from far and wide. But it was a melancholy time; we all knew that Tim's brother Tommy—who managed to make the trip to be here with us—was very sick and that for many, it would be the last time to see him in this world.

Tom died a scarce two months later in cold and wintry Pennsylvania. We had hardly returned to Franklin from his memorial service in late January when Tim was diagnosed with the same type of cancer that had killed Tom. He immediately began chemotherapy and radiation, which was temporarily successful.

After Tim's treatment was completed, Peanut and her boyfriend Cricket set off for Southern California to thru-hike the 2,600-mile Pacific Crest Trail. In mid-July, Tim and I joined them for a few days in Truckee to see their faces and give them a break. But by this time, Tim was obviously still sick and getting sicker.

Peanut successfully finished her thru-hike in late September in time to be home for Tim's sixty-first birthday.

Through the rest of 2018 and all of 2019 and into the spring of 2020, Jen and I took occasional weekend trips to hike sections of the Mountains-to-Sea Trail or to closer venues, such as Land Between the Lakes in Kentucky or the hills of Chattanooga in Tennessee. I did not want to leave home for more than a few days at a time or be further than a few hours' drive away. These trips were times of solace and rejuvenation for me, even though my heart wasn't really in it. I am forever grateful for Tim's constant awareness of my need to walk in the woods and for Jen's unquestioning company.

During the summer of 2020, Tim's condition worsened, and on September 2, a typically warm, sunny Franklin day, he died, a month shy of his sixty-third birthday.

ACKNOWLEDGMENTS

The author would like to gratefully acknowledge Gerald D. Swick, her original editor, and Sheri England, who introduced them to one another.

Grateful acknowledgments are also extended to those who read first drafts of the manuscript and offered intelligent insight and kind support.

Finally, acknowledgments must be extended, reverentially, to the Appalachian Trail Conservancy and the selfless volunteers who maintain the Trail from Georgia to Maine.

ABOUT THE AUTHOR

DIANE "STICKS" HARSHA retired as a Special Agent from the FBI in 2014. She lives in Franklin, Tennessee.

Made in the USA
Monee, IL
18 April 2022